CW00735999

ELC

ISBN 1 898432 15 5

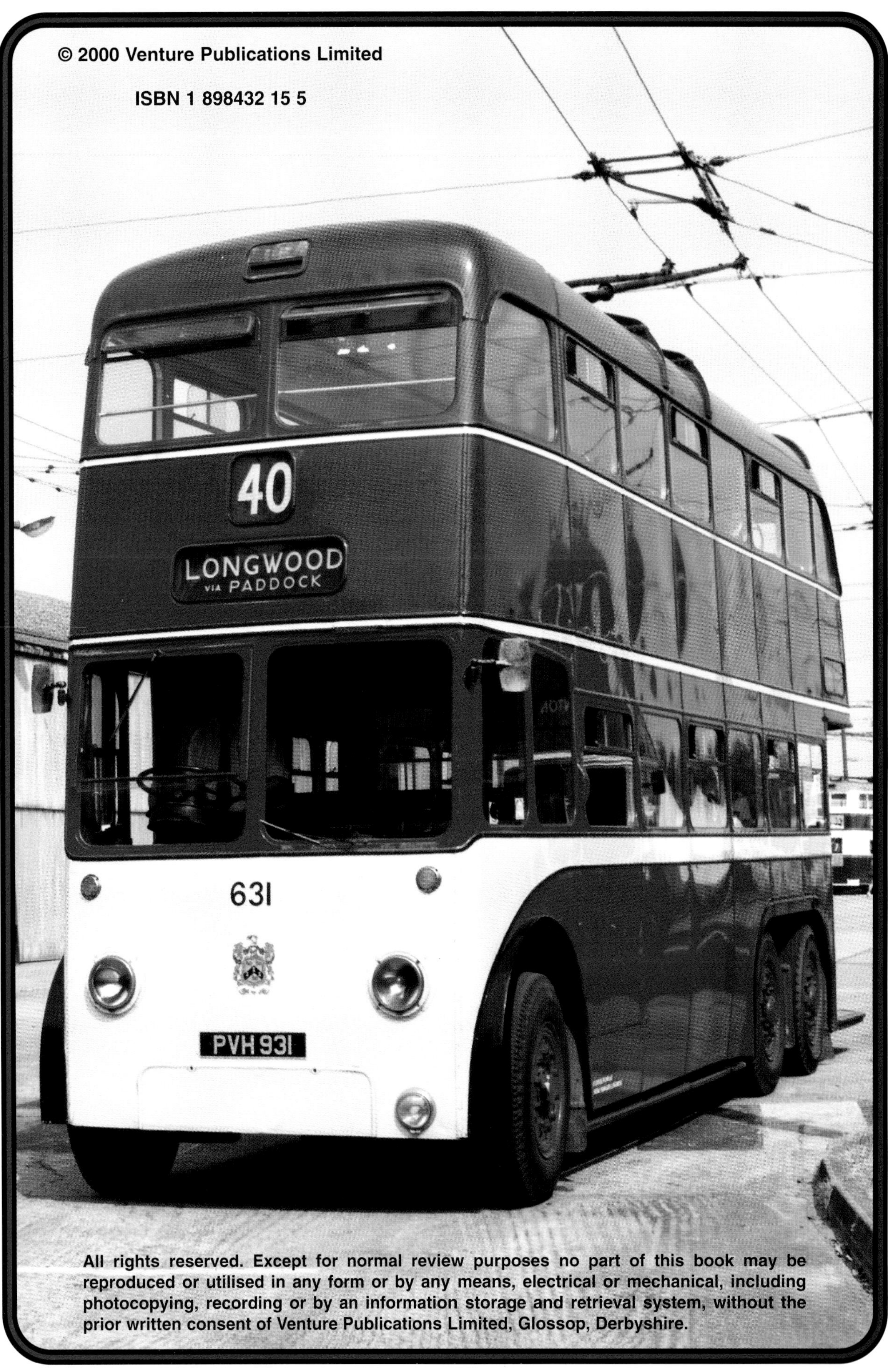

East Lancashire Coachbuilders

Harry Postlethwaite

Table of Contents

Foreword

Having been employed by East Lancashire Coachbuilders for the past forty years, and having witnessed monumental changes in the manufacturing and operational sides of our public transport services in the United Kingdom, I feel it is time that the bus industry should be able to share in our Company's past, and indeed its future, and the changes that have taken place over the years.

Venture Publications kindly agreed to print our story. Harry Postlethwaite was tasked with coordinating information from various sources to collate the history of East Lancashire Coachbuilders. The following chapters trace the story of East Lancs from conception to the new Millennium.

I would personally like to thank Harry for his efforts over the twelve months he has spent scouring our archives and interviewing numerous employees past and present. I would also pay special thanks to George Alcock and John Bufton along with Joe Hutt, all three of whom you will read about in the following pages.

Final thanks go to our customers, without whom there would be no history. I sincerely hope every reader derives as much enjoyment from this book as I have had working for East Lancs over the past forty years. Here's to the next forty!

Philip Hilton
Deputy Managing Director
East Lancashire Coachbuilders Limited

There are many old East Lancashire vehicles to be seen flying the flag for the Company in the ranks of the preservation movement. The Aldershot & District Dennis Lance, opposite, dates from 1948 whilst the Burnley Colne & Nelson Leyland above is a 1967 model. The Huddersfield trolleybus seen on page 2 is one of many built by East Lancashire Coachbuilders, several survivors being located at the Sandtoft Trolleybus Museum.

Preface

My first recollection of East Lancashire Coachbuilders goes back to around 1940 when, as a six years old already taking a great interest in the local bus scene in Whitehaven, I noticed that two of the four Leyland TD5s, delivered to Cumberland Motor Services in 1939, were quite different from the others. Further investigation revealed that two had bodies built by Massey Brothers and the other two had bodies built by East Lancashire Coachbuilders. I then noticed that some of the Leyland TD1s in the fleet carried flywheel cover plates embossed with the name East Lancashire Coachbuilders Ltd, Blackburn. I assumed, wrongly as it happened, that they too had been bodied by the Blackburn firm and it was many years later that I discovered that they had been re-built by East Lancashire Coachbuilders. In 1941 five further East Lancashire bodies arrived in the fleet on Leyland TD7 chassis and they were the last bodies to be supplied to Cumberland by East Lancashire but my interest in the firm continued.

For fifteen years I lived on the north side of Manchester and renewed acquaintance with the Company through the bodies supplied to Rochdale Corporation who were joint operators with Manchester on the local 17 service. Further afield I took great interest in the fleets of the Lancashire Municipals, many of whom had East Lancashire-bodied vehicles. Later, on the other side of Manchester, Stockport turned to East Lancashire and standardised on the make for all their buses, mostly on Leyland PD2 and PD3 chassis. Shortly after I moved to Blackpool the local undertaking turned to East Lancashire for their first and subsequent bodies on Atlantean chassis, turning again to the Company when new trams were required.

When John Senior mentioned to me that he believed there was the possibility of publishing a book on East Lancashire Coachbuilders, I had little hesitation in volunteering for the job as author. However, a book such as this could not have been written on personal recollections alone, no matter how vivid those memories may have been, and I am indeed grateful to all who have assisted in any way.

Philip Hilton gave the project the green light and has given of his time in the midst of a heavy work load to provide information from his 40 years with the Company. George Alcock, son of one of the founders, has provided information and photographs whilst John Bufton, who commenced work with the Company in 1941, has provided invaluable information and memories. There has also been assistance from Chris Clarke, Bernard Hunt, Tony Newbould, John Horn and Joe Hutt.

Outside the Company there has been help from many directions. John Senior and Bob Rowe from Venture Publications have been invaluable as has John Banks in translating my text into a book. Jeff Johnson, who has taken an interest in East Lancashire Coachbuilders for many years, has provided information and read the text. There has been some difficulty in compiling a full and accurate body list due mainly to records having been lost in the works fire, about which you will read. However, Bob Smith has made available his detailed records as have Jeff Johnson and Mike Sutcliffe and reference has also been made to the records of the PSV Circle. These have all been combined and presented in a more compact form to save space. Without these records the book would have been very much the poorer.

Roy Marshall provided information from his many years in the industry whilst Brian Pritchard and Mark Bailey have both read the text and made useful suggestions. Howard Talbot, the photographer, assisted in providing copies of photographs taken by himself and by his father. Geoff Lumb and Eric Ogden provided items from their archives and cuttings which clarified dates and other details. The staff at Companies House were very helpful in providing information to verify the original formation and shareholdings. Acknowledgement is also gratefully made to other publications consulted including Motor Transport Yearbook, Who's Who in the Motor Industry, Who Owns Whom, Coach and Bus Week, Buses Magazine, Bus Fayre, Diesel Railway Traction and the excellent fleetbooks published by British Bus Publishing. Thanks also to the many photographers who have contributed and who are acknowledged individually elsewhere and to those photographers whose prints are not marked with their name but have been used.

Harry Postlethwaite.
Blackpool, March 2000.

Photo Credits

G.Alcock Collection - 15 (upper) 36 (upper) 42 (top) 57 60 (top left) 62 63 91 (upper) 132.
Stephen Armstrong - 66 (lower).
Author - 53 (lower left) 55 (lower right) 60 (all except top left & bottom right) 65 69 73 86 88 89 94 95 96 (upper) 97 98 (bottom) 99 (bottom) 101 (top & centre) 104 108 113 (except bottom right) 114 (top) 115 (bottom) 118 (top right & centre left) 119 (upper & lower centre) Dustjacket flap.
Author's Collection - 22 (upper) 30 (bottom) 51 (top).
Mark Bailey - 60 (bottom right) 70 71 72 76 80 (lower) 81 (lower) 85 103 (upper) 105 111 (lower) 113 (bottom right) 114 (centre) 115 (top left & centre) 118 (top left) 120 (bottom).
John Banks - 96 (lower) 98 (top & centre) 106 (upper) 107 (top left & right) Dustjacket flap.
John Barley - 120 (centre).
David Barrow - 81 (upper) 82 121 122 (lower) 133 135 (lower).
Bus & Coach Buyer - 107 (bottom) 127 (centre).
R.C.Davis - 17 33 (lower right) 107 (centre left).
Denis Clarke - 28 29 30 (centre) 31 (lower) 32 (upper left) 35 (centre & lower) 38 (upper right) 39 (centre) 41 (centre).
David Cole - 99 (top & centre) 106 (lower) 107 (centre right) 111 (upper) 114 (bottom) 115 (top right) 116 (bottom) 117 (upper) 118 (centre right) Dustjacket flap.
Bob Downham - 34 (lower) 35 (top) 36 (lower) 38 (left) 40 (upper left & right) 42 (centre & bottom) 44 45 47 49 51 (centre) 52 53 (lower right) 54 55 (lower left) 56 (upper) 77 103 (lower).

East Lancashire Coachbuilders - 11 13 14 18 (upper) 21 (top & centre) 22 (lower) 26 27 (top & bottom) 34 (upper) 37 38 (lower right) 39 (top & bottom) 40 (lower) 41 (bottom) 46 50 51 (bottom) 53 (upper) 55 (upper) 56 (lower) 67 68 78 79 80 (upper) 84 90 91 (lower) 92 (bottom) 93 101 (bottom) 110 112 122 (upper) 128 131 134 135 (upper) Front cover/rear cover (lower).
Philip Higgs - 66 (upper).
Jeff Johnson - 116 (top left & right) 118 (bottom left) 119 (bottom).
Jeff Johnson Collection - 116 (centre) 119 (top).
Roy Marshall - 15 (lower) 16 20 23 25 27 (centre) 33 (lower left) 41 (top).
Roy Marshall Collection - 12 24 (upper).
Bob Rowe - 120 (top).
John Senior - 2 4 5 6 7 8 9 10 24 (lower) 100 102 109 123 (upper) 160 Dustjacket flap and Rear Cover (upper).
Senior Transport Archive - 18 (lower) 21 (bottom) 30 (top).
Ken Swallow - 31 (upper) 32 (except upper left) 33 (upper left & right).
Howard Talbot - 92 (top & centre).
David Toy - 118 (bottom right).
Tony Wilson - 117 (lower) 123 (lower) 124 125 126 127 (top).
Russell Young - 1 127 (bottom).

Photographs from the East Lancashire Coachbuilders Collection were taken by Wally and Howard Talbot, Blackburn; David Barrow, Bury; David Bennett, Brighton; Norman Thompson, Taunton; DSB, Glasgow and London Transport.

Stockport operated many East Lancashire-bodied buses and had the distinction of placing in service the last rear-entrance double-decker in Britain. One of a batch similar to this example, it is today to be found, superbly restored, in the Manchester Museum of Transport.

1 IN THE BEGINNING

Barton and Danson were coachbuilders based in Orrell near Wigan, and the Danson of the company was the father of George Danson who later became a Director in the reconstituted East Lancashire Coachbuilders company in 1938. George is seen here, without hat or cap, alongside the doorway of this Leyland C7 model registered TD 296. It was supplied to Blue Line of Great Eccleston in 1925.

For many people the County of Lancashire, particularly in the historical context, is synonymous with the cotton industry and 'dark satanic mills'. Much of this industry is no longer in evidence and since local government reorganisation in 1974 the county has become largely rural with attractive rivers, canals, woodland and villages together with a number of important towns with

This view of TD 296 shows that it was No. 5 in the fleet. Note the 'Built by Barton & Danson' plate which was proudly placed alongside the bus.

The first buses produced by the reconstituted East Lancashire Coachbuilders in 1938 comprised a batch of 10 on Leyland TD5 chassis for Bolton Corporation. One of these, thought to be No. 148, is seen on completion. The similarlty of style to current Massey Brothers double-deckers is evident.

considerable character and thriving modern industries. This book is centred on such a town - Blackburn.

For those involved in the transport industry, the county will long be remembered for its connection with the heavy vehicle industry. The once mighty Leyland Motors had its origins in the county and most of its activities took place in the small town of Leyland, just south of Preston. Seddon Vehicles commenced in Oldham and Crossley Motors in Manchester, whilst Gardner made their famous diesel engines at Patricroft, in the days when all of these places were in Lancashire. Atkinson Lorries manufactured lorry and bus chassis in Walton le Dale on the outskirts of Preston. There were also major body building organisations in the county. These included H V Burlingham of Blackpool, later taken over by Duple, another firm which no longer exists. In Wigan there was Northern Counties Motor and Engineering Company Limited and Massey Brothers both manufacturing bus bodies. In addition to a host of smaller manufacturers there was and still is East Lancashire Coachbuilders of Blackburn, the subject of this book. In 1967 Massey Brothers was taken over by Northern Counties and with the local government reorganisation of 1974, Wigan found itself out of Lancashire and in the Metropolitan County of Greater Manchester. In 1999 Northern Counties was renamed Plaxton-Wigan.

The nett result of all this is that East Lancashire Coachbuilders is now the only major bus body building firm in the County of Lancashire where once there were so many organisations connected with the manufacture of buses. The Company has not only survived but has, in recent years, expanded to the extent that a move to more modern premises in a prominent position on the outskirts of Blackburn became necessary, but more of this later.

The name East Lancashire Coachbuilders was first registered on 27 October 1934, the registration number being 293485. The directors were Mr Walter Smith, Yarn Agent, 18 Aldwych Place, Blackburn; Mr John Johnson, Coachbuilder, 22 Bank Hey Lane, Blackburn; Mr Edward Ainsworth Eastwood, Cabinet Maker, 390 Whalley New Road, Blackburn and Mr William George Bell, Coachbuilder, 15 Whalley Old Road, Blackburn.

The share capital was £500 and there was a loan from Walter Smith in the sum of £1180. The

Chester Corporation received two East Lancashire-bodied AEC Regents in 1938, numbered 29 and 30. The bodies were very similar in outline to those supplied to Bolton, but of five- bay construction. These were the only new bodies supplied by East Lancashire to Chester who remained faithful to Massey Brothers for most of their subsequent orders until such time as Massey products were no longer available. Many years later, second hand examples of East Lancashire-bodied Dennis Dominators were acquired.

Above: The lower saloon of Chester No. 29 shows the lighting fittings mounted on the window pillars and typical ceiling straps for standing passengers. The 'East Lancashire Coachbuilders' cast plate on the flywheel cover is just visible whilst in the bottom right hand corner is the transfer used by the Company for many years.

Below: Rotherham Corporation Transport was to become a major customer and the first bodies supplied were nine centre entrance single-deckers on Bristol L5G chassis in 1939. Number 106 is shown when new and the inclusion of a roof mounted luggage rack can be seen.

Rotherham also placed orders for single-deck trolley bus bodies, the first to be built by East Lancashire Coachbuilders and No. 26 on Guy BTX chassis supplied in 1939 is shown when new.

Articles of Association quote the business activity as:-

"To carry on business as coach and carriage builders, body builders, tyre manufacturers and repairers, motor, mechanical and general engineers, electricians, fitters, tube makers, vulcanisers, annealers, enamellers, electro-platers, painters, varnishers, upholsterers, wood and timber merchants and joiners." A whole host of other activities, directly or indirectly associated with the motor industry, are quoted.

The first Directors' Report and Profit and Loss Account on 29th June 1935 covered the first thirty five weeks of trading and showed a loss of £83 16s 9d. Prior to the formation of East Lancashire Coachbuilders, Walter Smith had operated East Lancashire Motors from premises on the opposite side of Whalley New Road to Brookhouse Mill.

The coachbuilding business was mainly concerned at this time with lorries and vans, whilst lorry cabs were built for Walker Brothers of Wigan, but some coachbuilding work was also undertaken. Generally during the winter months the work would be on lorries and vans but as the spring months approached and coach operators prepared for the coming season, orders for coach bodies would be received. Coach bodies were supplied to Weardens of Blackburn, Ribblesdale of Blackburn and Battersbys of Morecambe, a firm which is still operating at the time

The then largest single order to date, for 20 bodies, and the first for double-deck trolleybus bodies was supplied to Kingston upon Hull Corporation Transport in 1939/40. This view shows the characteristic East Lancashire treatment of the rear.

of writing. There is also evidence of two Albions being bodied for East Lancashire Motors in 1934 and a Bedford WTB for T Helliwell and Sons, Nelson in 1935.

Mr Eastwood resigned in December 1935 and Messrs Johnson and Bell resigned in August 1937, Mr Bell being replaced by Lilian Smith, the wife of Walter Smith.

Mr Joe Hutt joined the Company as an apprentice coachbuilder at the beginning of 1936 and was employee number 18. In late 1999 he still recalled working in part of Brookhouse Mill at that time under the supervision of Messrs Johnson and Bell. Mr Bell's parents lived in a house next to Brookhouse Mill and his mother was employed to brew the tea. Joe Hutt recalls that the tea never tasted very good and on one occasion he was sent by Mr Smith to ask Mrs Bell to brew a pot of tea for some visitors. It was then that he discovered the reason for the poor taste, for the tea was stewed! Billy Bell and John Johnson were both coachbuilders but Walter Smith was not and the reaction of the work force to this was that every time Walter Smith entered the workshop the men downed tools and stopped work until he departed.

During this period the Company had a contract with Atkinson Lorries of Walton le Dale, Preston to build cabs and lorry bodies. A local firm Scales Funeral Service had a Rolls Royce with a timber body and this body was stripped off and replaced by a new hearse body. Another 'one off' was the building of a car body on a Bentley chassis for the son of a local millowner, the design being based on that of a new Standard car which Walter Smith had recently purchased. Following the resignation of Messrs Johnson and Bell, Joe Hutt worked under the supervision of a Mr Pickard who told him that he should be able to produce three flat back wagons in a week but the most he ever achieved was two and a half.

At this time, Alfred Alcock and George Danson worked for Massey Brothers. Mr Alcock, who had previously worked for Northern Counties, was the Designer and General Manager whilst Mr Danson was the Works Foreman. Alfred Alcock had received his further education at Manchester College of Technology whilst living at Heaton Mersey, Stockport and in the 1919 City and Guilds of London Institute examination in Road Carriage Building (Final) was awarded the 2nd Prize of £2 10s 0d. and the Silver Medal. A copy of the examination paper is reproduced in the Appendices.

Above: **Kingston upon Hull No. 48 is shown on tilt test at the works. Alfred Alcock, wearing the trilby hat which he never removed, even when working at his drawing board, stands at the left of the trolleybus.**

Below: **The first bodies supplied to the local municipal operator in Blackburn were two on AEC Regent chassis supplied in 1939 and numbered 54/5. Number 54 is parked at the town's bus station, adjacent to the railway station, on 10th June 1951. The ornate lining out of the livery is a reminder of times past.**

Whilst with Massey Brothers he patented a staircase which became known as the Alcock Staircase and which was unusual in being fitted at the front nearside of the bus ascending through the front bulkhead and partly over the bonnet. The

Above left: **In 1940 Darlington Corporation Transport received four single-deck trolleybus bodies on Leyland TB5 chassis and one of these, No. 65, is shown in service in the town on 14th April 1952.**

Above right: **A repeat order calling for eight single deck trolleybus bodies on Sunbeam chassis was delivered to Rotherham in 1940 and 1941. One of these, No. 73, is shown in service in Effingham Street on 8th May 1949.**

staircase was featured on a Tilling-Stevens vehicle supplied to Merseyside Touring Company in 1929 and also on an AEC Regent supplied to Bury Corporation in 1931. It may well have been fitted to four dual-doorway Massey-bodied Leyland TD1s supplied to Bury in 1930. Similar staircases were provided on two Massey-bodied AEC Renowns supplied to Warrington Corporation in 1930.

George Danson gained his training and experience in the coachbuilding industry with the family firm of Barton and Danson, of Orrell, Wigan and had also spent some time with H V Burlingham of Blackpool and later with Crossley Motors.

Alfred Alcock, as Massey's designer, wanted to produce steel framed bodies but Massey Brothers would not agree and arising from this he and George Danson decided to form their own company for the manufacture of bus bodywork. Mr Danson borrowed money from his father and they originally intended to locate the new business in Bolton thinking that it was close enough to Wigan to enable them to attract labour from there. However, some difficulty was encountered in finding premises which they could afford and they reached agreement with Walter Smith, of East Lancashire Coachbuilders, to join him in his business. Mr Smith had the premises for he owned Brookhouse Mill, part of which he was using for coachbuilding at that time. Messrs Alcock and Danson had the technical expertise for bus body manufacture, including double-deckers, and with effect from 9th May 1938, the Company was reconstituted with the following directors:-

Mr Walter Smith, Company Secretary, Oakfield, Billinge End Road, Blackburn; Mrs Lilian Smith, Oakfield, Billinge End Road, Blackburn; Mr Alfred Marsden Alcock, Manager, 2 Sycamore Road, Blackburn; Mr George Danson, Works Manager, 28 Furness Avenue, Little Harwood, Blackburn. The Share Capital was increased to £6000 of which £5000 was issued (1939 figure). Lilian Smith resigned in March 1943.

The reconstituted Company was based at Brookhouse Mill where it was to remain until September 1994. The mill was thought to be the oldest weaving mill in Lancashire and when they moved into it, alternate vertical pillars of the structure were removed in order to provide space to manoeuvre vehicles. It had originally belonged to Lord Hornby and a plaque bearing his crest was on the fascia of the building. When rebuilding work was undertaken following the fire of 1970, it had been intended to incorporate this crest in a wall of the new building but unfortunately it disappeared overnight.

It was decided that the reconstituted Company would concentrate on the manufacture of bus bodywork. Alfred Alcock assumed the dual role of Designer and Sales Manager, spending part of his time in the drawing office and the remainder out of the works visiting customers and prospective customers. George Danson became Works Manager and spent most of his time in the works. Other staff who transferred with them from Massey Brothers included Jack Thompson who became Fitting Shop foreman, Gerry Cunliffe who became Sheet Metal Shop foreman and panel beater Harold Disley. In view of the founders' previous employment with Massey Brothers, it is perhaps not surprising that early orders were received from operators who had experience of Massey Brothers bodywork. Among these was Bolton Corporation Transport Department who ordered ten double-deck highbridge bodies for fitting to Leyland TD5 chassis. These were of six-bay construction with sloping front and well-rounded rear roof dome bearing, not surprisingly, some resemblance to the current Massey Brothers designs. Delivery of this, the first order for new bodies, was completed in November 1938.

In the meantime further orders were received, one from Chester Corporation for two highbridge bodies for AEC Regent chassis and the other from Leigh Corporation for two lowbridge bodies (where the upper-deck gangway protruded into the lower saloon to reduce the overall height) for Leyland TD5 chassis. The bodies for Leigh were to a new design with outswept skirt panels and were the first lowbridge examples to be built by the Company.

Register of Directors or Managers

Of East Lancashire Coachbuilders Limited,

And of any changes therein.

No. 9a. Shaw & Sons Ltd., Fetter Lane, E.C.4. Ph.32 82809 (8)

(1) †The present Christian Name or Names and Surname	(2) ‡Any former Christian Name or Names or Surname	(3) Nationality	(4) Nationality of Origin (if other than the present Nationality)	Date of Birth	(5) Usual Residential Address	(6) ‖Other Business Occupation (if any). If none, state so	(7) Date of Appointment	(8) Changes *In the case of a new Director the words "in place of—" should be placed against his name and the word "deceased" or "resigned" against the name of the former Director. The date upon which a Director ceases to act should be shown in this column.
Walter Smith.		British			18 Aldwych Place. Blackburn	Yarn Agent.	1934 Oct 27th	Deceased 15th January 1958
Edward Ainsworth Eastwood.		British			390 Whalley New Road Blackburn.	Cabinet Maker.	-Do-	Resigned 13th December 19[illegible]
John Johnson		British			22 Bank Hey Lane Blackburn	Coachbuilder	-Do-	Resigned 7th August 1937
William George Bell.		British			15 Whalley Old Road Blackburn	Coachbuilder.	-Do-	Resigned 7th August 1937
Lilian Smith		British			Oakfield Billinge End Rd Blackburn		1937 August 7	(Notice of Change of Directors filed 29/12) in place of W.G. Bell. (Notice of Change of Directors filed [illegible]
Alfred Marsden Alcock	–	British	–	[illegible]	281 Whalley Old Road Little Harwood Blackburn; ~~2 Sycamore Rd Blackburn~~	Manager.	1938. May 9th	Resigned 31 Dec 1966. Additional. Resigned Sept 1984 (Notice of Change Directors filed May 31st 19[illegible])
George Danson	–	British	–		~~30 Fortefford St Blackburn~~	Work Manager	May 9th	Additional

Above: **This extract from the Director's Register shows that when the Company was reconstituted in May 1938 Alfred Alcock, who was described as Manager, and George Danson who was described as Works Manager, became Directors. At this stage the former owned 40% of the shares of the Company and the latter owned 10%. This was increased to 20% in 1943 following the reignation of Lilian Smith and additional shares, some from Walter Smith being transferred to George Danson. The Directors of the Company and their shareholdings were then to remain unchanged until the death of Walter Smith in 1958, see Chapter 3.**

Below: **Although supplied in the second half of 1941, well into the wartime era, the five bodies on Leyland TD7 chassis for Cumberland Motor Services were entirely to peacetime standards with regard to external appearance and interior finish. Number 164, the first of the batch is shown parked at Whitehaven in the postwar period. A notable feature is the rearward sloping windscreen, not repeated on other East Lancashire bodies of this period. It is unlikely to have been specified by the operator as the five bodies received from Massey Brothers at the same time did not have this feature.**

Burnley Colne and Nelson Transport had, at this time, some English Electric-bodied Leyland TD3s the bodies of which had deteriorated and new lower decks were provided by East Lancashire. Similarly Rotherham Corporation had experienced problems with some Cravens bodies and new frames were supplied for these.

Cumberland Motor Services Ltd had been a regular customer of Massey Brothers since 1923 and between December 1938 and April 1939 sent a total of fifteen 1931 Leyland-bodied TD1 double-deckers to East Lancashire for rebuilding and refurbishment. This work included the fitting of half drop opening windows, in place of the full drop type fitted when the vehicles were new, but the original 'piano front' outline was retained. The author recalls that embossed flywheel covers bearing the East Lancashire Coachbuilders name were fitted to these buses. In 1939 Cumberland split its body order for fitting to Leyland TD5 chassis between East Lancashire Coachbuilders and Massey Brothers, receiving two from each supplier. Those from East Lancashire were very similar to the bodies supplied to Leigh but with the front and rear destination apertures protruding slightly from the body outline.

Other 1939 orders were from Rotherham, Kingston upon Hull and the local Blackburn Corporation Transport Department. The two double-deck bodies on AEC Regent chassis for Blackburn bore considerable resemblance to Cravens bodies and the reason for this was that Len Barradell had moved from Cravens to East Lancashire Coachbuilders as a draughtsman, later becoming Chief Draughtsman. The order from Rotherham was for single-deckers, the first to be built by the Company, and comprised nine on Bristol L5G chassis and eight trolleybuses, four on Guy BTX chassis and four on AEC 664T chassis. These were also the first trolleybus bodies built by the Company. The order for Kingston upon Hull was the largest order received to that date and also the first for double-deck trolleybus bodies, a total of twenty being supplied on Leyland TB7 chassis.

The willingness of the Company to build what the customer wanted was established at an early stage in its history. This AEC Regent *(above)*, one of seven supplied to Cardiff Corporation in 1940, was virtually a Northern Counties design as supplied by that concern to Cardiff, Stalybridge Joint Board and others, including Birkenhead as illustrated *(below)*. The fact that one of the new East Lancashire directors had earlier worked for Northern Counties might also be considered significant.

Rotherham Corporation Transport became a regular customer for many years and in the early days had purchased a large quantity of teak for the framing of trolleybus bodies and stored this at the East Lancashire works. The connection with Rotherham had been established during the First World War when Alfred Alcock was a motor cycle rider in the Royal Engineers and became friendly with T P Sykes who was similarly employed and who later became General Manager at Rotherham.

The fact that Brookhouse Mill had a low roof dictated the method of production for double-deckers in that the lower and upper saloons were built separately and joined together later. One section of the mill had the roof raised so that it could accommodate eight complete double-deckers. This method of construction was continued until the introduction of the Alusuisse system. It was however a practice that was normal in the industry at that time and was followed by others including Leyland Motors Ltd.

The bodies for Bolton were timber framed but after this steel framing was adopted though, initially, timber framing was used for trolleybuses, there being a reluctance to use steel for trolleybus bodies for electrical safety reasons. However, the vertical timber framing sections were grooved to take a tee shaped steel section in order to add strength. The steel framing comprised a tee section vertical member used in conjunction with angle section horizontal rails. The vertical tee was in fact the 'Brake Shoe Tee' section as manufactured for the brake shoes of motor cars and because of its extensive use for this purpose it could be obtained at a competitive price. Initially and for many years timber inserts were used to accept wood screws for the fixing of panels and these inserts were held in a supplementary folded sheet steel section rivetted to the main tee section. Later the wood screws were superceded by pop rivets and an alternative sheet steel folded section was rivetted to the main tee section to accept these. Initially the framing of upper saloons was also in steel but lighter angle sections were used for the horizontal rails. Those for the upper saloon were 1.25" x 1.25" x 14 gauge and those for the lower saloon 1.5" x 1.5" x 0.125". Aluminium alloy was later adopted for the upper saloon framework.

The Company carried out its own in-house tilt testing of vehicles from early days until 1962. Company employees would watch the proceedure with interest but the directors normally arranged for this to be carried out after 5pm so that if the employees did watch they did so in their own time!

Demarcation lines between trades were strictly observed in the early days and for many years to come. For instance, if a body builder was fitting a ceiling panel to a bus, a sheet metal worker would be standing by in case it was necessary to trim the panel with sheet metal cutters. There were up to seven trade unions active in the works, each protecting the interests of its members.

Complete information relating to early body numbers is not available but there was a consecutive series which, as far as buses are concerned, terminated with the number 2978, allocated in June 1945 to Plymouth Corporation. This was No. 208, a 1938 Leyland TD5c with Weymann body, completed by Mumford, and rebuilt by East Lancashire Coachbuilders at that time. However the series extended to 2989 to cover a railcar cab and nine crane cabs all built for Walker Brothers of Wigan, the last of the crane cabs being delivered in February 1946. A new series commenced at 4001, this number being allocated to St Helens Corporation No. 71, a Leyland TD7c rebuilt in December 1945 following a fire. Some records do show this body number allocated to Cardiff CBO 702 but the same records also show body number 2919 allocated to this vehicle. A summary of the various body numbering systems is included in the Appendices at the back of this book.

An important character in the works for many years was Jim Broad. In theory he would have been classed as 'unskilled' but he tended to the coke fired boilers, kept the place clean and tidy, opened up in the morning, locked up at the end of the day and walked round the site at weekends just to make sure that everything was in order. A very valuable type of employee for any organisation.

There was very limited heating in the works in the early days and empty five-gallon paint drums with holes in the side would be filled with coke and used as braziers next to the work benches to provide additional heating.

The advent of the second world war in 1939 could have had a serious detrimental effect on the development of a new company but in fact the reverse was the case as we shall see in Chapter 2.

2 WARTIME

The Second World War was declared on 3rd September 1939 and the effect on bus services was more or less immediate, brought about largely by restrictions on the supply of fuel. The effect on vehicle supply was not as dramatic and the changes which were to come took some time to evolve. Initially manufacturers delivered vehicles which had been ordered prior to the outbreak of hostilities and these were to peacetime standards. The full story of buses in wartime is told in the book *The Best of British Buses No.8 - Utilities* by Alan Townsin published by Transport Publishing Company.

As far as East Lancashire Coachbuilders was concerned, it continued to deliver vehicles to peacetime standards in the early years of the war. Cardiff Corporation Transport was to become a major customer in years to come and their first order, calling for seven double-deck bodies on AEC Regent chassis was delivered in 1940. These were unusual in being produced to a design previously supplied to Cardiff by Northern Counties and incorporating wide corner pillars to the front of the upper saloon. Cumberland Motor Services was purchasing secondhand double-deckers at this time to cater for an increased demand brought about by the war effort and sent four Leyland TD1s with Leyland bodies to East Lancashire Coachbuilders for rebuilding. A repeat order was received from Rotherham again calling for nine single-deck bodies on Bristol L5G chassis and eight single-deck trolleybus bodies on Sunbeam MS2C chassis. New customers were Darlington Corporation Transport for four single-deck trolleybus bodies on Leyland TB5 chassis and Barrow in Furness Corporation Transport for whom three bodies were provided on Leyland TD7 chassis. These were unusual in being built to the design of English Electric Company Ltd who had previously supplied bodies to Barrow. This arose because in the early days of the war English Electric was instructed to cease building buses and concentrate on the war effort. Partially completed vehicles were taken to East Lancashire Coachbuilders for completion. At the time someone in English Electric discovered that there was one top deck which did not have a bottom deck to go with it. The outcome of this situation is not clear and it may be that East Lancashire Coachbuilders provided a bottom deck for it. Someone certainly did!

The author has clear memories of the batch of five lowbridge vehicles on Leyland TD7 chassis delivered to Cumberland Motor Services Ltd between July and October 1941. They were entirely to peacetime specification being attractive and well finished vehicles, very much a development of the body style provided to the same operator in 1939. Other bodies produced at this time on new chassis were single-deckers on Bristol L5G chassis for Aberdare Urban District Council, Caledonian Omnibus Company, and yet more for Rotherham. There were also two lowbridge bodies for Brown, Tunstall, on reconditioned AEC Regent chassis. The Company was to become deeply involved in this sphere of work in the immediate future.

Birkenhead No. 206, a 1935-built Leyland TD3 was extensively damaged during an air raid and was provided with a new East Lancashire body in 1942. It has a mix of styles, retaining the D shaped windows of the lower saloon as supplied on bodies to Leigh, Chester and Cardiff which followed Northern Counties design, but with the now distinctive East Lancashire front dome treatment.

Right: **The prewar East Lancashire lowbridge body design featured heavily rounded top corners to the front domes as shown on this example on a Leyland chassis for the Cumberland fleet.**

The period which followed this is often referred to as the era of the 'unfrozen' vehicle. The simple explanation to it is that restrictions had been placed by the Government on the supply of new vehicles with the result that manufacturers found themselves with stocks of materials which they could not use, these having been 'frozen' by Government Regulation. It was then realised that buses were still required to get people to work, many of whom had been directed into the war effort and who had to cover greater distances than before. The 'frozen' material stocks were 'unfrozen' thus and manufacturers were allowed to build vehicles from materials in stock - hence the term 'unfrozen vehicles'. Generally speaking vehicles built under this dispensation were to the manufacturers' prewar outline but often with a simplified interior finish, a common effect being the omission of interior lining-panels.

The vehicles built under this scheme were allocated by the Ministry of War Transport and the result was that many operators received vehicles which were non-standard in their fleets. The same principles were later applied to the allocation of the utility vehicles which followed, and about which more will be said shortly.

The Government easing of restrictions resulted in some 373 double-deck chassis being unfrozen, of AEC, Bristol and Leyland makes, but the great majority - nearly 200 - were Leyland TD7s. Whilst other body makers were allocated two or even all three of the available chassis types ELCB seemed favoured by only being allocated Leylands. Thirteen TD7s were sent to Blackburn and of these three were fitted with highbridge bodies clearly to East Lancashire's prewar design and finish. Since all bodybuilders were allowed to use up stocks of components previously 'frozen' this is unremarkable.

Seven unfrozen Leyland TD7 chassis were bodied by East Lancashire with lowbridge bodywork and this example *(above)* for Wigan - the only body ever supplied by the Company - was clearly a Leyland derived product, almost certainly based on Leyland frames. Whilst the wartime body differed from the Leyland product in detail finish the overall shape was unmistakeable. A true Leyland body for the same operator, in this case a postwar model, is shown *(below)* for comparison.

Much more interesting were the other ten, fitted with lowbridge bodywork of a type clearly very different from the earlier ELCB design as supplied to Leigh and Cumberland.

Above: Lancaster No. 41, later renumbered 298, was a Leyland TD7 supplied to Lancaster in 1942 under the wartime allocation system. The Lancaster fleet was then mainly Daimler and when three Daimlers were allocated to the mainly Leyland fleet of Cumberland in 1943, discussion took place regarding a possible exchange, though nothing materialised. It may be that Lancaster took a look at the wartime Brush bodies on the Cumberland Daimlers and decided to stick with their East Lancashire bodied Leyland. It is shown at Lancaster bus station in the postwar period. It could never have been imagined, in those days, that in years to come Lancaster would be covered by the Cumberland operation.

Below: Ribble received two East Lancashire bodied-Leyland TD7s in 1942 numbered 2388/9. One of them is shown when new before entering service. The design may have been Ribble's own: similar bodies were supplied by Roe and ECW.

Examination of the photographs accompanying this chapter will show just how similar this lowbridge body was to that supplied by Leyland to its customers. The Wigan vehicle is probably the best example. The body design is pure Leyland of the type introduced by that Company at the 1937 Commercial Motor Show in November of that year. It is inconceivable that ELCB would have had the time or resources to design a body for these ten unfrozen chassis, especially when they were going to five different operators, three of whom had never previously bought ELCB products. It therefore seems most likely that ELCB was allocated - or purchased - parts from Leyland when the unfrozen TD7 chassis were diverted to its works.

Leyland would undoubtedly have been left with stocks of part-manufactured components when its body building programme was suddenly curtailed and whilst it is known that some components went to the Alexander concern for incorporation into its wartime bodies it now seems clear that both Alexander and East Lancashire adopted Leyland's lowbridge body design 'for the duration'. At least one chassis was sent to Falkirk with a skeleton frame, and it seems that another one at least went to the Blackburn factory. Whether ELCB then borrowed Leyland's tools, or had purchased sufficient parts to last it for some time, or had some arrangement with Alexanders is not at present clear but the outcome is there to be seen through the photographs.

Whilst Alexanders were obliged to fit the prescribed angular wartime domes to the Leyland frames East Lancashire were able to continue fitting domes of the 1938 Leyland design as recorded elsewhere in this narrative.

It has long been a matter of conjecture as to how or why ELCB managed to avoid building buses to the wartime specification and whilst conclusive proof still eludes the researchers it would appear that the reasons stemmed partly from ELCB's method of construction - metal instead of wooden framing as specified in the utility body - but also from the combination of metal framing techniques and availability of Leyland frames. Perhaps its two panel beaters were also exempt from war service for some reason? It should be noted that Northern Counties, who also used metal framing, were given dispensation to build their utility bodies with metal instead of wooden framing. East Lancashire's dispensation was not to build utilities at all.

It is often said that it is an ill wind which blows no good and this saying can certainly be applied to the Company in the wartime situation. As previously mentioned operators bought vehicles from manufacturers who could supply or to whom they were directed by the Ministry of War Transport. Under this arrangement double-deck bodies were supplied to the South of England for two large company operators, Aldershot and District Traction Company and Southdown Motor Services and to one municipal operator, Eastbourne Corporation, all of whom placed substantial orders with the Company in the postwar period. Nearer to home one-off double-deck bodies were supplied to Lancaster and Warrington Corporations on Leyland TD7 chassis and both operators became regular postwar customers.

Other unfrozen vehicles were supplied by East Lancashire Coachbuilders on Leyland TD7 chassis to Ribble Motor Services, Barrow Corporation, Wigan Corporation, Western SMT and Lancashire United Transport, the only vehicles ever supplied to this local operator. Those bodies were reliable and long-lived, but despite that no further orders were received from Wigan Corporation. With two major bodybuilding organisations established in the town that is perhaps not surprising.

It was further realised that new buses would be required during the wartime period and a specification was drawn up by the Ministry of Supply, Ministry of War Transport and the National Federation of Vehicle Trades and Operators Joint Technical and Advisory Committee.

The aim was to produce a no-frills vehicle without the use of scarce material such as

Another case of allocation of non-standard vehicles arose with the two Leyland TD7s with East Lancashire bodies supplied to Aldershot and District in 1942. Whilst the order for Leyland chassis was not repeated, the company preferring to support local industry through Dennis, East Lancashire did become the main supplier of double-deck bodywork to this operator in the postwar period. One of the pair, ECG 943, is shown in service after the war.

A single-deck trolleybus body was supplied on a Sunbeam chassis to the Tees-side Railess Traction Board in 1942 and numbered 14. The open rear platform is visible in this view.

aluminium and of simple outline devoid of curves which required expensive and highly skilled panel beating, skills which were unlikely to be available because men had been called up for war service. The body specification was applied to new vehicles and to existing chassis which were often rebodied during this time to give them a new lease of life when complete new vehicles were difficult if not impossible to obtain.

The allocation of work to manufacturers was strictly controlled by the Ministry of War Transport and East Lancashire Coachbuilders was allocated work in connection with the rebodying of existing double-deck chassis.

Lancashire United Transport received two East Lancashire-bodied Leyland TD7s in ,1942 numbered 260 and 261. The latter is shown in this view at Swinton Church. These bodies also bore distinct Leyland-like styling though the two side ventilators above the lower-deck windows were a distinctive East Lancashire feature. The flat panelling between the lower-deck window and the beading also served to illustrate that it was not a true Leyland product.

As mentioned earlier, East Lancashire were allowed to produce vehicles in accordance with their own methods of construction. As a result of this agreement, bodies to the prewar outline were produced incorporating curved front and rear profiles as against the angular design of the Wartime Standard Specification. Standard window pans were included with radii to the bottom corners very much in accordance with peacetime standards.

It was something of a mystery to men on the shop floor at this time as they were fitting curved domes, manufactured by their panel beater Harold Disley, and yet local operators in the Blackburn area were introducing buses with very angular outlines. At that time some of the men were apparently not aware of the Wartime Specification to which other coachbuilders were working. Harold Disley produced up to three rear domes per week

During the war the rebodying of single-deckers was normally allocated to the Blackpool coachbuilder H V Burlingham but in 1943 East Lancashire Coachbuilders rebodied seven Leyland TS3 and TS4 chassis for Barrow in Furness Corporation Transport. There is a similarity in the frontal appearance with the Burlingham bodies but the use of window pans is clearly evident in this view of No. 3 in its home town on 26th May 1953 10 years after rebodying.

whilst Tommy Abbott produced up to three front domes. However, it is understood that there was in the works one angular type rear dome to show to Ministry of War Transport inspectors when they visited. Northern Counties also included their standard window pans but this was within the angular outline of the standard specification. Other major bodybuilding concerns allocated work in connection with rebodying double-deckers included Northern Coachbuilders of Newcastle upon Tyne, Willowbrook of Loughborough and Brush of Loughborough, all producing bodies to the austerity Wartime Specification.

There was some simplification of the front domes during the later years of the war in that the style where the front corners were tapered down to meet the corner pillars was not used after the Lancaster vehicle of 1942. Following this front domes with the horizontal lower edge were used until the rebodied London Transport trolleybuses were commenced in 1945 and these incorporated a version of the earlier design which was also reintroduced for all postwar production, initially on new chassis, but later on rebodies. This arrangement of the front dome provided an identification feature of East Lancashire Coachbuilders bodies for many years.

Wartime bodies were sometimes finished in battleship-grey flat paint with white edgings to the black mudguards. Operators were often able to supply quantities of paint in their standard colours from stock and this would be used, whilst some operators painted vehicles themselves, prior to them entering service.

Bodies supplied under these arrangements went to Aberdare Urban District Council, Aldershot and District, City of Oxford, Eastern National, Mayne of Manchester, Southdown and Venture of Basingstoke and to the Corporations of Birkenhead, Bolton, Bradford, Cardiff, Eastbourne, Grimsby, Leigh, Northampton, Plymouth and St Helens. A surprising order was for the rebodying of seven Leyland TS3/TS4 single-deckers for Barrow in Furness Corporation as the coachbuilder allocated to rebody single-deckers was H V Burlingham of Blackpool. In addition to the building of complete new bodies, work was undertaken on the rebuilding for Plymouth, Birkenhead and Rotherham Corporations of bodies which had suffered war damage.

Grimsby Corporation No. 62 was one of three AEC Regents rebodied by East Lancashire Coachbuilders in 1943 and it was still looking presentable when photographed 14 years later on 4th August 1957 in its home town.

Not only did the Company get away during the war without manufacturing bodies to the Standard Wartime Specification, they were able in this case to provide a front entrance with doors when Maynes of Manchester had this AEC Regent rebodied in 1942. It had been acquired from Exeter Corporation in 1938.

Vehicles for rebodying would generally be driven to the works in various states of disrepair, some having suffered damage by enemy action. Former Works Manager John Bufton recalls Albert Crook, a wartime dilutee, i.e. a semi-skilled man brought into a factory and trained to do a particular job. He was a resourceful character and he purchased the old bodies from the Directors for something like £7 each and would take them to the spare ground at the rear of the works and on Sundays, with assistance from John Bufton and Jack Wilkes, would dismantle the bodies, burning anything that was of no use and selling the steel as scrap. There was always a demand for good secondhand timber during wartime and he had no difficulty in selling this. The intermediate floors formed from tongue and grooved timber would be removed in two sections and found a ready market for use in garden sheds and poultry cabins. A figure of £7 may sound very cheap for a damaged bus body but it has to be realised that in those days it would represent something between one and two weeks' wages for most people.

In 1943 the Company undertook the assembly of a number of American Army trucks which had been sent over to this country in kit form and this work continued into 1944. The Company also built rescue vehicles for towing tanks out of ditches, these comprising little more than a chassis with a winch on the back.

There was little time for social activities during wartime but there were Christmas concerts in the canteen on the afternoon prior to the commencement of the Christmas holiday. George Danson would sing, Frank Doxey, the Trimming Shop foreman would play the violin and Alfred Alcock would come in with a nine-gallon barrel of beer which he would place on the servery and the men would help themselves, filling their tea mugs with beer. His contribution was doubtless the most appreciated!

At this time the four storey building on the site, which then had not been occupied by East Lancashire Coachbuilders, was taken over by the American Army and used for the accommodation of personnel. John Bufton recalls seeing American negroes, the first coloured men he had ever seen, in the basement, whilst in the top storey, on the large brick pillars, there were painted silhouettes of men which were used for rifle practice. They were still there, and doubtless many people wondered why they were there, when this building was later taken over by East Lancashire Coachbuilders and used as follows:-

Ground Floor - Sawmill.

First Floor - Trimming Shop and wood polishing.

Second Floor - Pipe Bending and window pan manufacture.

Third Floor - Spraying Shop for ceiling panels.

There was no wartime bomb damage to the Works, although there was in other parts of the town.

London Transport suffered considerable damage to its fleet during wartime and sent 25 trolleybuses to East Lancashire Coachbuilders for rebodying. These were returned to London from 1945 to 1948 and it seems that some delay was incurred due to unforseen increases in cost which took some time to resolve between East Lancashire Coachbuilders and London Transport. These bodies were of course built to London Transport specification. Ten were delivered without seats and secondhand seats

Above: **One of the 25 London trolleybuses which were rebodied by East Lancashire Coachbuilders following war damage was 801B which was completed in August 1946.**

Right: **The only Crossley Condors which the Company rebodied were for Northampton Corporation and one of them, No. 62, is depicted in service in its home town.**

Below right: **Only the white edging to the mudguards suggests the wartime scene in this view of one of seven AEC Regents rebodied for Eastern National in 1943. Apart from the outline not complying with the Wartime Specification, the elaborate destination indicator arrangement over the rear platform is visible. Wartime bodies did not normally have side destination equipment and that at the front was usually limited to a single aperture. The similarity to the Aldershot & District body seen in the photograph on page 28 is most noticeable.**

removed from war damaged trolleybuses were fitted at Fulwell. A number were delivered in a brownish red livery which they retained until their first overhaul.

This period which had started with the uncertainty of a new business and the added complexity of a wartime situation ended with an optimistic outlook for the future with new customers and a business on which great demands were to be made in the forthcoming years.

At the end of the war Leyland prepared to resume bus building and East Lancashire ceased building its Leyland look alike body, putting its own new designs into production. Most significantly in addition to continuing production of its traditional five bay designs the opportunity was taken to develop a four-bay body, improving the appearance whilst reducing the weight. This was some years before such designs became common apart from the London Transport RT family bodies being built by Park Royal and Weymann and was a major coup for East Lancashire Coachbuilders. It clearly demonstrated the Company's intention to be at the forefront of good design in the postwar period.

Above: In 1944/45 Aldershot and District sent ten 1937 Dennis Lances for rebodying. One of them, 746 (CCG 343), is shown on service 30 to Onslow Village leaving Farnham Road bus station.

Left: The first East Lancashire bodies supplied to Southdown Motor Services were ten on reconditioned Leyland TD2 chassis in 1944/45. One of these 950 (UF 8850) is shown at Worthing Dome on service 31 to Portsmouth. This was an unusual working for a petrol engined vehicle allocated to Portsmouth Depot. A side destination box had been added by this time and the body was later transferred to Guy Arab No. 402.

The registration number brings back memories to the author who recalls travelling to school in Whitehaven on sister vehicles UF 8844, 8845 and 8848 after they had been sold to Cumberland Motor Services.

3 THE POSTWAR PERIOD

Many coachbuilding firms would have no difficulty in drawing a clear demarcation line between wartime and postwar production for it would be the time when they ceased manufacture of bodies to the angular outline of the wartime specification and resumed production of bodies to their own design and outline. In the case of East Lancashire Coachbuilders there had been no production to the wartime specification and the demarcation is much less clear. It is proposed therefore to commence this era of the Company's history with the delivery of the first bodies on new chassis following the cessation of hostilities. This comprised a batch of six double-deckers on Leyland PD1 chassis for Eastbourne Corporation delivered between October 1946 and May 1947. In addition to orders received from established customers at this time there were export orders undertaken in conjunction with Leyland Motors Ltd. These included double-deckers for Madrid, Cuba, Golden Arrow Bus Company of Capetown and Consolidated Near East Trading Company of Palestine. The bodies for Palestine were finished in aluminium paint and were the first bodies to be spray painted, this work being carried out during the night when the works were otherwise unoccupied.

An interesting report in the *Leyland Journal* dated March 1946 describes the rebuilding by

Above right: **The first postwar East Lancashire bodies of four-bay construction on new chassis were six Leyland PD1s for Eastbourne Corporation numbered 13 - 18. Number 17 is pictured at work on service 1 heading for Old Town. The open windscreen suggests that it was a hot summer day and shows a facility which the drivers of modern buses do not have. Several East Lancashire characteristics are visible including the 'D' shaped end windows to the lower saloon, the curved lower edge of the nearside window of the front bulkhead and the corners of the front dome tapering to meet the front corner pillars.**

Right: **Rebodying continued in the postwar period and a total of 51 double-deck bodies were supplied to Southdown Motor Services on reconditioned prewar Leyland TD3, TD4 and TD5 chassis. One of the TD4s, BUF 224, was completed in February 1946 and is shown at Worthing Dome en route to Arundel Park Road. The body style is similar to that produced in wartime. Later rebodies for Southdown were to the postwar style.**

Left: **In the immediate postwar period a number of export orders were obtained through Leyland Motors Ltd, including one for five bodies on Leyland OPD1/A chassis supplied to Madrid in 1947. They were unusual in having right-hand drive and right-hand entrances as shown in this view of one of the quintet taken when newly built.**

Centre left: **One of the later rebodies for Southdown was Leyland TD5 206 (FCD 506), completed in June 1949. It is shown at Broadwater Church in March 1950 working on service 1 to Worthing Pier. This bus later passed to Brighton Corporation.**

Bottom left: **Warrington was one of a number of municipal operators which favoured Bristol chassis in the immediate postwar period. Number 61 shown in the Town Centre was one of 29 received between 1947 and 1950. Twenty-seven of the bodies were produced by Bruce Coachworks, Cardiff using four-bay construction framework supplied by East Lancashire Coachbuilders.**

Leigh Corporation of two Leyland TS7 single-deck chassis dating from 1937 to TD4 double-deck specification and the fitting by East Lancashire Coachbuilders of double-deck bodies using parts supplied by Leyland Motors Ltd.

This was a boom period for bus manufacturers brought about by a number of reasons. There had been a shortage of new vehicles during wartime, skilled maintenance staff had been called up for military service resulting in reduced maintenance standards and it was clear that some new bodies supplied during wartime were not going to last for long without major rebuilding or replacement. These factors combined to place great pressure on coachbuilders to supply new vehicles and also new bodies on existing reconditioned chassis. As a result of this, the established coachbuilders could not cope with demand and many new suppliers entered the market. This postwar shortage of skilled labour caused Walter Smith to write to John Bufton's CO in the Grenadier Guards in 1947 asking if John could be released 12 months early. John had other ideas. He was enjoying his sport in the army, taking part in the 400 metres and tug o'war teams and looking forward to participating in the Royal Tournament. He appreciated Walter's interest in him, but declined the offer of early release.

In his book *The British Bus Story - The Fifties* published by the Transport Publishing Company, Alan Townsin lists 39 bodybuilding firms that began production between 1945 and 1950, most of which were no longer in the business by 1960.

Even during this boom period, the Company showed a willingness to diversify and meet the special requirements of customers. Between 1945 and 1947 a total of seventeen crane cabs were manufactured for Walker Brothers of Wigan. A number of railcar bodies were also manufactured for this firm and details of these are given in Chapter 5.

East Lancashire Coachbuilders formed an association with two newcomers to the business. In 1946 Cardiff Corporation Transport entered into a contract with a local firm, Air Despatch Ltd, to rebuild their East Lancashire- and Northern Counties-bodied AEC Regents using parts supplied by East Lancashire. Forty-five vehicles were dealt with and this led to East Lancashire supplying frames to Air Despatch Ltd for completion in their works, an arrangement which was of mutual benefit. In 1948, the name Air Despatch Ltd was changed to Bruce Coachworks Ltd and this arrangement continued until 1951 when Bruce ceased trading. The Bruce works were housed in three aircraft hangers and vehicles moved through these from start to finish in an 'S' formation in a very tidy and orderly manner. In addition, East Lancashire supplied frames to Yorkshire Equipment Company Ltd of Bridlington and in 1950 took control of this company, renaming it East Lancashire Coachbuilders (Bridlington) Ltd. This operation remained in existence until 1953 when it closed. It is said that it had 'cost the directors a lot of money'.

Around the time of closure the order for the rebuilding of three Coventry wartime Daimler double-deckers was diverted from Bridlington to Bonds of Wythenshawe, the first two vehicles of the batch of five having been completed at Bridlington. Another order undertaken by Bond at this time was for five rebodies on Bristol L5G chassis for

Top: **Another user of Bristol chassis in this period was Cardiff Corporation Transport who purchased 20 KW6G models in 1948/49. They were bodied by Bruce Coachworks, using East Lancashire frames. Number 132 is shown operating on Cardiff's service 30 in a typical scene of the era with the crew having a chat and the driver's door open, ready for a resumption of duty.**

Above: **The only postwar Crossley double deckers bodied by East Lancashire comprised a batch of eight delivered to Eastbourne Corporation as fleet numbers 32 - 39 in 1949. Number 34 (JK 9991) is shown at Eastbourne Pier heading for the Foot of Beachy Head on 14th August 1949.**

Top left: **Aldershot and District No. 989 (GAA 625) on a Dennis Lance III chassis was built in 1949 by Yorkshire Equipment Company at Bridlington on frames supplied by East Lancashire. The drop-down windows to the front of the upper saloon are noteworthy as a typical Aldershot & District feature of that time.**

Above left: **Cardiff Corporation No. 238 was one of five single-deck trolleybuses delivered in 1949 on BUT 9641T chassis. It was photographed operating in Cardiff's City Centre.**

Top right: **This style of single-deck East Lancashire body with half canopy was peculiar to Rotherham who continued to specify centre entrances for single-deck bodies. Number 116 on a Bristol L5G chassis was supplied in 1950.**

Above right: **Rotherham was another user of single-deck trolleybuses and regularly bought bodies from East Lancashire for them. Number 77 was one of eight on Daimler CTE6 chassis supplied in 1949, the batch eventually totalling 44.**

Rotherham Corporation. The frames for these were supplied by East Lancashire.

The provision of frames for these two additional works placed great pressure on the works in Blackburn and an additional building was occupied in Hollins Bridge Street, Blackburn. This was used for the assembly of frames for Bruce and Bridlington, the parts having been made at the main Whalley New Road works. Following assembly, the frames would be partly dismantled into sections, i.e. sides, roof, bulkheads, etc., for transportation to Bridlington and Cardiff. The Company had a petrol-engined Austin flat back lorry for this purpose. George Alcock remembers this vehicle well as he learned to drive in it.

A notable feature of the Company's activities in the immediate postwar period was the number of bodies produced for Bristol chassis. This make of chassis was traditionally associated with Tilling Group operating companies and bodywork by Eastern Coach Works. However a number of other operators developed a liking for the rugged simplicity of the Bristol chassis and it so happened that some of these were East Lancashire customers. Included among them were Rotherham Corporation who had standardised on this chassis, Warrington Corporation and Cardiff Corporation, in addition to operators such as St Helens Corporation and others who took small batches. As a result of this, a total of 150 bodies were built on

Top left: **Rotherham's use of Bristol chassis continued in the postwar period until such time as they were no longer available. Number 200 on a K6B chassis was one of six bodied by Yorkshire Equipment using East Lancashire frames in 1949.**

Above left: **Ribble purchased 20 double deck coaches with East Lancashire bodies on Leyland PD2 chassis in 1950/51. The general style of the body is similar to the 25 Burlingham bodies on Leyland PD1 chassis purchased by Ribble in 1948 except that the Burlinghams were of five-bay construction. They were used on Limited Stop services and No. 1233 is shown at Blackpool Coliseum Coach Station in August 1959.**

Top right: **St Helens Corporation purchased its last new trolleybuses in 1951 comprising eight on Sunbeam F4 and eight on BUT 9611T chassis, originally numbered 174 to 189 but later renumbered 374 to 389. The last of the batch is shown en route to Rainhill with a St Helens RT behind. The bodies for the Sunbeams were built at Bridlington and those for the BUTs at Blackburn.**

Above right: **On closure of the St Helens trolleybus system the eight BUTs 382 to 389 passed to Bradford Corporation and the Sunbeams 374 to 381 to South Shields Corporation where they became the only 8ft-wide trolleybuses in the fleet and the last trolleybuses to be purchased. Former St Helens 381, now numbered 209, is shown at South Shields Market.**

Bristol chassis up to 1953, some of the later ones being rebodies for Rotherham Corporation who seemed to be reluctant to part with their Bristols. As late as 1956 framework was supplied to Rotherham to enable them to rebody another Bristol L5G chassis. The Company did receive an order from St Helens Corporation for eight single-deck bodies on Bristol L-type chassis but due to pressure of work asked to be relieved of this contract and the order was transferred to Charles Roe of Leeds. No doubt the total would have grown further had it not been for government regulation which prevented Bristol from taking orders from non-Tilling Group operators following the nationalisation of that group in 1948. This was an agreement to safeguard the interests of non-state-owned manufacturers.

With regard to the bodies supplied during this period, these generally followed on from designs established in the prewar period with typical characteristics of the firm. These included a well rounded rear dome, a flat sloping front and, in some cases, 'D' shaped window outlines at the front and rear lower saloon side windows. Although the firm had a standard design it continued being prepared to build what the customer wanted.

Above: Rochdale's blue and cream livery would have looked good on almost any double-decker of the early nineteen-fifties and it certainly suited the East Lancashire body very well. Number 235 was one of five supplied in 1951 on AEC Regent III chassis. The author recalls them on service 17 between Rochdale and Manchester. If it was a cold day one could be assured of a more comfortable ride on one of these vehicles with their saloon heaters, rather than on their unheated Manchester counterparts.

Below: In 1951 Burnley Colne and Nelson Joint Transport purchased 16 Guy Arab III chassis with East Lancashire bodies. Number 207 was being driven hard in the centre of Burnley en route to Rosegrove in October 1971 when 20 years old.

Right: **In 1952/53 Bradford City Transport purchased 40 AEC Regent IIIs with East Lancashire bodies. The Birmingham style 'new look' fronts to the bonnets were fitted by Crossley Motors. Number 84 was still operating 18 years later and still looked smart and respectable when photographed in the City Centre on 30 August 1970.**

Centre right: **The first Blackburn-built bodies on Leyland Royal Tiger chassis were ten for Southdown Motor Services numbered 1500 - 1509 built in 1952. They were unusual in having rear entrances and a further batch of 30 supplied in 1953 were also unusual in having central entrances. In those days the question of one-man-operation with full-sized single-deckers had not been addressed. All 40 were later rebuilt to front-entrance specification. Number 1503 of the first batch is shown returning to Hillsea Garage, after operating as a duplicate on the London to Portsmouth express service. The attractive style of these early bodies for underfloor engined chassis is evident, with gently sloping front, recessed windscreen and lower edge of the front side-windows curving down to the level of the bottom of the windscreen. Another early order was for five bodies on Royal Tiger chassis ordered by Cardiff from Bruce and completed at Blackburn in 1952.**

Bottom right: **This view of one of the second batch of Royal tigers for Southdown, No. 1520 with centre entrance, shows the elaborate rear destination display still specified by Southdown at that time.**

Another example of this was a batch of twenty double-deck coach bodies on Leyland PD2 chassis for local operator Ribble Motor Services Ltd of Preston. These vehicles, delivered in 1950/51 were of similar outline to a batch of earlier bodies by H V Burlingham on Leyland PD1 chassis for the same operator. They were fitted with full fronts and semi coach seating and were used regularly on medium distance express services such as those between Manchester and Blackpool and between Manchester and Burnley, Colne and Skipton. A further one-off non-standard contract involved the provision of a new upper saloon on a St Helens Corporation London Transport type RT double-decker following an accident with a low bridge in Southport in 1959.

It was during this period that the Company established its

Above: **Illustrating again the Company's willingness to build what the customer wanted is this single deck trolleybus, one of ten built for Glasgow Corporation in 1953 on BUT chassis to the design of Mr E R L Fitzpayne, the undertaking's General Manager. This one is No. TSB6 and it is illustrated at work in its home city.**

Below: **Showing the typical East Lancashire lowbridge body of the era is Leigh Corporation AEC Regent III, numbered 45 when supplied in 1952. It had received its Selnec No. 6945 when photographed outside the Lancashire United bus station in Leigh on 3 September 1970. The bus depot at Leigh was of insufficient height to accommodate highbridge buses, hence the need to standardise on the lowbridge design.**

reputation as a major supplier to the municipal market. At this time there were ninety-seven municipal operators in the country ranging in size from the tiny Colwyn Bay operation to the largest of them all, Birmingham City Transport. However, as mentioned in Chapter 2, the company did also become a major supplier to two large company fleets in the South of England.

Aldershot and District returned to East Lancashire as its main supplier of double-deck bodywork in the postwar period, these being unusual in generally being mounted on Dennis chassis built at Guildford in Aldershot and District's operating area. This helped to establish a relationship between East Lancashire Coachbuilders and Dennis which was to prove significant in the future. Southdown Motor Services Ltd, of Brighton, one of the largest bus companies in the south of England and held in high esteem throughout the industry, purchased a total of 61 new double-deck bodies for fitting to reconditioned prewar chassis together with 40 single-deck bodies for Leyland Royal Tiger chassis and 24 double-deck bodies for Leyland PD2 chassis. Both these companies had pleasing liveries which enhanced the already attractive lines of the East Lancashire bodies.

The changes in design of the Company's double-

Another example of postwar rebodying was the supply in 1954 of 30 double-deck bodies on wartime Daimler CWA6 chassis for Glasgow Corporation and numbered DR1 - 30. This one was photographed after completion by East Lancashire Coachbuilders. Thirty similar bodies had been supplied for the same operator on reconditioned Albion CX19 chassis in 1952/53 and numbered BR1 - 30.

deck body during this period were gradual involving a more curved frontal profile and the adoption of window pans with radii at the top as well as at the bottom. The traditional polished timber window finishers gave way to melamine plastics in anodised aluminium alloy frames and this material also replaced leathercloth as the finish on interior lining panels. The Company offered window pans with either a flush interior finish or a flush exterior finish, to suit customer preference.

The production of traditional single-deck bodywork on front-engined chassis was rather limited in the postwar period but examples with rear entrance were built for Burnley Colne and

Right upper: **This view of Colombo Trolleybus No. 34 shows the characteristic East Lancashire rear profile which was so familiar at this time. The export orders came through East Lancashire's contacts at Leyland Motors.**

Right: **This interior lower saloon view of one of the 1954 Colombo double-deck trolleybuses shows the polished timber finishers to the window surrounds, also the polished timber cover to the bulkhead ventilator and the polished trim to the ceiling panels. Also evident are the rectangular lighting fittings which were a feature of East Lancashire (and Massey Brothers) bodies for many years. The author recalls this type of lighting fitting being provided on the bodies supplied to Cumberland in 1939 and 1941. These may have been the last bodies to be provided with polished timber trim as the single-deck trolleybus bodies supplied later to Colombo had laminated plastic trim.**

Above left: **Foden was never a common make of bus chassis. Warrington Corporation purchased three batches in 1949, 1954/5 and 1956. The 1949 and 1956 examples had East Lancashire bodies and one of the 1956 deliveries, No. 110, was photographed arriving at Arpley bus station on the joint, with Lancashire United Transport, service 78 in August 1970.**

Top right: **Cardiff purchased its last East Lancashire-bodied trolleybuses in 1955, a total of 14 on BUT 9641T six-wheeled chassis being supplied. Number 282 is shown in the city.**

Above right: **As late as 1955 Burnley Colne and Nelson Transport purchased three Leyland PS2/14 front-engined single-deckers with rear entrances to add to eleven similar vehicles purchased in 1953 and 1954. This was at a time when front-engined single-deckers, particularly with rear entrances, had lost favour. They were converted to front entrance by East Lancashire Coachbuilders in 1959.**

Nelson Transport as late as 1955, when three bodies were supplied for Leyland PS2/14 chassis following eleven similar bodies supplied earlier on the same type of chassis. These bodies were later converted to front entrance by East Lancashire.

This traditional design was made out of date by the introduction of the underfloor-engined single-deck chassis which gave greater seating capacity within a given length and was therefore much more attractive to operators. It did offer better facilities for one person operation, although the days of this being the norm were still some years away. The first such bodies from the Company were seven on AEC Regal IV chassis for Rochdale Corporation Transport delivered in 1951. These were followed in 1952 by a batch of five, on Leyland Royal Tiger chassis, originally ordered from Bruce Coachworks but completed at Blackburn, for Cardiff Corporation Transport and the previously mentioned batch of 40 also on Leyland Royal Tiger chassis for Southdown Motor Services delivered in 1952 and 1953. The first ten Southdown bodies had rear entrances and the remaining 30 had centre entrances.

A similar body to those for Southdown was built on a Guy Arab LUF chassis for Aldershot and District, being the only single-deck body supplied to this regular customer. George Alcock recalls that after delivery the bus was returned to East Lancashire Coachbuilders with the claim that it was too heavy. George describes the chassis as 'a real monster' and he and John Bufton were given the task of investigating the weight. Parts were stripped from the body and weighed and then George, who was an apprentice at the time, was given the task of remaking them using lighter gauge metal. The patterns were already available and it was therefore considered that the remaking could be undertaken by an apprentice and it was said 'our George will do it'. The seats were also rebuilt using shallower cushions and the desired weight reduction was achieved.

After this time, apart from the deliveries to Burnley Colne and Nelson, all single-deck bodies were built on underfloor-engined chassis until the arrival of the rear-engined chassis and minibuses covered later.

Unlike the double-deck bodies where, during this time, changes were of a minor nature, the single-deck body design for underfloor-engined chassis underwent a number of fundamental design changes from the early designs for Rochdale,

Above: In 1956 and 1957 24 bodies fitted with 'Eastlanco' single-piece sliding doors were supplied to Southdown Motor Services on Leyland PD2/12 chassis. The hinged flap in the lower part of the front portion of the door is clearly visible. As the door opened and entered the body side this flap, guided by a curved track in the floor, turned through 90 degrees to avoid contact with the wheel arch.

Right: The last rear-entrance double-decker to be supplied to Southdown was fleet number 812 (RUF 212) which arrived in June 1957. Sister vehicle 800 is seen at Rottingdean. Sadly Southdown's orders for the next few years did not come to East Lancashire.

Below: One of the 35ft-long Colombo single-deck trolleybuses photographed on completion in 1957, showing the front and rear doorways and the high-level 'standee' side windows.

Top left: **Accrington Corporation had a very distinctive livery of dark-blue and red and this is displayed on No. 144, a Guy Arab IV dating from 1957, seen in Peel Street, Accrington in August 1970.**

Top right: **In 1958 Darwen Corporation purchased three Reliances which were unusual in being badged as Crossleys rather than AECs. Number 20 is leaving Darwen Circus in September 1970. This photograph shows the arrangement of the second generation of bodies for underfloor engined chassis from East Lancashire. It is a squarer design than the first generation of such bodies but still well-proportioned and attractive.**

Above: **In traditional Bolton livery of maroon and three cream bands and set in moorland scenery on the outskirts of Blackburn is No. 130 on a Leyland PD3 chassis, one of a batch of five supplied in 1959.**

Cardiff and Southdown up to the period of rear-engined vehicles. An appreciation of these changes is best obtained from reference to the photographs and the associated captions.

During this period an important part of the Company's activities was the manufacture of single and double-deck bodies for trolleybuses with examples supplied to Bradford, Cardiff, Glasgow, Huddersfield, Rotherham and St Helens Corporations. The single-deck bodies for Glasgow were built to the design of the General Manager, Mr E R L Fitzpayne, and seated 27 with provision for 40 standing passengers. They were totally different in appearance from previous East Lancashire products. An export order for trolleybus bodies was received from Colombo Municipal Transport of

Right: **The only one of its kind... In 1959 St Helens Corporation No. 62, a London Transport-type RT double-decker, was in collision with a low bridge in Southport. East Lancashire Coachbuilders built a new upper saloon and made such an excellent job of it that to the uninitiated no difference could be detected.**

Centre right: **The first Dennis Lolines were bodied by East Lancashire Coachbuilders for Aldershot and District in 1958. The first to be completed was No. 336, shown here in Farnham en route to Aldershot bus station and illustrating the informative intermediate route blind used by Aldershot and District for many years.**

Bottom right: **This lower saloon interior view of Aldershot No. 336 shows the rearward-facing front seat which was a feature of this type of vehicle, required to provide housing for the offset transmission. Also evident is the distinctive moquette for the seat trim and the traditional enclosed lighting fittings.**

Ceylon, the first being for 15 double-deck bodies on BUT chassis supplied in 1954, followed by an order for 26 single-deck bodies on Sunbeam chassis, 20 of which were 30ft-long and six to a length of 35 feet, all supplied in 1957.

After the initial postwar boom period for bus travel there came a period of decline as passenger numbers reduced, mainly because of the increase in car ownership. This began to take effect in the mid fifties and this period saw the introduction of the lightweight double-decker and to a lesser extent, the lightweight single-decker in an attempt to reduce fuel costs. There was little scope for weight reduction in the double-deck chassis and the emphasis was therefore on weight reduction in the bodywork. This was the era of frameless domes to the front and rear of upper saloons and the omission of window finishers with the bare steel framework being paint-finished, particularly in upper saloons. This move seems to have been encouraged by the BET Group through its engineering chief, S C Vince, who is alleged to have held the view that the bus was inherently ugly and therefore appearance did not matter. One of

Left: In 1960, North Western Road Car Company took delivery of Dennis Lolines with East Lancashire front-entrance bodywork. One of them is shown whilst on loan to Aldershot and District to demonstrate the front entrance layout.

Centre left: Blackburn 169 on a Guy Arab IV chassis with 'Johannesburg' style of bonnet was one of 12 supplied in 1961 and is shown in Blackburn in April 1971. Walter Lowe was the Rolling Stock Superintendent at Blackburn and it is said that his idea of an ideal bus was a Guy Arab chassis, Gardner engine and East Lancashire body.

Bottom left: Stockport bought its first East Lancashire bodies in 1961 and standardised on this make until the takeover by Selnec in 1969, taking the last British-built rear-entrance double-decker to be built. Number 59 was one of 30 supplied in 1967, 15 of which including No. 59 were built at Neepsend. It is shown in Mersey Square, Stockport in October 1970, the classic lines being well set off by Stockport's attractive red and ivory livery.

the famous expressions of all time in connection with such vehicles came from an Edinburgh baillie who described the vehicles delivered to his city as 'ungainly, inelegant, monstrous masses of shivering tin'. The author recalls travelling to work in Manchester in the late fifties on unheated examples of similar vehicles in the depths of winter. It was not a pleasent experience. Happily, they were not East Lancashire products!

During this period East Lancashire Coachbuilders had declined to get involved in the production of such vehicles and continued to produce their attractive, well proportioned and well finished bodywork which provided an answer to anyone who was of the opinion that a double-deck bus was inherently ugly. As far as can be ascertained, no regular customers were lost by this action, indeed the reverse was the case. When, in 1958, Park Royal used up unwanted stocks of parts from the unpopular Bridgemaster design and produced what many considered really was the ugliest double-decker of modern times, East Lancashire Coachbuilders picked up orders from operators who had previously standardised on Park Royal bodywork. Notable among such operators were Ipswich Corporation and Southampton Corporation, both placing regular orders for many years to come. The change at Southampton may also have been influenced by the appointment as General Manager of Mr Gilbert Armstrong who had experience of East Lancashire Coachbuilders in his previous appointments at Accrington and Burnley Colne and Nelson. John Owen, Managing Director of Thamsdown Transport in his response to *The Customer's View* (see Chapter 10) wrote, "My experience of East Lancashire goes back to the mid-sixties when I started at Southampton as a management trainee. Just before I started 30 East Lancashire-bodied AEC Regent Vs in two batches had been delivered. These followed about 40 Park Royal-bodied vehicles with 66 seats and tiny upstairs windows. You had to be a midget to get your legs between the seats and if you were you couldn't see out! The East Lancashire bodies with their white (rather than cream) laminate interiors, which looked far brighter, attracted much favourable comment."

Trolleybuses had been part of East Lancashire's core business since 1939, but the electrically propelled vehicle gradually fell from favour and the last trolleybus body to be built in this country was provided by the Company to the order of Bradford Corporation Transport in 1963. This was the last of a long line of trolleybus bodies supplied to Bradford going back to 1956. Bradford was the last operator of trolleybuses in this country and as other systems had closed down, had purchased vehicles from them and had some rebodied by East Lancashire Coachbuilders together with a number of their own vehicles which had time-expired bodies.

PLATFORM DOORS

During the early-fifties a number of operators who were concerned at the number of accidents involving rear-platform vehicles specified platform doors for double-deckers. Some of these were manually operated but this meant that the conductor had to be on the platform at the appropriate time to operate them. Alfred Alcock saw possibilities for the provision of doors which could be operated remotely, or by locally placed controls, and patented two types of door, the 'Southlanco' and the 'Eastlanco'. The problem with sliding doors on rear entrance double-deckers was wheel arch intrusion and in the case of the Southlanco door this was overcome by making the door in two sections. By using two different sizes of gear wheel on the motor shaft, the inner leaf which was the one which extended to the rear of the platform, was arranged to travel at twice the speed of the outer leaf, with the result that both leaves reached the open and closed positions simultaneously. This was covered by patent No. 771,672 applied for on 26th January 1953. The complete specification was published on 3rd April 1957. The first bus to be provided with this type of door was a lowbridge-bodied AEC Regent III for Bamber Bridge Motor Service. An unusual application was that fitted to Southdown Motor Services No. 547 which had a Park Royal body.

The disadvantage of the Southlanco door was that it required two leaves and two sets of tracks, and because of the overlap between the two leaves it was impossible to provide the drive at a position about half way up the door. It was for this reason that Alfred Alcock designed the Eastlanco version covered by Patent No. 813,272 for which the initial application was made on 26th March 1956 and the complete specification published on 13th May 1959. In this case the door was made in a single leaf with a hinged flap in the forward portion extending part way up the door. The bottom track was curved in front of the rear bulkhead so that as the door opened the hinged flap turned through 90 degrees to clear the wheelarch. The patents were taken out in the joint names of East Lancashire Coachbuilders and Alfred Marsden Alcock. Drawings illustrating these patents are included in the Appendices.

LOW FLOORS - 1950s STYLE

The concept of the low floor double-decker tends to be associated with the 1990s but in 1949 Bristol Tramways and Carriage Company introduced, in conjunction with Eastern Coach Works, the Bristol Lodekka. This allowed a normal upper saloon seating arrangement with centre aisle to be accommodated within the constraints of a lowbridge vehicle having a height of 13ft 5ins. Because Bristol and Eastern Coach Works were part of the state-owned Tilling Group they were only allowed to supply to the Tilling and Scottish Bus Groups and the Joint Omnibus Committees where British Rail had a share. Other operators were denied the benefits of this vehicle. This was the situation until 1957 when agreement was reached with Dennis to allow that company to manufacture a similar vehicle, to be known as the Dennis Loline, under licence.

The first vehicles produced under this arrangement comprised a batch of 34 for Aldershot and District and these were bodied by East Lancashire Coachbuilders and delivered in 1958. The bodies were fitted with an Eastlanco sliding door to the rear platform, the first time such a facility had been specified by Aldershot and District. In 1971 two of these vehicles passed to Tumilty, one of the participants in the AA Motor Services of Troon operation and later in 1972 passed to another AA participant, Dodds, when one of them, SOU 460 received the front cowl from a Bristol Lodekka, thus giving the appearance of being an East Lancashire-bodied Bristol Lodekka. There is a photograph of it in the book *British Bus Systems No. 8 - Dodds/AA Motor Services*, by Bill McGregor, published by Transport Publishing Company.

Bodies on the Dennis Loline chassis were also supplied to Hutchings and Cornelius, North

Bradford City Transport was the last trolleybus operator in Britain and purchased many vehicles from other operators as their systems closed down. Number 845 was a Sunbeam F4 which came from the Mexborough and Swinton Traction Company and was rebodied in 1962 by East Lancashire Coachbuilders. It is shown in Bradford City Centre in August 1971. The last normal scheduled trolleybus journey on 24th March 1972 was worked by sister vehicle 844.

Western, City of Oxford, Leigh, Luton and Reading Corporations. The bodies for North Western were the first East Lancashire bodies to have the exterior panels fixed by pop-rivets.

Following the success of the Dennis Loline, AEC introduced its Bridgemaster of integral construction and then a separate chassis version named the Renown and East Lancashire provided bodies on AEC Renown chassis for Leigh Corporation, Leicester City Transport and West Bridgford Urban Distict Council. Leyland then seemed to think it was time to get involved in this type of chassis and introduced its Lowlander, generally sold as an Albion in Scotland. This created a problem for some body builders due to the retention of the high bonnet line associated with the PD2 and PD3 chassis and some rather ungainly body designs were produced for it with varying window heights and limited space for destination displays. However, East Lancashire managed to succeed where others had failed and produced attractive vehicles for Luton Corporation. All East Lancashire front-entrance bodies of this type had rearward ascending staircases.

There was a problem with the rear entrance AEC Renowns supplied to Leicester with regard to the rear air bags of the air suspension system which was in its infancy at that time. When the vehicle was loaded and the air bag was compressed there was no problem, but with a lightly loaded vehicle the rear suspension rose lifting the platform to a height of 19.5 inches above the ground with the result that elderly people and ladies in tight skirts found it very difficult to board. Although the problem was not of East Lancashire's making, the Company worked closely with AEC to resolve it. The problem was not as acute on front-entrance examples as the weight of the engine and gearbox kept the front suspension supressed although it still resulted in a high rear end when lightly loaded.

After the Dennis Loline was withdrawn and prior to its reintroduction Leigh turned to the AEC Renown taking four in 1963 numbered 25-28.The body design can be seen to be attractive and well-proportioned. When photographed at Leigh bus station on 3rd September 1970, this one had received its Selnec number as 6925.

By now the rear-engined double-decker with its greater seating capacity was becoming more popular, particularly with traffic departments and the appeal of the low floor front-engined chassis was limited. No doubt if it had been introduced earlier to non-Tilling Group companies it would have proved popular and many more would have been produced.

The Company had the distinction of building the last body on a rear entrance conventional double-decker, this being Stockport Corporation No. 91 delivered in 1969, and also the last body on a conventional front-engined double-decker, this having been ordered by Ramsbottom Urban District Council but delivered to Selnec also in 1969. Happily both have been preserved and can be seen in the Manchester Museum of Transport.

This was not however to be the end of front-engined double-deckers as many operators were still not happy with rear-engined buses. The companies within the Scottish Bus Group were particularly unhappy with rear-engined designs and worked closely with Ailsa Bus Ltd in the development of the Ailsa B55 double-deck chassis. Ailsa was closely linked with Volvo and the chassis utilised the compact Volvo 6.7 litre turbo charged engine mounted at the front but positioned towards the offside so as to allow an entrance ahead of the front axle as on rear-engined vehicles. The first example was exhibited at the Scottish Motor Show in November 1973. East Lancashire Coachbuilders bodied only one batch of these vehicles comprising the 25 supplied to Tayside in 1983/84 referred to in Chapter 4.

THE GUY WULFRUNIAN

Whilst the rear-engined double-decker was becoming popular with traffic departments, their enthusiasm was not always shared by engineers who were concerned at the increased complexity of the vehicle. Such concern was voiced to the author on one occasion by an engineer of many years standing when he said, "In the old days we placed the engine alongside the driver and if anything went wrong he heard it and took action. Later we placed the engine under the floor in the middle of the bus, but even then the driver could hear it and take action in the event of a problem arising. Now we place the engine at the rear and the driver hasn't a clue as to what is happening until very often it is too late." This philosophy provides the background to another inovation of this period, the Guy Wulfrunian, a vehicle for which East Lancashire

Above: **The two Guy Wulfrunians supplied to Accrington Corporation in 1961 were unusual in having rear entrances. The heavy corner pillars to the front of the upper saloon, which were in contrast to the slender pillars normally found on East Lacashire bodies, are thought to have been brought about by the need to accommodate ducting for the Cave-Browne-Cave heating and ventilation system. The intake grilles associated with this system are also visible.**

Below: **One of the two bodies supplied to Wolverhampton Corporation on Guy Wulfrunian chassis was also unusual in having a forward entrance behind the front wheels rather than a front entrance ahead of them. This vehicle was exhibited at the 1962 Commercial Motor Show.**

Right: **Southampton City Transport turned to East Lancashire Coachbuilders in 1963 and thereafter standardised on this body make. Number 365 was one of the second batch of 15 bodies on AEC Regent V chassis delivered in 1964/65 and which were built at Neepsend. It is shown in the City Centre on 11th November 1972.**

Centre right: **Prior to local government reorganisation in 1974, Widnes was in Lancashire and its Transport Department made no secret of its support for Lancashire products. This Leyland PD2/40, built in 1964 with traditional East Lancashire rear-entrance body, was at Widnes Town Hall in June 1971 en route from Hough Green to Runcorn. Following reorganisation Widnes was transferred to Cheshire and the extended borough renamed Halton. At the time of writing it still operates its own transport department.**

Bottom right: **As part of the same local government reorganisation in 1974 Lancaster was amalgamated with the Borough of Morecambe and Heysham and the transport departments were combined. Prior to this Lancaster used an attractive livery of maroon and cream and this is displayed by No. 206, a 1965 Leyland PD2 with East Lancashire front-entrance body, photographed in the city centre in June 1971.**

Coachbuilders was to provide a number of bodies.

This chassis was an attempt to provide the advantages of the rear-engined chassis with regard to seating capacity and access whilst retaining a front mounted engine. It is generallly considered that the chassis was too sophisticated, being 20 years ahead of its time, and that it suffered from under development. The majority of bodies for it were supplied by Charles H Roe Ltd of Leeds to the order of West Riding Automobile Company Ltd who had been involved with Guy Motors Ltd in the development of the chassis. East Lancashire Coachbuilders did however build five bodies on the chassis, two for Accrington Corporation, two for Wolverhampton Corporation, one of which was exhibited at the 1962 Commercial Motor Show at Earls Court, and one for West Wales Motors. The two for Accrington were unusual in being the only Wulfrunians with rear entrances and one of the Wolverhampton bodies was provided with the entrance in a forward position behind the front axle rather than the more usual arrangement of the entrance being in front of the front axle. The Wulfrunian was not a success, most being withdrawn after short lives and no further East Lancashire bodies were built for it.

START OF A SHEFFIELD CONNECTION

As recorded in Chapter One the Directors remained unchanged from 1943 until the death of Walter Smith on 15th January 1958 when his shares passed to Martins Bank Ltd, 4 Water Street, Liverpool, as executors of his estate. At this time Walter Smith had owned two fifths of the shares, Alfred Alcock owned two fifths and George Danson one fifth.

On the death of Walter Smith the Danson family were interested in buying more shares but would not pay the current rate and the family of Walter Smith were not prepared to sell them at a reduced price. As a result of this lack of agreement, Martins Bank Ltd sold these shares to Bishopgate Nominees Ltd, 15 Bishopsgate, London EC2 in January 1963.

Around this time Alfred Alcock had met Joseph Edward Owston, the Managing Director of Cravens Ltd and had discussed with him Cravens interest in getting back into the bus body building business and Alfred had said 'Why don't you buy us?'

Cravens, of course, was an old established Company with a long pedigree of railway, tramcar, trolleybus and motor bus bodybuilding. Among their previous orders had been trams for Sheffield, buses for Bolton, Portsmouth and Sheffield, and trolleybuses for Hull and Portsmouth.

The negotiations with Cravens, and the sale of Smith's shares, culminated in February 1963 with the sale of Messrs Alcock and Danson's shares to Bishopsgate Nominees Ltd and in September 1963 three additional East Lancashire directors were appointed, all resident in Sheffield.

They were Joseph Edward Owston, a Managing Director, Edward Thomas White, an Engineer and Henry Booker, a Chartered Accountant. Mr Booker had been with the John Brown Group of Companies since 1951, Secretary of Cravens Homalloy (Sheffield) from 1953 to 1961 and a Director of this firm from 1961. In addition, from 1963 he was Director and General Manager of Cravens Homalloy (Preston) Ltd and also from the same date, Director and General Manager of Transport and Commercial Aluminium Ltd

In January 1964 Bishopsgate Nominees Ltd sold all the shares to Cravens Ltd, Darnall, Sheffield 9. The name Cravens Ltd was changed to Cravens Industries Ltd in February 1964 and the shares were accordingly transferred. The agreement for the sale of East Lancashire Coachbuilders to Cravens included a two year contract for Alfred Alcock, a five year contract for George Danson and directorships for the two sons, George Alcock and Arthur Danson.

The new Directors did not interfere with the operation of the Blackburn plant but considered that there was scope for expansion by the establishment of a subsidiary Company in Sheffield. This materialised as Neepsend Coachworks Ltd on Pennistone Road, which was not a subsidiary of East Lancashire but of Cravens. A Management Committee was set up to be rersponsible for policy and general guidance and to ensure the close relationship between the two Companies on manufacture and sales. This Committee comprised Messrs J E Owston, (Chairman); A Alcock; H Booker; G Danson and E White.

Tom Kenny, who had left his position as Works Manger at East Lancashire in the later fifties with Alan Brettle, the bodyshop foreman, to form KB Coachworks in Darwen, came back to the Company to become Works Manger at Neepsend. Initially frames were supplied from Blackburn for incorporation in bodies built at Sheffield but later frames were also manufactured at Sheffield. All the bodies produced at Sheffield were however to East Lancashire Coachbuilders' designs and drawings.

There was limited enthusiasm in Blackburn for this venture in the fear that Neepsend Coachworks might have been built up at the expense of East Lancashire, leading to possible closure of the Blackburn plant. However, the fears were eliminated for production at Neepsend ceased in February 1968, the last vehicles built being a batch of ten single-deckers on Leyland Panther chassis for Chesterfield Corporation.

There were two main reasons for the closure of Neepsend. One was that the quality of build was not as good as at Blackburn and the other that costs were much higher than at Blackburn.

4 THE REAR-ENGINED ERA

The prototype rear-engined Leyland Atlantean double-decker appeared at the 1956 Commercial Motor Show and a considerably modified first production example was displayed at the 1958 Show. Early examples gained a reputation for unreliability and many operators preferred to remain loyal to the traditional front engined vehicles which were to remain in production until 1969. Nevertheless there was considerable interest in the Atlantean with its easy access together with increased seating capacity and a number of substantial orders were placed for the new model.

Early body designs were disappointing, lacking in style, being very box-like in outline and with what seemed like vast expanses of metal between the lower and upper saloon windows brought about by the retention of deep lower saloon and shallow upper saloon windows as introduced on some conventional double-deckers just prior to the introduction of the Atlantean. This was a period when new trolleybuses with attractive full fronted bodies were still being produced by East Lancashire Coachbuilders and others, yet there seemed to be a reluctance by the early body builders to follow suit with the Atlantean. Daimler introduced its rear engined double-decker, the Fleetline, in 1960 but again early body styles were disappointing and generally followed the styles used on the Atlantean. During this time, East Lancashire Coachbuilders continued to build attractive well finished double-deck bodies on conventional front engined chassis and trolleybus bodies for its regular customers.

In May 1960, Ralph Bennett was appointed General Manager at Bolton Corporation Transport Department. He had some firm ideas about vehicle design and livery and in addition to introducing a brighter livery entered into discussions with East Lancashire, who had been supplying traditional bodies to Bolton for many years. His first influence brought about the provision of translucent roof panels and full fronts for a batch of Leyland PD3 double-deckers bodied by East Lancashire Coachbuilders. He was also involved in the design of a new single-deck body produced by the Company for Bolton. He then turned his attention to the design of a body for rear engined double-deckers, again working closely with East Lancashire to produce a design which was more acceptable to him than those previously available.

The first batch comprised eight vehicles delivered from April 1963 and thereafter regular orders were received from Bolton until the time when that operator became part of Selnec. The bodies were to a well-proportioned angular design with peaked domes which was later to form the basis of the standard East Lancashire body on rear engined chassis supplied to many operators. It was for the manufacture of these peaked domes that fibreglass was first introduced by the Company. Fibreglass was also used for what became known as the

Bolton No. 22 on a Leyland Leopard L2 chassis was not a rear-engined vehicle but was very much part of the rear-engined era. It was the first body designed in conjunction with Ralph Bennett when he became General Manager at Bolton in 1960. It was delivered in 1962 and had a crisp contemporary look to it which was enhanced by the attractive application of the traditional Bolton maroon and cream colours and it was provided with high backed seats. In 1964 four similar bodies were provided but with bus seats and dual doorways, two being on L2 chassis and the other pair on the longer PSU3/4 chassis. Number 22 is shown in service in April 1971 after being renumbered 6012 by Selnec.

Following on from the single-deckers came the first Leyland Atlanteans for Bolton, also designed in conjunction with Ralph Bennett and with a similar application of the maroon and cream colours. The design showed a considerable improvement on many of the bodies which had been available up to that time for rear-engined chassis and formed the basis of what became the standard East Lancashire body for rear-engined double-deckers for the next 20 years or so. Number 185 was the first of a batch of eight supplied in 1963. Later versions had a curved windscreen to assist in keeping the vehicles' windows cleaner through improved air flow. The angled 'peak' of the domes had been influenced by the contemporary Ford Anglia motor car.

'Bramley' cowl. This was a cowl in the driver's cab for the housing of the instruments, designed by Alf Bramley, the Works Manager.

However, alongside this Bolton-inspired design, a different design on rear engined chassis was supplied to other operators. This was very much a development of the style used for conventional front engined double-deckers at the time with a similar outline to the front of the upper saloon and with deep windows to both lower and upper saloons. The first bodies to this design were supplied on Daimler Fleetline chassis to Warrington Corporation from September 1963. Further examples went to Sheffield Transport on Atlantean chassis and to Bury and Coventry Corporations on Fleetline chassis.

The rear engined double-decker was followed by the rear engined single-decker and the first on the scene was the Bristol RE, introduced in 1962.

Initially, sales were restricted to the state-owned Tilling and Scottish Bus Group companies, as explained on page 33, but there was growing concern in many quarters over this restriction. Among those showing concern was Tony Benn MP who, at that time, represented a Bristol constituency. A plan was therefore launched which allowed Leyland to purchase a 25% share in Bristol and Eastern Coach Works in return for a 30% share in the ordinary capital of Park Royal Vehicles Ltd passing to the Tilling Group. In the short term this released Bristol and Eastern Coach Works from the restriction and allowed them to compete on the open market. The long term effect was somewhat different for, later, Leyland took complete control of Bristol and Eastern Coach Works and eventually closed both firms, but that is another story, as told by Venture Publications in its histories of those companies.

The agreement did mean that East Lancashire and indeed other coachbuilders were able once again to offer bodies for Bristol chassis. The first East Lancashire bodies on Bristol RE chassis were provided in 1968, two being on RELL6L chassis for Warrington Corporation and three RESL6Gs for Accrington Corporation. Thereafter regular orders followed, mainly from small and medium sized municipal operators in the North West who were established East Lancashire customers.

Next came the Bristol VRT double-decker which was Bristol's answer to the Atlantean and Fleetline and attracted the attention of many operators and substantial numbers were bodied by East Lancashire for Sheffield, Merseyside, South Yorkshire, Burnley, Northampton and Lincoln. The last VRT bodied by East Lancashire was delivered to Northampton in 1982.

Ralph Bennett moved from Bolton to Manchester City Transport, as General Manager, in 1965 and took with him his interest in vehicle design, introducing the 'Mancunian' double-deck body designed specifically for one person operation. The initial body order went to Park Royal Vehicles but

Right: Contemporary with the order from Bolton for Atlantean bodies was an order from Warrington for bodies on Daimler Fleetline chassis which were completely different from the Bolton bodies. They were based on the current East Lancashire design as fitted to front-engined double-deckers. Another well-proportioned, attractive design was produced. Flat windscreens were provided for the first batch which was delivered in 1963. Later similar bodies for Warrington had curved windscreens.

Lower right: The first rear-engined vehicles to be built at Neepsend comprised a batch of 20 on Leyland Atlantean chassis for Sheffield Transport delivered in 1964/65. They were built to the same design as the Daimler Fleetlines for Warrington but incorporated two-piece curved windscreens. A further batch of 20 numbered 162 to 181 was built at Neepsend in 1966 and No.165 is shown in service on 29th September 1970.

Below: The Company built eight bodies on AEC Reliance chassis in 1964/65 for Reading Corporation to the operator's specification incorporating large windows. George Alcock recalls going to Reading to collect the glasses for these bodies and returning with them in the boot of his car only to find that some had broken en route. He had to go back to Reading for replacements. The bodies were built at Neepsend and No. 48 is shown before delivery.

Left: **Following the Daimler Fleetlines Warrington returned to front-engined double-deckers and received seven on Leyland PD2/40 chassis in 1964/65. In 1965 this operator also took 12 Leyland PD2/40 specials built to a width of 7ft 6ins for operation through parts of the town centre where there were width restrictions. East Lancashire provided front-entrance bodies for these and one of them, No. 47, is shown crossing the bridge over the River Mersey at the south end of the town centre on service 10, operated jointly with North Western Road Car Company, to Thelwall in August 1970.**

Lower left: **Burnley Colne and Nelson No. 70 was one of four Leyland Tiger Cubs supplied in 1967 just before the change in single-deck body design from the 'square'-type body shown here to the later type. It is shown arriving in the Yorkshire market town of Skipton operating the mid-day journey from Colne on a Saturday in May 1973.**

the 1969/70 order was split between Park Royal and East Lancashire, the latter receiving an order for 24 on Leyland Atlantean chassis. The first twelve of these differed from previous Mancunians in that they were of single rather than dual door type. The tender for these vehicles was submitted and the Company quoted a very competitive price as they were keen to supply to a large operator such as Manchester and also to maintain the excellent relationship which had been built up with Mr Bennett during his time at Bolton. Following submission of the tender George Alcock and Arthur Danson were called to a meeting at Ralph Bennett's office in Manchester and advised that their price was the lowest and asked if they would stand by it. Bennett suggested that George and Arthur go for lunch and come back in the afternoon to tell him if they would stand by their price. They telephoned George Danson to discuss the matter with him and they were told that if they stood by the price it was 'on their heads'. They were keen to have the contract so they stood by their price and in the afternoon the contract was signed. It was very carefully supervised internally and also by regular visits from Manchester personnel. The decision of George and Arthur to stand by their tender was justified and a small profit was made. The final order for Mancunians was placed in 1969 for delivery in 1971/72 and East Lancashire received an order for 34 bodies. However, the disastrous fire of 1970, mentioned later, caused the Company to ask to be relieved of the order, because they could not have completed it in the required time. The order was transferred to Charles Roe of Leeds.

At this time, George Alcock was still a young man and he speaks of the excellent relationship which was established with Mr Bennett who seemed to take a fatherly interest in him and at conferences would always ensure that George was included in any social gatherings.

Top: **The only bodies supplied by East Lancashire on Daimler Roadliner chassis were three for Eastbourne Corporation in 1967 and 1968. The first of these is shown when new and illustrates the style of body developed for rear-engined single-deckers as a replacement for the previous single-deck 'square' design. This design incorporated longer window bays, curved front screen and flat rear window.**

Above left: **The single-deck body style used for rear-engined chassis was also supplied for underfloor-engined chassis. Barrow in Furness Corporation received five, built at Neepsend on Leyland Leopard chassis, in 1967 which were numbered 55-59. Number 56 is passing the railway station on Abbey Road in April 1985 followed by No.61, one of five similar vehicles delivered in 1968 and with bodies built at Blackburn.**

Above right: **In 1969 Lancaster City Transport purchased three Leyland Leopards numbered 110-112 to which East Lancashire fitted the current style of single-deck body. This view in Lancaster bus station shows the rear and front views as 111 passes 112 in May 1970. Where high-backed seating was fitted, the rear window was lifted vertically so that its top edge was just below roof level.**

The high demand for the Bristol RE may have influenced Seddon to introduce the RU and the Company bodied on this chassis for Blackburn and Accrington Corporations and later for Accrington's successor, Hyndburn Borough Transport.

AEC had followed Bristol with a rear engined single-decker, the Swift, and Leyland followed with the Panther and the Panther Cub, but neither of these makes was as popular as the Bristol RE. East Lancashire did however provide bodies on both and also on Daimler Roadliners for Eastbourne Corporation. In addition single-deck bodies were provided on Daimler Fleetline chassis for Barrow in Furness and Bury Corporations.

The bodies provided for these rear engined single-deckers were very similar to the then current design for underfloor engined vehicles with long bays, single piece curved windscreens and peaked domes to the front and rear, the rear having the characteristic flat curved top window. A variation on this design was that provided on the Daimler Fleetlines for Barrow which featured a low driving position, flat double windscreens set lower than the side windows and a rather heavy looking front dome. This design was later superceded by a more angular design, with stepped waistrail and flat windscreens which bore considerable resemblance to the current double-deck design. There was still a

Left: **Merthyr No. 147 was one of ten short Leyland Leopards supplied in 1967/68 and is shown in May 1976.**

Centre left: **This view taken in May 1973 shows two versions of the Bolton style of body on Leyland Atlantean chassis. The bus on the right was formerly Bolton 277 but is displaying its Selnec number 6777. That on the left was ordered by Bolton as its No. 296 but was delivered to Selnec as No. 6796. Evident are the larger side-windows and sloping window-pillars introduced by Jim Batty when he took over as General Manager at Bolton after Ralph Bennett had moved to Manchester. Both vehicles show the curved windscreen.**

Bottom left: **Manchester No. 1154, one of the dual-doorway Mancunian bodies on Leyland Atlantean chassis is shown at Piccadilly bus station in July 1970 on service 100 to Woodhouse Park. Woolworth's store would later be destroyed by fire.**

demand during this period for service bus bodies on underfloor engined chassis and variations on this design were produced to suit this type of chassis, some bodies having the BET style of windscreen. These variations are shown in the photographs.

In 1974 a luxury coach body was produced on a Seddon RU chassis to the order of Hyndburn Borough Council and the following year, two similar bodies were supplied to Halton Borough Council on Leyland Leopard chassis.

By the late sixties and early seventies there were two important developments in the industry which could have adversely affected East Lancashire Coachbuilders, beginning in 1969 with the first PTEs coming into operation and covering Greater Manchester (Selnec), Merseyside, Tyneside and West Midlands. Among them they took over a number of municipal operators who had been East Lancashire customers for many years. However, the PTEs were generally managed by people who had come from the constituent municipal operators, many of whom were aware of and had previous experience of the products of East Lancshire Coachbuilders. The result was that orders continued, generally being for larger quantities from a

Top: **In the early seventies a revised design of single-deck body was introduced which retained the long bays, peaked front dome and flat rear window, but incorporated twin flat windscreens similar to those used on the then current double-deckers which brought about a considerable change in appearance. This design was used to body five AEC Swift rear-engined chassis for Ipswich Corporation in 1973. The stepped waistrail is visible in this view of No. 92, photographed in front of the new factory building, a location used for many official East Lancashire Coachbuilders photographs.**

Above left: **Warrington Borough Transport became a regular user of the Bristol RE chassis and became in 1999 the last undertaking on mainland Britain to operate such vehicles which had been supplied new to them. This example, No. 65, was one of five supplied in 1972 on the short RESL version. Similar vehicles supplied in the same year had dual-purpose seating.**

Above right: **Nottingham City Transport has been a regular customer of East Lancashire Coachbuilders since 1973, the first order being for 46 bodies on Leyland Atlantean chassis, built to the operator's design. These were numbered 540-585. High seating capacity has always been a Nottingham strong point, these dual-door vehicles seated 77.**

smaller number of separate customers. Of particular note are the large orders received at this time from Merseyside PTE. There was, of course, still a sizable municipal market and orders from this sector were not only maintained but the customer base expanded to include such operators as Coventry, Nottingham, Brighton, Preston and Plymouth, all of whom placed substantial orders with the Company. The vehicles supplied to Nottingham were to the operator's characteristic design and provided yet another example of the willingness of the Company to meet specific requirements of customers. Orders for this operator were generally shared with Northern Counties but the East Lancashire bodies could be identified by the large window to the upper saloon rear emergency exit.

The second event was the establishment of the National Bus Company and the formation of a partnership between that organisation and Leyland to produce the Leyland National single-decker. This was of integral construction rather than of the

Above: One of two coach bodies supplied on Leyland Leopard chassis to Halton Borough Transport in 1975 was photographed in Widnes on a local service in August 1976. Both were rebodied with service bus bodies by East Lancashire Coachbuilders and later entered service with Hyndburn Borough Transport. A similar coach body was supplied on a Seddon RU chassis in 1974 to Hyndburn Borough Transport. No other examples were built.

Left: During the time that the first Dominator was under construction, Dennis required photographs for publicity purposes. East Lancashire Coachbuilders had just completed some Leyland Atlanteans for Brighton. A front grille and a 'Dennis' name plate of the type fitted to Dennis fire engines were fitted to the front of one of the Atlanteans and photographs taken, no doubt confusing enthusiasts.

traditional body on chassis construction, and Leyland saw this as becoming the standard single-decker in this country superceding the separate body on chassis arrangement in which East Lancashire and other body builders had been involved for so long. However, there was a distinct lack of enthusiasm for this vehicle for reasons discussed in Chapter 7 and in an attempt to increase sales of it, Leyland withdrew the Bristol RE and Bristol LH single-deck chassis together with the AEC Swift and the Leyland Panther. Nevertheless, operators, particularly those outside the National Bus Company, made it clear that they would not be forced into buying something they did not want, some buying underfloor engined chassis which they then had bodied by firms such as East Lancashire Coachbuilders whilst others turned to Dennis who introduced a rear engined single-deck chassis named the 'Falcon', a model which East Lancashire bodied for a number of customers.

In the midst of this upheaval in the industry a third event threatened the Company for at Easter 1970 the Works was virtually destroyed by fire. The fire started in the area below the electricians' shop and two theories were put forward as to the cause. The first that it was due to an electrical fault and the second that it had started in fibreglass waste stored in the area concerned. Extensive damage was caused to the premises and staff were called in to carry out salvage work. No member of the work force was laid off as a result of the fire and the Company was grateful for assistance and understanding received from customers during this crisis. Mr Chadwick, the General Manager of Accrington Corporation Transport, and Mr Oak, the General Manager of Blackburn Corporation Transport both made available sections of their premises and production was undertaken at both of these locations.

Dennis and East Lancashire Coachbuilders in Downing Street. The sight of a double-decker bus outside No. 10 is a rarity: this one, indeed, may well have had no precursor. The first Dennis Dominator was photogaphed outside the Prime Minister's official residence on the occasion of the presentation of an award made by Mr James Callaghan to John Smith, Managing Director of Hestair, in official recognition of Hestair's contribution to Great Britain's export drive.

Reconstruction work commenced in May 1970 and was completed by March 1971. This included the provision of a new building, isolated from the remainder of the works, which had been planned long before the fire and this explains why it was possible to make an early start on this building following the fire for construction was already programmed to commence in May. The reason for the isolation is that it was considered that if ever the work load reduced and the Company found itself with too much space, it would be easier to sub-let or sell an isolated building than one which was connected to the works. This did however create a large amount of personnel traffic between the main works and the new building and on one particular day Philip Hilton recorded something like one thousand man movements between the two sections of the works. The new building which was designed on the basis of 15-ft-wide bays was positioned so that it could be extended, if necessary, in the future by the addition of three bays which could be contained within the confines of the site.

It had not been intended to alter the layout of the existing works but one evening George Alcock and Arthur Danson were on site with John Bufton and it just so happened that the gable wall collapsed. Rumour has it that the collapse was influenced in some way by those on the site! When George Danson arrived the following morning he was aghast to see the collapsed gable wall. Arthur suggested that the collapse had probably been initiated by all the water applied during the fire. However, it was decided to rebuild the gable with doors which meant that buses could be driven from the old works to the new works without going on the main road.

As far as vehicles in build were concerned a batch of ten Bristol VRT double-deckers for Stockport was destroyed together with a Bristol VRT chassis for Merseyside PTE. A Leyland Atlantean for Southampton was damaged and the chassis was later exported to the Seven Hills Bus Company in Australia receiving a Pressed Metal single-deck body. Reference has already been made to the second order for Mancunians which had to be diverted to C H Roe because of the fire and another diverted order was that from Lancaster City Transport for six single-deck bodies on Leyland Leopard chassis which went to Pennine.

In 1974 further changes in Local Government took place which led to the establishment of two additional Passenger Transport Executives covering West Yorkshire and South Yorkshire, the former taking over two long established East Lancashire customers at Bradford and Huddersfield, and the latter incorporating Sheffield which had become an important customer in more recent years. Selnec became Greater Manchester Transport, taking in Wigan whilst Merseyside took over St Helens, another East Lancashire customer, and Southport. In addition the Tyneside Passenger Transport Executive was extended to include Sunderland and, of more significance for East Lancashire Coachbuilders, the West Midlands Passenger Transport Executive was extended to include one of their main customers, Coventry. It is interesting to note that following this takeover, the General Manager at Coventry, Derek Hyde, moved to Blackpool as General Manager and Blackpool became, for the first time in its history, an East Lancashire customer.

By the mid seventies Leyland was in a very strong position despite the general lack of enthusiasm for the National and had a virtual monopoly as far as double-deck chassis were concerned. Some operators were not satisfied with the standard of service received from Leyland and were keen to see another make of chassis being made available. Among these operators were the West Yorkshire and South Yorkshire Passenger Transport Executives. When Geoffrey Hilditch moved from West Yorkshire PTE to Leicester City Transport he took with him his desire for an alternative chassis and recalls the situation in his contribution to the 'Customer's View' from which we quote:-

"I wanted to buy some Fleetlines and sent an order to Leyland but the response was 'Sorry we are not making any more, you can have Titans or Atlanteans.' I suggested that this might lose them business only to be asked the question 'Well, where can you go ?' It made me cross, so I began to investigate alternative possibilities and my search led me to Guildford and Dennis, then part of the Hestair Group, and not - as a chassis builder - thriving. In actual fact it did not take long to come up with a chassis design but by this time Dennis had a history of coming into the PSV market and then quickly leaving it and many prophets were of the opinion that Dennis and the automobile industry were scheduled for an early divorce. Despite this adverse reaction chassis construction of what was to become the Dominator began but who would take a chance and accept our body order? Some of my contacts would have done but were told they could not, others felt there was little point in developing a body design to fit a chassis that could well follow the established Dennis format of here to-day, gone tomorrow, but in this they missed a significant feature. Expecting such a reaction I had indicated to Dennis that as far as possible, the wheel base, front and rear overhang, and top of frame contour should be as close as possible to the Fleetline so that a body for the latter would fit the Dominator and this was done.

At this point Arthur Danson came into the picture. He had been told by a Leyland executive that he would be well advised to look for alternative employment for what would East Lancashire do when there were no independent chassis available on which to mount their products?

The result was that Arthur wanted chassis and I wanted bodies and in the Leicester Centre Hotel one night a deal was struck. This was the starting point for the delivery of East Lancashire-bodied Dennis Dominators to Leicester."

The Guildford and Blackburn companies were no strangers to each other, of course. East Lancashire already had considerable experience in providing bodies for Dennis chassis notably in the postwar period for Aldershot and District and later on the Dennis Loline chassis.

On 22nd June 1977 Arthur Danson submitted a quotation to Hestair Dennis Ltd in the sum of £14,320 for the supply of the body for the prototype Dominator. Hestair Dennis Ltd responded with their official order No. 325087 dated 1st July 1977.

At this time the Company had an order for 15 bodies for Southampton on Leyland Atlantean chassis and increased this to 16 to provide a body for the first Dominator. There was some mystery among the works employees as to where the missing chassis was but eventually it arrived and was not an Atlantean but the first Dennis Dominator.

On completion the bus was inspected by John Hood of Dennis and Norman Kay of South Yorkshire PTE and was purchased there and then by South Yorkshire PTE. It spent some time as a demonstrator before entering service with its owner. Agreement had been reached with British Aircraft Corporation Ltd for testing to be carried out at their Samlesbury Airfield near Blackburn. Following this, substantial orders were received for the Dominator and East Lancashire built a total of 371 bodies by the time production ceased in 1996. The production included two batches bodied as single-deckers, one for Hartlepool Corporation and one for Barrow in Furness Corporation.

The choice of the name 'Dominator' for the new chassis could be said to have been prophetic. Although it did not achieve the sales figures of the Leyland Olympian, no one could ever have envisaged in those days that 20 years later, Dennis would dominate the bus chassis manufacturing scene in this country.

The other experimental vehicle produced at this time, also in an attempt to break Leyland's stranglehold, was the Foden NC and one example was bodied by East Lancashire for South Yorkshire PTE. However, it did not have the success of the Dennis Dominator and only seven were built.

Apart from the single-deck trolleybuses and some rebodies supplied to Glasgow Corporation Transport in the postwar period, mentioned in Chapter 3, the Company had not supplied to the Scottish municipal market until 1979 when the first order was supplied on Dennis Dominator chassis to Tayside Transport.

In the meantime the standard East Lancashire body for rear engined double-deck chassis which had evolved from the 'Bolton' design continued in production with minor variations. One of the most noticable was the introduction of deeper upper saloon front windows and with the foremost side windows sloping down on the bottom edge to match. A further change was the adoption of a more vertical front profile to meet the requirements of operators who requested the same size of side window throughout the bus. During this period a number of municipal operators specified coach seating for double-deckers to make them more attractive to a growing private hire market.

The early eighties saw Scania making an attempt to enter the British double-deck market with two demonstrators, both bodied by East Lancashire, appearing at the 1980 Motor Show, one on the Scania stand and the other in the demonstration park. The chassis was designated BR112DH and the body of the vehicle on the Scania stand featured bonded glazing. Scania worked closely with East Lancashire and after the chassis arrived in Britain a total of nineteen modifications were made at the suggestion of the bodybuilder, one of these being the inclining of the offside radiator to allow a lower floorline. The first of these vehicles was later purchased by Nottingham City Transport, becoming their No. 400. The other entered service with Gibson Brothers, the Leicester City Transport subsidiary, on 20th November 1980 but was sold to Singapore Bus Service in March 1982 and became an 84-seat dual-door vehicle. It was reregistered SBS 7000E. Another demonstrator appeared on the Scania stand at the 1982 Motor Show, again bodied by East Lancashire, but the chassis designation was changed to N112DH.

A further new double-deck chassis was the Dennis Falcon V. The first example was bodied by East Lancashire to the order of Dennis Vehicles for use as a demonstrator and was to the coachbuilder's standard outline. It was presented to operators at a 'drive in' held at the Lucas Girling test track near Warwick immediately after completion of the body in late 1981. The vehicle, which was not registered until August 1982 when it became XPD 659Y, went to Stevenage Borough Council in January 1984 for use as a playbus. A further example was displayed at the 1982 Motor Show and was one of two built to the order of Nottingham City Transport as their fleet numbers 396 and 397, the body being to their characteristic outline. An unusual feature of this body was that in addition to incorporating bonded glazing, it also incorporated bonded between-decks panelling, the first time such a feature had been provided in a double-decker. The chassis did not become popular and no further examples were bodied by East Lancashire.

ALUMINIUM FRAMING BECOMES MORE SIGNIFICANT

The well established East Lancashire Coachbuilders body continued in production until 1984 when two new designs were introduced. The first of these designs is sometimes referred to as the 'Alexander Lookalike' and it arose as a result of a request from South Yorkshire Passenger Transport Executive for bodies which had interchangeable parts with those of the operator's Alexander 'R' type bodies. In his book, *South Yorkshire's Transport, 1974 to 1995* published by Venture Publications Ltd, D Scott Hellewell, who was the PTE Controller of Operations and Planning at the time, records that they were concerned over Alexander's high prices and sought alternative sources of supply, i.e. East Lancashire Coachbuilders and Northern Counties. South Yorkshire obtained permission from Alexanders for their design to be used by others and provided samples to East Lancashire Coachbuilders for the manufacture of parts. Not only did the body look like an Alexander body but it used the same structural aluminium alloy sections which were standard sections available on the market and not peculiar to Alexanders. Following

completion of the initial order of fifteen bodies for South Yorkshire, examples of the same design were supplied to a number of other operators. It became known as the 'E' type. There are however two main features which distinguish the East Lancashire bodies from those built by Alexanders. One is the characteristic East Lancashire large window to the upper saloon emergency exit and the other is the lack of visible rivets at the waist and cant rail levels made possible by the use of the East Lancashire-designed aluminium alloy section illustrated in the Appendices.

The other design which was produced at the same time was introduced initially to meet the requirements of Sandy Strachan, General Manager at Tayside Transport. An order had been received for 30 double-deck bodies, the first 25 being on Volvo B55 front engined chassis and the remaining five comprising three bus-seated bodies and two coach-seated bodies on Volvo B10M-56 chassis. Incidentally, this was the first and only time that East Lancashire Coachbuilders built bodies on the Volvo B55 chassis. Mr Strachan stated that for the coaches he wanted something different from a flat fronted body. It was arising from his request that this version of body was developed, starting with a mock up in George Alcock's office. The angular type of body was provided with curved windscreens and curved front upper saloon windows. The windscreen was the same as that used on the

<< *Opposite page top left:* **The first of many... Leicester No. 233 is handed over to the operator by John Hood of Dennis and George Alcock of East Lancashire Coachbuilders in October 1977. Geoffrey Hilditch is standing to the left of the photograph with his back to the vehicle entrance.**

<< *Opposite page top right:* **The Company provided single-deck bodies on Dennis Dominator chassis for Hartlepool and Barrow Corporations. The Barrow examples were numbered 18 and 19 and No. 18 was photographed on Abbey Road, Barrow heading for Biggar Bank in April 1985. The unusual arrangement of the rear end is just visible. Jim Chadwick, General Manager at Accrington, is alleged to have told George Alcock that they looked like dust carts from the rear!**

<< *Opposite page centre left:* **The Dennis Falcon V was not a successful chassis and very few were built. East Lancashire bodied a demonstrator in 1981 and two for Nottingham City Transport to a version of Nottingham's characteristic body design in 1982. One of these, No. 396, was in the City Centre on 1st May 1985. It had been exhibited at the 1982 Motor Show.**

<< *Opposite page centre right:* **Another exhibit at the 1982 Show was this East Lancashire-bodied Scania N112DH. It is shown in service with Nottingham City Transport, numbered 395, in the city centre, on 1st May 1985.**

<< *Opposite page bottom left:* **Preston was one of the operators which took delivery of coach-seated bodies on Leyland Atlantean chassis, taking two in 1982 numbered 1 and 2. The bodies incorporated the deep upper saloon front windows and the sloping lower edge of the foremost side-windows. Number 1 is shown in the town in April 1985 returning to the bus station from Moor Nook. In those days Preston buses tended to operate with the destination blinds set for the outer terminus regardless of direction of travel. A revised livery was applied to these vehicles.**

<< *Opposite page bottom right:* **The only Volvo B57 to be bodied in this country was this example from East Lancashire in 1985. It is shown in service with Raisbeck at Bedlington in August 1995.**

Mancunian double-decker for Manchester City Transport and the upper saloon front window was the same unit as used for the windscreens on the Atlanteans for Bolton. The design was supplied to a number of other customers and the structure was in aluminium alloy, identical to the 'E' type.

A low-height version of this body came in 1989 with a height of 13ft 7½ins, principally to meet the requirements of former National Bus Company subsidiaries who had operated low height Bristol VRTs and Leyland Olympians. The first four were mounted on Leyland Olympian chassis for Midland Red North and they were followed by a further fourteen on Dennis Dominator chassis, eight for North Western and six for Midland Red North.

The other factor which had influenced the change from steel lower-deck framing to aluminium alloy was that the 'brake shoe tee' which had been used by East Lancashire from the outset for its vertical metal framing became unavailable as motor car manufacturers moved towards disc brakes. An alternative section had been tried by splitting an 'I' section to form two tees but this was heavier than the brake shoe tee and not as successful.

A one-off body produced during this period was a 53-seat single-deck service bus body on a Volvo B57-60 chassis, the only occasion when a body has been provided in this country for this chassis. It was completed in July 1985 and entered service with Raisbeck of Morpeth, Northumberland.

We conclude this chapter with reference to two double-deck designs which, although not rear engined, were intended as alternatives to the rear engined designs and were very much part of the rear engined era.

Volvo had shown a reluctance to become involved in rear engined vehicles and after only limited success with its front engined B55 double-deck chassis decided to offer an underfloor engined double-deck chassis named the 'Citibus', based on its highly successful and popular B10M single-deck chassis. The first bodies for this chassis were built by Marshall of Cambridge but these were followed by two demonstrators with bodies built by East Lancashire Coachbuilders in 1983. The first of these passed to Docherty of Irvine in February 1985 and the second to Singapore Bus Service as SBS 4961B. Although the underfloor engine necessitated a higher floor level it did allow the full length of the bus to be used for passengers giving, if required, a higher seating capacity compared to rear engined vehicles. Further orders were received from a number of operators and as mentioned earlier it was on this chassis that East Lancashire built the first of the double-deck coach type bodies for Tayside.

At the 1986 Motor Show, Leyland introduced its double-deck underfloor engined chassis and christened it the 'Lion', thus reviving a chassis name from years gone by, applied to a very different type of vehicle. It had a very short life, its demise being brought about by the Volvo takeover of Leyland in March 1988. During the short time that the Lion was available East Lancashire built ten bodies, all for Nottingham City Transport - five standard service buses and five with coach seating.

5 RAILCARS AND TRAMCARS

The adaptability of the firm is well illustrated by its involvement in the manufacture of bodies for railcars, tramcars and a railway carriage.

RAILCARS

Reference was made in Chapter 1 to the early connection between East Lancashire Coachbuilders and Walker Brothers Ltd. The Wigan based firm was involved in the supply of railcars to operators in various parts of the world and it was through them that East Lancashire became involved in the provision of bodies for such vehicles. The bodies were built on stillages in the Blackburn works and then delivered on low-loaders to Walker Brothers who mounted them on their underframes and bogie units.

Full details of all the railcars built and referred to in the list of body numbers are not available and it is suspected that the records for some of these were lost in the fire of 1970. There are also references to railcar cabs and cabs for mobile cranes built for Walker Brothers. However, in 1947 a single car was supplied to the Sligo, Leitrim and Northern Counties Railway in Ireland. This was a 48¼-miles-long, 5ft 3ins. gauge line linking the Great Northern Railway (Ireland) at Enniskillen with Coras Iompair Eireann (Irish Transport Company) at Sligo. The line was notable for its sharp curves and heavy gradients and the car was arranged to take account of these. It was designed in conjunction with Mr G F Egan, Locomotive, Carriage and Wagon Superintendent for the Sligo, Leitrim and Northern Counties Railway.

The body was steel framed with 18-standard-gauge aluminium exterior panels. The main coach-body was 47ft 1½ins long with an outside width of 9ft 6ins and an interior width of 8ft 11ins Seating for 59 passengers was provided with straps for 15 standing passengers and the coach was divided into smoking and non-smoking compartments plus a luggage compartment 8ft 6ins long situated at the end of the coach next to the power unit. Three-and-two seating was provided with an offset centre walkway between. The seats comprised tubular frames with single top rail fitted with Dunlopillo cushions covered with turquoise blue leather. The floor was covered in blue linoleum to match the seating. Horizontal double sliding ventilators were provided to the windows and the bottom ledges of the windows were arranged as armrests.

The passenger section was connected to a short power unit via an articulated connection giving an overall length of 54ft 11½ins with driving controls at both ends. Passenger access was by double sliding doors and, because at some halts there were

Shown at Walker Brothers' works in Wigan just prior to delivery is the railcar built for the Sligo, Leitrim and Northern Counties Railway.

Above: This view of one of the Peruvian Railcars parked on the sidings near the works of Walker Brothers shows clearly the swivelling headlamp, the bird-protection bars to the windscreen and the animal-catcher bars below the windscreen.

Below: An interior view of one of the railcars for Peru shows the slatted wooden seats in the second-class section of the car. These will bring back memories to those who travelled on similar seats in this country on buses built to the utility specification during the Second World War. Ironically, of course, East Lancashire didn't build any utility bodies.

no platforms, a hinged step was provided at each door that could be folded down as necessary and then, when not required, securely fixed by a locking bar. The external colour scheme was white roof, eau de nil from the lower edge of the windows to the roof and deep chrome green below the windows. The engine was the Gardner 6LW, well-known and respected in the bus world, driving through a four-speed Wilson epicyclic gearbox and separate reversing gearbox. Of the 102bhp available from the engine, 6bhp was used for auxiliaries leaving 96bhp available for traction. During a test run a speed of 42 miles per hour was maintained and a fuel consumption of 13.3 miles per gallon was recorded.

Walker Brothers had supplied railcars to the British-owned Peruvian Coastal Railways since 1936, ten having been supplied up to 1940. As a result of customer satisfaction, only one failure having been recorded in 176,000 miles, an order for a further six cars was received to be built to a similar design to that used on the car for Sligo, Leitrim and Northern Counties Railway. The cars were to be suitable for operation either as single units or as coupled twins, two being for operation on the Pacasmayo and Guadalupe line, two for the Paita - Piura line and two for the Trujillo line. The first two were of standard gauge but the Trujillo line was of 3ft gauge. The first pair of cars coupled as a twin unit was tested from the Wigan Works of Walker Brothers with a full complement of passengers on 30th January 1949 and reached a speed of 50 mph. This pair of cars was for the Paita - Piura line.

These cars were 53ft 4ins long overall with a width of 9ft (8ft 5½ins internally). The passenger section was 45ft 7ins long and was connected to the power unit in a similar way as on the car for Ireland. There were 18 seats in the first-class section, laid out two on each side of a central walkway, and 46 in the second-class section, arranged in a two-and-three formation with an offset central walkway. In both sections, seats were arranged in a back-to-back formation. A toilet was provided within the area of the second-class section but with access from the vestibule between the first and second-class sections. Double sliding doors were provided for passenger access and windows were of the half-drop pattern.

The engine was again the well-tried Gardner 6LW unit driving through a Wilson epicyclic four speed gearbox with separate reversing box to give four speeds in both directions and driving controls were provided at both ends. An unusual feature, necessitated by the acute curves on the lines, was the provision of a swivel-mounted headlamp at high level, operated by a foot pedal. In order to give protection against large birds, bars were fitted over the windscreen and in front of the radiator and a catcher was fitted at low level to protect against mountain lions.

The reason for the separate power unit was to minimise noise and vibration intrusion to the passenger compartment and reports indicate that this was successful. In both cases access was available between the power units and the passenger compartments by means of a flexible vestibule.

One Friday afternoon during the construction of one of the railcars Len Barradell, the Chief Draughtsman, climbed into it to inspect something and someone switched off all the factory lights thinking everyone had left the premises. The railcar was of course up on stillages and he could not get out. He was eventually rescued by the arrival of Jim Broad, the night watchman!

TRAMCARS

The Blackpool tramway is well known, being the last traditional tram system in the country as distinct from the modern systems more recently introduced in Manchester, Sheffield, Birmingham and Croydon. There had been considerable in-house rebuilding of rolling stock over the years, notably the conversion of 13 English Electric rail coaches dating from 1934/35 to make them suitable for one-man-operation. This work was undertaken in the early seventies and it was decided in 1975 to rebuild one of the double-deck 'Balloon' cars to make it suitable for one-man-operation, work that commenced in April 1976. Following completion a similar rebuild was undertaken on a second double-deck car which re-entered service in June 1982. By this time it was clear that further improvements to the rolling stock had to be made and whilst Blackpool's own work was satisfactory it was realised that, with the limited resources available and the amount of work required, the assistance of outside contractors would have to be sought. Accordingly the Transport Committee authorised the construction of a new prototype single-deck tramcar and tenders were invited from a number of bus body builders.

The body specification called for a seating capacity of approximately 52 in a body 50-ft-long and 8ft-wide and tenders were received from Duple (Metsec) Ltd, Leyland Bus, Walter Alexander (Coachbuilders) Ltd and East Lancashire. At this time East Lancashire had supplied a number of bus bodies to Blackpool and was therefore able to offer a tram body with identical doors, windows, pillar sections, seats, lights and other fittings to those supplied on the bus bodies. This had an initial cost saving in reducing the number of special parts required for the tram body and also provided a potential saving with regard to spares.

The contract was agreed and the order placed for the initial tramcar body. The building of a tramcar body was a new venture for East Lancashire and the Company acknowledges the assistance and guidance provided by Blackpool Transport Department during the execution of the contract. For the initial car, the chassis was manufactured by the Primrose Third Axle Company of Blackburn. Some chassis were also manufactured by Wickham of Ware and prior to the first of these being built George Alcock and Philip Hilton went to the

On 24th April 1985 Blackpool 'Centenary' tram 641 travels south through Victoria Square, Cleveleys en route to Starr Gate, the southern terminus of the famous tramway system. This was at the time of the Blackpool Tramway Centenary and the sign on the front of the pantograph tower reads 'East Lancashire Coachbuilders are proud of their contribution to 100 years of transport.'

Wickham works to discuss the project and provide a plywood mock up of the chassis. Entrances were provided at the extreme ends of the body opposite the driver but in the light of experience gained from the second double-deck rebuild, No. 762, the exits were staggered. This arrangement gave the driver a better view of alighting passengers and provided a stronger body section. The framework and general construction was the same as used for bus bodywork and the frame was zinc-phosphated and given three coats of Hammerite paint. The vertical pillars were of the steel tee-section as used in the bus bodies at the time of construction and the cant and vent rails were of galvanised steel. The waistrails were of aluminium alloy channel section and these and the aluminium seat rails and truss panels were treated to protect against di-electric effect. After assembly the whole structure was given a carbolistic coating. External panels were aluminium pop-riveted to the framework and the area of the roof in the vicinity of the centre exits was strengthened to support the pantograph tower and illuminated advertising panels.

It was known that passengers prefer to ride on forward-facing seats near the entrance and this had in the past led to congestion in that area. In view of this the seats behind the entrance were arranged as rearward facing and those in the rear of the saloon as forward facing. Internally the tramcars were finished to the same specfication as the bodies on the Leyland Atlanteans with laminated plastic-faced internal panels and window pillars with anodised aluminium window trims.

The Railway Inspectorate required the tramcar to be designed to withstand an impact load on the ends of something in the order of 60 tons and to have carried out tests to prove this would have been too expensive, particularly as the initial order was only for one tramcar. Contact was made with an engineer who worked in the aircraft industry and who had experience of calculations of this nature. He acted as consultant and undertook all the necessary calculations which were accepted by the Railway Inspectorate.

The tramcars had to be built on stillages in the works and obviously could not be moved around during manufacture in the same way as a bus on a chassis. This created a problem with painting, which had to be done during the night when the remainder of the works was inactive. The tramcars were delivered by lorry and the height of the stillages was such that the lorry could be driven under the tramcar after it had been slightly raised on jacks.

Following satisfactory completion of the prototype a further six bodies were built for

Top: **The body of the engineering car was transported to Blackpool for mounting on the bogies and fitting out with the diesel generator and other equipment. It is shown in the tram sheds at Blackpool whilst undergoing this work in August 1992.**

Above: **The engineering car in action on the tracks at Cleveleys.**

Blackpool Transport and another to the same body design was built for GEC Traction Ltd. This car incorporated a new design of propulsion equipment and was operated on loan to Blackpool Transport carrying fleet number 651 for two years for in-service evaluation. The car was later taken over by Blackpool Transport and given the fleet number 648. The trams are known as the 'Centenary' cars.

These tramcars operate throughout the twelve months of each year in what is, without doubt, the most hostile environment for any public service vehicle in the United Kingdom. The first one, fleet number 641, had its inaugural run on 14th June 1984. After 15 years satisfactory and demanding service, equivalent to the full life of many buses, the batch of trams became due for a full overhaul. Major rebuilding work on tram number 642 was completed during 1999 and included repanelling, new front and rear domes with larger destination indicator, new window frames and ventilators, retrimming of the seats using the latest Blackpool moquette and a complete new interior finish similar to that used on the latest buses. The ceiling panels were retained and were refinished in Aquadex as used on the Alusuisse bodies built by East Lancashire Coachbuilders but in this case applied by roller. During the rebuilding no major defects were found on the main framework of the body. The fact that 642 looks like a new tramcar is testimony to the quality of the original structure and also to the skill of the bodyshop personnel at Blackpool Transport. All the other Centenary trams are to receive similar rebuilding and work commenced on 641 in November 1999. By courtesy of Blackpool Transport the author was able to look at 641 in its stripped down state and again there were no major defects on the main framing.

Blackpool Transport had for many years used an old tramcar adapted as an engineering car but decided to replace this with a new vehicle and an order was placed with East Lancashire. The provision of this car was another new venture for the Company and one in which they again worked in close cooperation with Blackpool Transport. By the time this body was built the Company had adopted aluminium alloy framing and this was used for the engineering car. The double-deck open top car is provided with a rotating working platform and two trolley arms, one at each end, to enable the tram to operate in either direction without the need to rotate the trolley arm, which would have been impossible because of the working platform. The lower deck houses a diesel generator set rated at 75hp driven by a Leyland O600 bus engine, which was fitted by Blackpool Transport Services after delivery of the car. The lower deck also contains a toilet, wash hand basin and work area. Double doors are provided in the side of the tram to enable the diesel generator set to be removed if necessary. The tram was delivered in 1992, finished in bright yellow livery and carries fleet number 754.

SNOWDON MOUNTAIN RAILWAY

In the late eighties a carriage was constructed for the Snowdon Mountain Railway in Wales, their first new item of rolling stock since 1897. This again was a new departure for the Company and George Alcock and Philip Hilton went to the railway company to discuss their requirements. They went along in their business suits and best shoes - as one would - and George seems to think that it was the 'coldest day on record'. They were taken along the track in the snow to see various aspects of the railway and discuss the specification for the carriage. The specification was agreed and an order was placed. The carriage had to be suitable for operation in sub-zero temperatures and be fitted with a braking device, provided by Hunslet of Leeds, which had to come into operation if the speed of the carriage exceeded 7 miles per hour. The doors were to be typical railway carriage type to be operated only from the outside and there was no heating. The Railway Inspectorate sent a representative to the works to look at the carriage and initially insisted on a 'crash test'. This seemed excessive as only one was being built. George Alcock contacted a man at British Rail in Derby who advised the provision at each end of a one-inch-thick steel plate about four- or five-feet-long welded to the chassis. Assurance was given that this would withstand any crash. East Lancashire's equipment would not cope with this type of welding and this aspect of the work had to be sub-contracted. It had been agreed that it would be good to have seats with hinged backs as fitted to tramcars so that passengers could face forwards regardless of the direction of travel. However, on tramway systems that normally operate on the level, this is a simple arrangement. In the case of a mountain railway operating on steep gradients the requirement is much more complex. Philip Hilton worked in conjunction with Vulcan Engineering, the seat frame manufacturers, and eventually they came up with a satisfactory solution.

The carriage, which has overall dimensions of 11.2 x 2.0 metres, was constructed utilising aluminium alloy framework as used in bus bodywork at that time, incorporating boxed top hat section vertical pillars in conjunction with the specially designed horizontal waistrail and top hat section roofrails. Cross bracing was provided by steel channel section and galvanised stress panels were fitted. The carriage had to be suitable for parking outdoors in sub-zero temperatures for prolonged periods in winter and this meant that the normal laminated plastic interior finishes could not be utilised and a material called 'Lamiplate' bonded to aluminium sheet was used. A general arrangement drawing of the carriage is shown in the Appendices and it will be noted that this shows conventional bus type folding doors in the centre but, as the photographs show, it was delivered with typical railway carriage doors. It seems that there was some difficulty in getting the customer to reach a decision on details and this caused some delay in delivery. Furthermore the customer would not take delivery in winter, as they did not want to pay for it at a time when the railway was not in use. The carriage has given satisfactory service and to anyone familiar with the products of East Lancashire Coachbuilders, there is an 'East Lancs' look about it.

Having safely arrived at Llanberis, the carriage is carefully lifted off the low loader by crane and guided by railway staff on to the tracks.

Above: An interior view of the carriage for the Snowdon Mountain Railway showing the rather cramped seating arrangement brought about by limit of 2 metres for the width.

Below: With a job well done and the carriage safely on the tracks at Llanberis Station, Philip Hilton, more suitably clad for the occasion than on his first visit to the Snowdon Mountain Railway, can smile with relief. He is accompanied by Mr Rogerson, the railway's General Manager.

6 DEREGULATION AND INTO THE NINETIES

The 1985 Transport Bill contained many changes with regard to the operation of bus services in this country and within it there were two major issues. The first was the privatisation of the National Bus Company and in preparation for this a number of the larger subsidiary companies were divided into smaller units, or, alternatively, sections of the operating areas of such companies were transferred to adjacent smaller subsidiary companies. This part of the Bill had no immediate effect on East Lancashire Coachbuilders as they had not supplied bodies to the National Bus Company.

The other major issue was the deregulation of the bus industry which removed from established operators the protection from direct competition which they had enjoyed since the 1930 Transport Act. The immediate effect of this was to sow the seeds of uncertainty in the industry resulting in a reluctance to invest in new vehicles. Reference to the yearly outputs for the Company indicates the way in which this uncertainty affected East Lancashire Coachbuilders. The yearly output which in the seventies had been well above the hundred mark each year dropped to 44 in 1985, 68 in 1986 and 59 in 1987. This was a matter of considerable concern to the Directors and their concern became known to their regular customers. An indication of the high regard which these customers had for the Company is illustrated by the fact that some of them discussed the problem and were prepared for their own companies to inject capital into East Lancashire Coachbuilders to keep it going through this difficult period.

In the event this was not necessary for in 1987, as will be seen in Chapter 11, the Trafalgar House Group, who had by then become owners of East Lancashire Coachbuilders, decided to sell the Company and it became part of the Drawlane Group, with effect from January 1988. Drawlane was a growing organisation which had purchased a number of ex-National Bus Company subsidiaries and as a direct result of this takeover the customer base, which had earlier been threatened, now widened as the Company became the main supplier of bodywork to the Drawlane Group. For the first time since the fifties the Company had major customers outside the municipal sector whilst still continuing to supply its traditional municipal base.

Drawlane was later renamed 'British Bus' as also mentioned in Chapter 11. As part of its expansion policy it set up a consultancy in Warsaw. Three left-hand drive Dennis Lances were supplied as part of this operation. They were fitted with Duple Metsec bodies assembled by East Lancashire.

Minibuses were a feature of the period covered by this chapter and East Lancashire built 32, all coach-built on Dodge S56 chassis. Five were supplied to Barrow in Furness Corporation in 1986. Barrow's No. 85 had just turned from Abbey Road into Duke Street on 24th April 1989 en route to West Shore on Walney Island when photographed. This was just one month before deregulation took its toll on the undertaking which ceased to trade on 26th May 1989.

Left: **A variation on a theme. Islwyn Borough Transport preferred the Dodge GO8 chassis which already formed the basis of some of its commercial vehicles and East Lancashire Coachbuilders provided 25-seat dual-purpose bodies on six vehicles numbered 47-52. The photograph shows No. 49 at Blackwood in March 1992.**

Centre left: **Long-standing customers continued to place orders during this difficult period and among them was Nottingham City Transport who took delivery of 15 Volvo Citibuses numbered 315 - 329 in 1988. Number 323 is shown in the city in August 1998.**

Bottom left: **When Leyland brought out its answer to the Volvo Citibus in the form of the underfloor-engined 'Lion' Nottingham City Transport, as ever, was prepared to try it and took delivery of ten with East Lancashire bodies, five with bus seating and five with coach seating. One of the bus-seated versions, No. 390, is shown in the city centre, also in August 1998.**

The reluctance to invest in new vehicles continued for some time and this had its effect upon the Company. However there were at this time orders for further Blackpool trams, the railway carriage for the Snowdon Mountain Railway and in addition the Company showed its willingness to diversify in order to maintain work through the factory. This diversification took the form of rebodying existing chassis, usually coaches which were fitted with service bus bodies, and also a certain amount of rebuilding work. Included in this rebuilding work was the provision of new fronts and rear ends on four Leyland Tigers with the notorious Eastern Coach Works B51 coach body. The basic structure of these bodies had been designed for the Bristol RE chassis with plenty of rear end support. National Bus Company had however fitted them to underfloor-engined coach chassis with the result that they became known as the coaches with the detachable boots. The Company also built for the Lancashire Constabulary two personnel carriers, otherwise known as 'Black Marias'.

This was also the period of the minibus, with the style of such vehicles varying from van

Right: **Kingston upon Hull City Transport had not purchased bodies from East Lancashire Coachbuilders since the 20 trolleybuses of 1939 but became an important customer during this period. A total of 57 double-deck and six single-deck bodies was supplied between 1985 and 1990. Number 146 on a Dennis Dominator chassis was one of 20 supplied in 1988/89 and it was photographed in July 1993 in the City Centre. It carried the 'E' type body which continued in production during the early part of this period.**

Centre right: **In 1985 as deregulation approached, Thamesdown found itself short of double-deckers and purchased six East Lancashire-bodied Dennis Dominators from East Staffordshire. The East Lancashire body was no stranger to Managing Director John Owen, following his period at Southampton, and he speaks well of the service received from these secondhand vehicles. Number 235 is shown in Swindon in March 1994.**

Bottom right: **Following a management buy out, Brighton and Hove, delighted to be freed from the restraints of the National Bus Company with regard to vehicle policy, turned to Scania and East Lancashire Coachbuilders after a survey of the market. Ten double-deckers were purchased in 1988 followed by 20 in 1989/90. Number 729, one of the later batch is shown in Brighton in July 1997.**

conversions to purpose-built bodies on established chassis cowls. East Lancashire Coachbuilders ventured into this field with a coachbuilt body on the Dodge S56 chassis cowl. The body framework utilised the aluminium alloy sections as used for the upper saloons of double-deckers and the engine cowl was removed to be replaced by a flush front provided as part of the body. Thirty-two were built for a number of operators as indicated in the Body and Customer List, some of the bodies being provided with dual purpose seating. They were all completed within the period 1986 to 1987 and no further orders were received. In addition to these minibuses there was a batch of six 25 seaters with dual purpose seating provided on Dodge GO8 chassis for Islwyn Borough Council Transport Department but these were to an entirely different design, being more akin in style to a full size vehicle. The term 'Midibus' had not yet been introduced. The

Top left: **Following purchase of East Lancashire by the Drawlane Group, orders from Drawlane companies were to figure prominently. One of these companies was North Western which had been formed by splitting off the western section of Ribble. Following a batch of Dennis Dominators, North Western took 14 Volvo B10Ms with East Lancashire bodies in 1989/90 of which No. 641 was operating an excursion at Fleetwood in August 1995.**

Above left: **Rebodying was to be a feature of this period as operators endeavoured to make the best use of the limited finance available. One of the Drawlane companies which became engaged with rebodying was Midland Red North. Number 1725 was one of a number of 12-metre Leyland Tigers so treated with the East Lancashire bodies specially designed, as detailed in the text, to enable them to pass under the restricted railway bridge at Little Haywood on service 825. They were also used on other duties and No. 1725 is shown at Rugeley on 14th August 1998, operating service 823 to Stafford.**

Top right: **An unusual rebodying exercise was that carried out by Grey Green who had 16 Volvo B10M chassis, which had been built with coach bodies, rebodied as double-deckers by East Lancashire. This view of No. 167 taken at Finsbury Square, London in April 1998 shows that on the offside, the lower- and upper-deck pillars were not in line. This was because of the chassis arrangement with short rear overhang and the specified position for the emergency exit.**

Above right **Another ex-National Bus Company subsidiary which became a regular customer of East Lancashire Coachbuilders following privatisation was the Yorkshire Traction Group. In 1995 it had a number of Leyland Tiger chassis rebodied with EL2000 bodies for its Lincolnshire Road Car fleet including No. 455, shown at Gainsborough in August 1995. The chassis had been new to South Wales as RCY 121Y with Duple coachwork.**

choice of chassis had been influenced by the fact that the Dodge GO8 was used extensively on the Islwyn Council's commercial vehicles. A similar body design was provided on a Leyland Swift chassis which was later sold to the Lancashire Constabulary.

Once the operating side of the industry had recovered from the initial shock of deregulation, confidence began to return and orders for new vehicles increased. The yearly output of new bodies for 1988 was 84 compared to 59 the previous year and 1989 saw this increase to 102 with a further increase to 114 in 1990.

As far as double-deck body design was concerned the Company continued with the two designs which had been introduced in 1984. These were the 'E' type sometimes referred to as the Alexander lookalike, and the other design which was not given a type number or name, but sometimes referred to as the 'Droop Nose Design', which had been introduced as a coach body although often supplied with bus seating. On single-deck designs, although there had been what could be termed a standard design, there had not been the same degree of standardisation and designs were produced to suit customer's

Right: **This view of No. 1223 in the 'Cityplus' fleet of North Western taken in the centre of Liverpool in May 1999 shows the Van Hool-type rear as applied to the EL2000 body on Dennis Dart chassis.**

Centre right: **The coming of deregulation saw municipal operators' vehicles on services well outside their traditional territories and Lincoln No. 45 was photographed leaving Newark Bus Station in June 1988. This shows the more vertical front provided on later versions of the East Lancashire body to meet the requirements of operators who requested common window sizes.**

Bottom right: **An important event which took place during this period, in parallel with the development of low-floor single-deck bodies, was the design of a new double-deck body named the 'Citizen' for Scania chassis. A. Mayne and Son of Manchester took delivery of six in 1996/97 and No. 2 from the first delivery is pictured in June 1999 loading in Manchester Picadilly on Mayne's service to Mossley.**

requirements as illustrated in the accompanying photographs.

However, as the industry stabilized again, a decision was made to introduce a standard single-deck design and this materialised as the EL2000, the first example appearing in March 1990 on a Dennis Falcon chassis for London & Country. The design was also available for fitting to the Volvo B10M chassis. The structure was aluminium alloy framed, with front and rear sections in glass fibre. Non-structural impact-resisting plastic sections were used for lower skirt panels, wheel arches and bumpers. The front windscreen was a two piece unit of particularly neat design and was in fact the same screen as used on the Plaxton 3200 Paramount coach body. As an alternative, a BET style windscreen was made available and appeared on a number of bodies for various operators, although this did have an adverse effect upon the appearance. A notable feature of the rear was the similarity to the Van Hool design as used on their coaches.

The story behind this is that George Alcock the managing director and chief designer at the time, had often admired the Van

Hool design when driving behind their coaches on the motorways and had noted that they seemed to retain a clean appearance when other designs looked dirty.

SOME INTERESTING REBODYING CONTRACTS

An early version of the EL2000 body was used to rebody 27 Leyland Tiger chassis for fellow Drawlane Group company Midland Red North between 1989 and 1993. The operator was pleased with the performance of a number of Duple-bodied Leyland Tiger buses in the fleet and was looking to replace some ageing Leyland Nationals. A constraint on the new vehicles was that they had to be capable of operating through two railway bridges at Little Haywood, one of which had headroom of 3.05 metres and a width restriction of 2.5 metres with the further complication of a dip in the road on both sides. The opportunity arose to acquire eleven Leyland Tiger 11-metre coaches with time-expired ECW B51 coach bodies and discussions were entered into with East Lancashire Coachbuilders regarding the possibility of rebodying them as service buses. Detailed plans of the bridges and road layout were studied and the conclusion reached that there would be no problem with 11-metre vehicles. Nevertheless, to be absolutely sure, Rossendale No. 93, an East Lancashire-bodied Leyland Tiger, was borrowed and driven carefully through the bridges, without mishap, witnessed by officials of Midland Red North. The eleven coaches were then acquired and after the operator had stripped the old bodies and overhauled the chassis they went to Blackburn for rebodying.

There was also the opportunity to acquire a quantity of 12-metre Leyland Tiger coaches but it was recognised that the increase in wheelbase of 0.46 metres and increased length of one metre would present further problems. East Lancashire Coachbuilders solved this by modifications which allowed a lower floor level and lower gangway between the seats which in turn allowed a lower roof line to be incorporated. In addition roof ventilators were omitted and additional window ventilators were provided to compensate for this.

When Grey Green obtained the contract for London Transport Route 210 between Finsbury Park and Brent Cross, difficulty was experienced in finding suitable vehicles for the narrow roads and tight corners involved. The Optare Delta was too long and a trial with a Leyland Lynx presented manoeuvrability problems. London Transport had used 10.3-metre Leyland Nationals and Grey Green did not want to use these. The solution was to buy thirteen purpose-built short-wheelbase Volvo B10Ms with EL2000 bodies seating 41 passengers in the 10.3-metre length. The short length was achieved partly by a short rear overhang. In order to assist with spares, the bodies incorporated the same windscreens as used on the East Lancashire bodied Scania double-deckers for the operator and also the same size of side window. They were delivered in 1991.

In 1992 Grey Green found itself with a surplus of coaches as emphasis in its business moved from coach to bus operation and this surplus included 20 Plaxton bodied Volvo B10Ms dating from 1984-1986. Two were sold but of the remainder, sixteen were rebodied by East Lancashire Coachbuilders, nine as 10.3 metre 'E' type double-deckers for use on route 141 and seven as single-deckers similar to those provided for service 210. The double-deckers are readily identified by the short rear overhang and also, because of the specified position for the lower saloon emergency exit, the lower saloon pillars do not linc up with those of the upper saloon on the offside. East Lancashire Coachbuilders salvaged the glazing and body parts from the Plaxton bodies for sale.

MORE SUCCESS WITH DENNIS

The success story of the nineties as far as bus chassis are concerned must be the Dennis Dart, first introduced at the 1988 Motor Show. Much of the development work for the Dart had been carried out by Duple who were members, along with Dennis, of the Trinity Holdings Group. It had been intended, initially at least, that all Darts would be bodied by Duple but in July 1989 it was announced that Trinity Holdings had decided to close the Duple bodybuilding activity in Blackpool.

Following this, East Lancashire Coachbuilders was offered the option to purchase the designs and the jigs for the Dart body for the sum of £78,000 but this was considered excessive and subsequently in October 1989 it was announced that the Carlyle Group had acquired the Duple designs and jigs for the Dart body. Shortly after this, the Dart chassis was made available for bodying by other coachbuilders.

The first East Lancashire body for the Dart chassis appeared in 1991 and not surprisingly was based on the EL 2000 body design. Two bodies were produced, one of 8.5-metre length for Midland Red North and the other a 9.8-metre demonstrator with the standard East Lancashire windscreen for the EL 2000 body whereas the example for Midland Red North had the same style of windscreen as fitted to double-deckers for that company. These were to be the first two of many bodies produced for this popular chassis which was well received by companies of all sizes from London Transport and the major groups to municipalities and small operators. Among these was of course the Drawlane Group for whom many examples were produced.

The Plaxton type windscreen which was designed for wider bodies had to be reduced in width for fitting to the early Dennis Darts. Initially this was done by reducing the width of the offside screen by six inches, the thinking here being that damage generally ocurred to the nearside screens and in such an event the nearside screen could be replaced by a standard unit from stock, without the necessity to reduce the width. Later the tendency was to reduce both offside and nearside screens by three inches.

By the early nineties the gloom associated with deregulation had passed and the Company found itself with a much wider customer base than at any time in its history. This base was made up of its traditional but decreasing muncipal core, operating companies within the Drawlane Group, and other former National Bus Company subsidiary companies who were now freed from the restrictions imposed by NBC on vehicle purchasing policy. Notable among those who turned to East Lancashire Coachbuilders at this time were the Yorkshire Traction Group and Brighton & Hove Bus and Coach Company.

Alan Eatwell, the present Director of Engineering to the Go Ahead Group and a member of the management buy-out team for the Brighton and Hove Bus and Coach Company, recalls the situation well and writes:-

"For a manager within the nationalised industry, the approved latter day options were the products of Lowestoft and Workington, with little other choice, and only on freedom from the Victoria Offices did the opportunity present itself to examine the products of others. In 1987 five senior managers were able to acquire the Brighton business and among their first challenges was to consider the means of overcoming the backlog in vehicle replacement and the resultant inheritance of high engineering costs.

The acquired fleet consisted mainly of ECW-bodied Bristol VRs and Leyland Nationals which were obsolete. This led us to a consideration of the market, including those chassis and body builders who were previously prohibited to us. Beauty parades were held and the partnership selected was that of East Lancashire Coachbuilders and Scania, a winning combination, further acquisition of which continued through subsequent ownership of Brighton and Hove by the Go Ahead Group, until a fleet of 65 was accumulated and even now, despite a change of chassis, a further 20 new East Lancashire bodies have recently entered service.

Looking back at the mid-eighties the choices open to operators were somewhat utilitarian, particularly with double-deck. A potential order for ten new buses, whilst significant to the owners of a newly privatised company, probably with second mortgages, was inadequate to entice most of the bigger players from offering much more than the standard required by their established customers in Manchester, Edinburgh or Birmingham. To East Lancashire, an order for ten was their meat and drink and typical of the sort of order they were delighted to accept annually from many of the country's municipal operators, hardly any of which had comparable specifications. Our wishes were considered, advice given and the result was a product of which they and we were proud."

Dennis introduced a new single-deck bus chassis in 1991, named the Lance, and the first body provided on this chassis by East Lancashire Coachbuilders was for Ipswich Transport, completed in December of that year. Thereafter bodies were provided on this chassis for a number of operators but it did not achieve the level of popularity of the Dart due no doubt to the fact that as the Dart was developed longer versions became available and the need for the Lance was diminished.

MAJOR CHANGES IN THE COMPANY

The continuity of control at the top had been unbroken since the arrival of Messrs Alcock and Danson in 1938, and the subsequent appointment of their sons first as Directors and then as Joint Managing Directors. This changed when, in 1991, George Alcock, the Joint Managing Director, took early retirement and Chris Clarke was appointed Chief Executive with effect from January 1992.

Another link with 1938 was also to be broken. The old premises in Whalley New Road which, apart from the new Finishing Shop built in 1971, were becoming increasingly unsuitable for the production of modern bus bodywork and the decision was made in 1992 to look for new premises. The present site on an industrial estate on the outskirts of Blackburn was purchased. It is close to the M65 motorway which at the time of purchase was being extended to meet the M61 and the M6. The new factory was officially opened on 16th September 1994 and the first vehicle to emerge was a Dennis Lance single-decker for Ipswich Transport whilst the last vehicle from the Whalley New Road works was a Volvo Olympian for Nottingham Transport, these two vehicles being completed at the same time, as the move from the old to new premises had been undertaken in stages. The new premises afforded the opportunity to increase annual production and the Company responded to this as indicated in the customer and body lists.

With the new factory came new designs and the first of these appeared at the 1995 Coach and Bus Show in the form of the Cityzen double-decker on Scania chassis. This was produced in conjunction with Scania who met some of the tooling costs associated with certain parts of the new design and it is for this reason that the Cityzen body is only available on Scania chassis. The basic design was produced by John Worker Associates and the structure was in aluminium alloy using the same sections as used on previous double-deckers. The first vehicles produced to this design were for Northumbria Motor Services and these were followed by orders for Brighton and Hove and Maynes of Manchester as well as a number built for Scania stock.

Other East Lancashire exhibits at the 1995 Coach and Bus Show were either of low floor or of Alusuisse construction and information relating to these is given in Chapter 8.

Even more far-reaching changes followed when, in August 1996, British Bus was purchased by the Cowie Group but the purchase did not include East Lancashire Coachbuilders who, as will be seen in Chapter 11, had previously passed to a Trust of which Dawson Williams was the sole shareholder.

Nevertheless, within two days of completing the deal with British Bus, the Cowie Group cancelled all orders which British Bus had placed on East Lancashire Coachbuilders. It has to be emphasised that this was a political decison and had nothing to do with the quality of East Lancashire products. This was a major body blow to the Company for it represented 100% of scheduled production for the autumn of 1996.

The Company had faced problems in the past and faced this crisis with the same determination which they had shown on previous occasions and there were no redundancies as a result of this action. The old proverb states 'a friend in need is a friend indeed' and the Company very much appreciated the help which came from friends in this crisis. Dennis supplied eight Dart chassis on the understanding that they would receive payment after the vehicles had been sold and some operators brought orders forward to assist. These operators included Bournemouth Transport, Yorkshire Traction and Nottingham City Transport. In addition, the Company's readiness to diversify was again evident and other work such as refurbishment of existing bodies was undertaken including such work on minibuses for Peoples Provincial and of Leyland Nationals for Nottingham City Transport.

Another new double-deck body on a Dennis Arrow chassis for Capital Citybus was unveiled at the Brighton Coach Rally in April 1997. It bore a strong resemblance to the Cityzen body for the Scania chassis and in addition to being available for the Dennis chassis, it was also suitable for the Volvo Olympian. It was given the name Premyer but this name brought strong objections from Plaxton who considered that it was too close to their Premiere luxury coach name. Following this objection East Lancashire invited suggestions for a name and the name Pyoneer was suggested by Ms Ann Clark, the Finance Director at Eastbourne Buses. This was the name adopted and it maintained the trend of using mis-spelled names incorporating a 'y'. The body was of conventional aluminium alloy framed construction despite the fact that by then Alusuisse construction had been adopted for the Flyte and Spryte single-deck bodies. A low height version of the body was introduced in early 1998, the first two being supplied on Volvo Olympian chassis to Road Car of Lincoln in March 1998 to upgrade service 6 between Lincoln and Skegness.

Open top tourist services in this country are generally operated by older vehicles converted for the purpose but when Guide Friday planned their open top service for Paris they decided to purchase new vehicles. The 12-metre Volvo B10M chassis was chosen and East Lancashire Coachbuilders provided six open top double-deck bodies for these. The bodies, which feature dual doors and dual staircases, were based on the Pyoneer design but had of course to be suitable for left-hand drive.

Following the 'Citizen' body for Scania chassis came the 'Pyoneer' for the Dennis Arrow and Volvo Olympian. Capital Citybus took 28 on Dennis Arrow chassis numbered 427 to 454 in 1998. Number 438 is shown in the Capital heading for Waterloo on service 76.

With computer aided design, this presented no problem and drawings for the left-hand drive body were easily produced from the standard right hand drive versions. The vehicles were delivered in April and May 1998. Further orders were received for similar vehicles from Cityrama and Les Cars Rouge, six bodies being supplied to each operator in 1999. One of the Guide Friday vehicles was used to transport the victorious French football team on a tour of the city when they won the 1998 World Cup competition.

This period of Company history, which had commenced with uncertainty in the wake of Deregulation, ended with a new works, new products, new ownership, an increased customer base and optimism for the future as the industry moved into the 'Low Floor Era'.

Blue bus of Horwich took five Pyoneers on Olympian chassis in 1998/99 and No. 41 dating from 1999 is shown at Heaton Park, Manchester on 5th September 1999 at the Annual Rally held there.

7 THE NATIONAL GREENWAY

The first Greenway to be completed was JCK 852W which had started life with Ribble Motor Services and was transferred to North Western with the formation of that company from the western area of Ribble. It was finished in the livery of London and Country to whom it was delivered on completion and is shown here prior to delivery.

Reference has already been made in Chapter 4 to the introduction of the Leyland National single-decker and the effect that this could have had on independent bodybuilders such as East Lancashire Coachbuilders. However, it was not a universally popular vehicle and apart from the attempt by Leyland to force a very standardised vehicle on operators, the National suffered from a number of major problems. The first was the Leyland 500 series engine, developed from a goods vehicle engine for this bus, which soon gained a reputation for consuming far greater amounts of fuel than the engines it was intended to replace. In addition it needed serious attention at much shorter intervals than its predecessors. It was also noisy and dirty and the clatter of a Mark 1 National became a familiar sound on the streets of our towns.

Another problem was the rather spartan interior body finish, which soon became shabby in service, a problem for which there was no ready solution. There was also a very sophisticated heating system with high level outlets, which gave rise to complaints regarding cold feet. In addition there was a corrosion problem on certain panels and the fixing of exterior panels using huck bolts led to a complex procedure for panel replacement, involving the removal of interior panels and the cutting of the huck bolt from the inside using a special tool. The replacement panels had to be purpose made National panels rather than standard sheet metal. It was for these reasons that many municipal operators turned their backs upon it but National Bus Company subsidiaries did not have the choice and were forced by Group policy to purchase this vehicle. Despite its problems the National did have some virtues, not least the fact that it was a very strong box structure with good access for passengers and in later years it had been available with a Gardner or a Leyland 680 engine.

By the early nineties a number of ex-National Bus Company subsidiaries found themselves with large numbers of Nationals which they considered too good to scrap but which were in need of major refurbishment. In particular, companies that had become part of the Drawlane Group sought a solution to this problem. One of these companies, London Country (South West) Ltd based at Reigate addressed the problem and work commenced using one of its oldest Nationals, LNB50. This vehicle, registration number JCK 852W, had been new to Ribble Motor Services and had later passed to North Western following the split up of Ribble in preparation for privatisation. At that time East Lancashire Coachbuilders was part of the Drawlane Group and its expertise was drawn upon for the body refurbishment. Indeed it is ironic that a vehicle which could well have put East Lancashire Coachbuilders out of business should, 20 years later, provide work for the Company at a time when orders for new vehicles were few and far between.

The project was in the hands of Chris Clarke, who at that time was a consulting engineer and who later moved to East Lancashire Coachbuilders to become Chairman and Chief Executive, where he continued his involvement with the project. Initially all mechanical work was undertaken at London Country (South West) Ltd but as the project progressed and demand for the Greenway increased mechanical work on some vehicles was undertaken by Blackburn Borough Transport. The name Greenway was chosen because it was 'Green' in the recycling of old vehicles and coincidentally also because of the involvement of the London Country (South West) Ltd Eastern Division which had at that time had been named Greenway.

The replacement engine chosen for the project was the Gardner 6HLXB either brand new or a remanufactured unit from Gardner to the latest 'Green' specification carrying a three-year warranty. Operators could expect to obtain something like 500,000 miles from this before major overhaul, ie over three times that normally obtained from the Leyland 500 series engines being replaced. The exception to the replacement Gardner engines concerns vehicles for Blackburn Borough Transport which were fitted with Volvo units in order to provide standardisation in a fleet where there were already Volvo engined coaches and service buses. There was initially a reluctance on the part of Volvo to supply engines for this purpose but this was overcome and Volvo seemed to realise it was better to supply a quantity of engines rather than have no business at all. They later introduced a re-power package for Nationals.

A choice was offered with regard to gearboxes between the Pneumocyclic, Hydracyclic, ZF or Voith and substantial mounting facilities were provided for the replacement engine and gearbox. These included a new cross member used in conjunction with a mounting frame designed by Gardner and substantial gearbox mounts to take the considerable weight of the Pneumocyclic gearbox which, although lacking the sophistication of some more modern gearboxes, was generally considered to be adequate for the job.

In the case of rebuilt Mark 1 vehicles, the radiator was moved to the front of the bus bringing about an increase in length to 10.6- and 11.6-metres. The Mark 2 Nationals were of course built

Above: **These photographs of an ex-North Western National, thought to be JCK 852W, were taken after the mechanical work had been completed and after the fitting of the new internal galvanised stress panels.**

Below: **This view taken inside the East Lancashire works shows the engine and ancilliary equipment at the rear of the bus prior to rebuilding of the bodywork. The revised air intake ducting can be seen rising vertically to the roof of the bus.**

Above: **An interior view of a completed Greenway showing the revised arrangement of the cove panels, the cappings over the framework at cove level and the new melamine interior finish to the body sides.**

Below: **Blackburn Borough Transport carried out the mechanical work on some vehicles and was so impressed by the merits of the project that it decided to have some for its own fleet, despite the fact that it had not previously operated Leyland Nationals. Number 532 was converted in 1994, the base vehicle coming from Busylink, Hemel Hempstead in the same year. It had been new to East Kent Road Car Company Ltd. All the Blackburn Greenways were fitted with Volvo engines. Number 532 is shown in August 1994 at the town's bus station with East Lancashire-bodied Leyland Atlantean No. 21, dating from 1982, in the background.**

with front-mounted radiators. In order to avoid problems associated with leaks in pipework full length pipes in stainless steel were provided between the engine and the radiator and at the radiator end of the pipework heat sensors were provided to control the electrically operated fan, this type of fan replacing the hydraulically operated unit originally provided on the Mark 2 vehicles.

In order to improve the flow of air to the engine the original rear-mounted air intake was replaced by a new intake mounted in a central position on the roof comprising an intake scoop leading to three separate ducts manufactured from plastic pipework and passing through the roof structure. A stainless steel Eminox exhaust unit was provided with the outlet at a central position at the rear of the bus.

Consideration was given to the provision of a revised suspension system but it was decided that the existing design was adequate and it was retained. The axles were overhauled and if necessary, crown wheels and pinions were replaced. New kingpins, hubs, studs and brake drums were fitted.

BODYWORK

On completion of the mechanical work the vehicle was transferred to East Lancashire Coachbuilders on a low loader if travelling from Reigate or by towing from Blackburn Transport. Here the body would be completely stripped down, but the outer skin of the roof was retained. On vehicles which had roof pods associated with the original heating and ventilation system, these were removed, as they were no longer required for the replacement system. The next task was to inspect the structure, which would be cleaned back to bare metal for treatment with 'Miogard' rust preventative treatment supplied by Joseph Mason Limited.

New one-inch-thick plywood floors were provided and in the case of Mark 1 Nationals the floor line was reprofiled to match that of the Mark 2 models and raised at the rear to clear the Gardner 6HLXB engine. A new floor structure was provided at the rear to accommodate the higher floorline. The front portion of the floor was ramped slightly in order to reduce the step height to the rear section and reduce wheel arch intrusion. The floor was built in sections related to the size in which the one-inch-thick plywood sheets could be obtained and was covered with vinyl.

Above: A revised rear end was designed in conjunction with Ray Stenning of Best Impressions for the Red Arrow Greenways of London General, demonstrated by No. GLS1 prior to delivery. Other Greenway conversions received the Van Hool-style of rear end.

Below: Excellent reports have been received on the performance and reliability of Greenways in the Red Arrow fleet operating under arduous conditions in London. One of them, GLS467, was photographed at Waterloo in June 1997.

Whilst the Greenwaysingle-decks entrance was not step-free, it showed a great improvement over that of underfloor-engined vehicles. This is a Black Prince example.

Galvanised steel stress panels were fitted to the inside of the bus rather than outside as on the original design and plain aluminium alloy panels were fitted to the outside with an option of detachable fibreglass skirts. New side windows were gasket-glazed direct to the structure with square corners to the top of the windows and radiused corners to the bottom. Interior panels and window pillars were covered in light coloured laminate and the angle of the cove panels was changed to be more upright than on the original design to give a more spacious interior look. Because of this feature, part of the roof framing became exposed and black plastic covers were provided to cover this. New ceilings manufactured from wallboard laminate were provided.

Seating was provided for 41 passengers on 10.6-metre models and for up to 52 on 11.6-metre vehicles. The seat frames were reconditioned and provided with new upholstery, and a luggage pen was provided over the nearside front wheelarch. On later versions tracking was provided in the ceiling which enabled vertical handrails to be fixed at any point along the bus.

The existing front and rear steel domes were removed and replaced by fibreglass units, that at the rear being of the Van Hool type. The original design had relied on the steel domes contributing to the overall strength of the body and steel sub-structures were now added to the front and rear domes to add strength. The original windscreen was replaced, that on the prototype being replaced by a screen made up of four flat glasses, this being done to reduce reflection problems encountered with the original screen and also to reduce replacement costs.

In the driver's cab, the original steering wheel was retained and the gearbox and handbrake controls were retained in their original place. The control panel below the signalling window was discarded and push-button controls for Voith or ZF gearboxes were fitted in the instrument binnacle. A new heating system utilising convection radiators was provided for the saloon on a separate circuit to the fan-assisted heater in the driver's cab.

The prototype vehicle appeared at the Coach and Bus Show at the National Exhibition Centre, Birmingham in October 1991 and created considerable interest. The fact that it could be provided at little more than half the cost of a new vehicle appealed to operators and further conversions followed, initially for Drawlane Group companies but then other operators expressed interest, including some who had not previously operated Nationals.

One of these operators was Blackburn Borough Transport whose Engineering Director, Peter Iddon, was interviewed for an article in the January 1994 issue of *Transport Engineer*. In carrying out the mechanical work on some of the vehicles Mr Iddon recognised the soundness of the project and decided that they should have some themselves. The Gardner engine which had been such a favourite at Blackburn in years gone by no longer featured in the fleet but they did have a number of Volvo engined buses and coaches and it was for this reason that they chose the Volvo unit. The Volvo engines return a fuel consumption of around 8.5 miles per gallon and whilst this is less than that expected from a Gardner, it is better than the figure obtained from the original Leyland 500 series engines. The Volvo engine did however require fewer chassis modifications than were required for the Gardner engine. The existing front engine mountings were retained and special fabricated mountings provided for the rear but there was no need for the additional frame member as required for a Gardner engine. A modification that was carried out on the Volvo engine was the repositioning of the alternator from its standard position on the side of the engine to a new position on top. Volvo engines were also provided in the vehicles for Black Prince of Morley. Blackburn retained the rear-mounted radiator but found that on the 10.3-metre long buses the engine would not fit with the radiator in its original position. Consequently it was moved back slightly, turned round and the fan was positioned on the inside rather than the outside of the radiator. In this case a hydraulically operated unit replaced the original belt driven fan. Although Blackburn had not operated Nationals, obtaining suitable base vehicles for conversion was no problem as many operators were disposing of such vehicles.

The Greenway has been well received by the operators who either had vehicles of their own rebuilt or purchased base vehicles for conversion. In an article in *Buses* magazine dated June 1992 Stephen Morris, the editor, wrote favourably as a passenger on the prototype vehicle in operation in his locality and also wrote of favourable comments overheard from other passengers.

Generally the Van Hool-type rear was fitted to the Greenways but those for the Red Arrow fleet of London Transport were fitted with a different rear incorporating a more conventional rear window. This particular feature was designed in conjunction with Ray Stenning of Best Impressions.

A total of 176 Greenway conversions were undertaken and it is likely that this number would have increased had it not been for the development of lighter weight single-deck chassis generally referred to as 'midibuses' such as the Dennis Dart. This meant that operators could then buy a completely new vehicle for little more than the cost of a Greenway conversion. Indeed the popularity of the Dennis Dart was probably the success story of the decade as far as bus manufacture is concerned and East Lancashire Coachbuilders provided bodies for many of these as related in Chapter 6.

Up to the time of writing in December 1999 there had been no reports of significant problems with the conversions and the performance of the vehicles in the Red Arrow fleet, operating under arduous conditions in London, had been particularly praised by the operator.

8 LOW FLOORS, ALUSUISSE AND THE FUTURE

In 1993 East Lancashire Coachbuilders built two bodies to Scania design on Scania MaxCi low-floor chassis. One of these with appropriate registration number L3 LOW entered service with Tayside Transport, Dundee on 24th September 1993. Here, Mrs Vicky Newman with the help of her children and push chair, demonstates the easy access to the bus.

The low floor single-deck bus made its British debut at the 1993 Coach and Bus Show when three were exhibited. In addition to a Neoplan and a Wright-bodied Dennis SLF there was a Scania MaxCi with body built by East Lancashire Coachbuilders. This demonstrator was one of two similar vehicles, the other having entered service with Tayside Transport on 24th September 1993. The body was of Scania design and Scania had built framework for these two bodies in Sweden but subsequent bodies were fully built by East Lancashire Coachbuilders. The framework was of 'Cromweld' stainless steel. Scania provided East Lancashire Coachbuilders with the front and rear chassis modules, together with the lattice work floor framing for fitting between these modules. The body became known by the name 'European' and was supplied to a number of operators including Tayside, Yorkshire Traction and the Drawlane Group.

In the next two years interest in low floor single-deckers gathered momentum and 250 were built by various manufacturers. At the 1995 Coach and Bus Show there were thirteen complete vehicles and two chassis.

A surprise entry at the 1995 Show, amid the sophisticated low floor vehicles, was a very basic single-decker with East Lancashire body mounted on an American built Spartan TX chassis. Historically it became quite significant for East Lancashire Coachbuilders as it was the first body which they built using the Alusuisse system. The 53-seat body was code named Opus 2 and finished in the livery of Yorkshire Traction. The vehicle price was quoted as £83,000 complete, which showed a considerable saving over other exhibits at the Show. However, with the industry moving towards more sophisticated low floor vehicles interest in this high floor basic vehicle was limited and only two were built, both going to Yorkshire Traction.

The vehicle had provided East Lancashire with an introduction to the Alusuisse form of body construction, which was to prove significant with regard to future designs. As the emphasis in the

Above: In 1995 two batches of Scania MaxCis were supplied to Clydeside. The first five had the upswept rear as on the Tayside vehicle but the remaining eight had a horizontal waistrail as No. 519 shown here in Glasgow in April 1997. The name 'European' was adopted for this design of body.

Below: The Dennis Dart had proved to be a very popular chassis since its introduction and Dennis decided to develop it as a low-floor chassis, giving it the designation SLF - Super Low Floor. The first East Lancashire bodies for the SLF were five for Rossendale Transport delivered in July 1996 and numbered 106 - 110. Number 108 is shown in Bury the following month.

Above: At the same time a new body was developed for low-floor chassis, using 'Alusuisse' construction and named the 'Spryte'. This photograph taken inside the East Lancashire works shows the main feature of the side framework using the Alusuisse system. The view from the inside of the bus shows the vertical pillars bolted to the horizontal members using the radiused brackets as utilised when gasket glazing is specified. Also visible is the external extruded planking.

Below: Single piece intermediate floors for Alusuisse construction stacked at the works ready for use.

industry turned towards low floor vehicles the Company recognised that there was not the same degree of rigidity in a low floor chassis as there was in conventional chassis. It was therefore apparent that the body would have to provide some of this rigidity and various options were considered. The conclusion was that Alusuisse construction would provide this rigidity and the decision was made to standardise on it for low floor bodies.

ALUSUISSE CONSTRUCTION

The Alusuisse system, manufactured in Switzerland, comprises a kit of parts made up largely of aluminium alloy extrusions which are bolted together to provide the framework for the body. One major departure from conventional construction is that exterior side panels are not of sheet aluminium but comprise extruded aluminium alloy sections or planks which are stress bearing and which are bolted to the vertical and horizontal framework. The other major departure from convention concerns the roof and, in the case of double-deckers, the intermediate floor. These items are supplied by Alusuisse as one-piece units and comprise a sandwich construction made up of constructional foam between aluminium alloy sheets. The floor so formed is load bearing and the need for complicated supporting framework is therefore eliminated. Along the longitudinal edges are aluminium alloy extruded sections, which are utilised to bolt and bond the floor to the cantrail sections.

Further advantages are the reduction in time for erection and the increased floor to ceiling height that can be made available within the vehicle because of the reduced intermediate floor depth. Embodied within the floor are two lengths of aluminium alloy sections in positions corresponding to the inner fixing positions for the seats. These aluminium alloy sections are then drilled and tapped to provide seat fixings. Rigorous testing was carried out by Alusuisse to check the 'pull out force' which the fixings would withstand. Comparable testing using a plywood and steel test specimen resulted in failure of the specimen. An illustration of the test and testing rig is included in the Appendices.

If gasket glazing is specified radiused brackets are used to join vertical and horizontal sections of framework but where bonded glazing is specified, right angle brackets are employed. The gasket glazing is applied direct to the framework but the vertical pillars are capped with sheet aluminium to cover the joints in the framework and brackets. Vertical pillars are delivered cut to length and are continuous from skirt level to the underside of upper saloon windows with a lighter pillar from this point to the roof. This simplifies any modification required to provide an open top double-deck body and also minimises the amount of damage caused to the body below upper saloon waistrail in the event of collision with a low bridge or similar structure.

The system is expensive to purchase but the reduced labour costs involved in assembly compensate for this. The 12-year warranty on the structure is covered by Alusuisse who make regular inspections on body builders to ensure that assembly is maintained to their standard.

The first low floor Alusuisse body built by East Lancashire, apart from the 'Opus 2' previously mentioned, was named the 'Spryte' and was fitted to Dennis Dart SLF chassis for Rossendale Transport, a total of five being supplied in July 1996. Again John Worker Design undertook the conceptual design work and one of these chassis was the 100th Dart SLF to be built. Thereafter the 'Spryte' became the standard East Lancashire body for all low floor single-deck chassis. At this time there was still a demand for normal height single-deck vehicles and a modified version of the 'Spryte' body, named the 'Flyte', was developed for such chassis. The first examples, supplied on Scania L113CRL chassis, were for North Western in October 1996.

Following the success of the low floor single-decker, attention turned to low floor double-deckers and again Dennis was to the forefront introducing its 'Trident' chassis. East Lancashire Coachbuilders was quick to develop a body for this and other similar chassis and it was not surprising that the Alusuisse system of construction was decided upon. An article describing the new body appeared in *Coach and Bus Week* magazine dated 23rd June 1998 and initially the body was code-named ADD99. The significance of this code was: A = Alusuisse, DD = double-deck, 99 = for 1999 production. As with other recent bodies, John Worker Design undertook the basic design work and in outline the body bore strong resemblance to the Cityzen and Pyoneer bodies.

With the Alusuisse construction, incorporating the composite load bearing floor and composite roof construction, it was possible to provide upper saloon headroom of 1830mm within an overall body height of 4300mm. The reduction in weight brought about by this form of construction allowed a seating capacity of up to 82 on the 10-metre version and 90 on the 10.55-metre. The upper and lower saloon ceilings are supplied ready primed for finishing with Aquadex, a coating that is used for the refurbishment of aircraft interiors. The roof structure has only four components including the bonding agent, compared to around 250 components with traditional construction. Another feature of the body is the large panoramic windows to both saloons and these can be either gasket glazed or bonded to suit customer choice.

The body was given the name 'Lolyne' and a further new feature was the incorporation of the East Lancashire Multi Signal System to provide distribution and control for the body electrical circuitry. The system, which is designed to give operators reliability and simple diagnostics, was developed in conjunction with ASL of Gateshead, using state of the art electronics, and operates using two ring main cables from the driver's cab to

Above: Bournemouth Transport took delivery of eight Dennis Dart SLFs with Spryte bodies in June 1998 numbered 475 to 482. Number 478, photographed in the town centre in May 1999, shows the signwriting for 'Super Route 6', branded for operation by these advanced vehicles.

Below: A Myllennium single-decker, intended for use on the Millennium Dome service, under construction at the works on 20th September 1999. As mentioned in the text on the facing page this was a very prestigious project. A Myllennium in service is illustrated in chapter 10.

four zones in the bus. Low voltage signals are transmitted along a 50 core ribbon cable to operate transistors to provide switching of loads and there is sufficient spare capacity within this cable to allow for the inclusion of warning signals back to the driver's cab. As part of this system miniature television cameras can be provided to give the driver a view of the upper saloon and also to assist in the setting of destination blinds. A comprehensive manual with diagrams is provided to operators to assist with maintenance of the system.

The first pre-production Lolyne body was completed on a Dennis Trident chassis in December 1998 and was the first of an order for Nottingham City Transport. The body received its first public showing at the United Kingdom Coach Rally held at Brighton in April 1999 when an example for Brighton & Hove Bus and Coach was exhibited. Thereafter regular orders have been received for the Lolyne.

During 1998 there had also been the construction of 30 double-deck bodies on Dennis Trident 3 axle chassis for export to Hong Kong Citybus. This contract was undertaken for Duple Metsec Ltd, the bodies incorporating their frames.

In December 1998 it was announced that the Company had won a prestigious contract to supply 17 low floor single-deck bodies on DAF chassis to the order of London Central to operate on the high profile Millennium Dome service. John Worker undertook the basic design work for the body, which was to a completely new design. East Lancashire Coachbuilders worked closely with London Central and London Transport on the development, which incorporates a low-cost Clayton air conditioning system. The first example was completed in September 1999 and given the name 'Myllennium'.

THE 1999 COACH AND BUS SHOW

This show took place at the National Exhibition Centre, Birmingham from 5th to 7th October. The Company exhibited on its own stand a Myllennium single-decker and a Lolyne-bodied Dennis Trident double-decker for First Bristol. Outside in the demonstration park was a Spryte-bodied Volvo B6LE for London Traveller and a Lolyne-bodied Dennis Trident for Blue Triangle, built to the London Transport specification with centre staircase. There was also a Scania with double-deck Cityzen body in dealer white. A further Myllennium single-decker appeared on the British Telecom stand in connection with the adaptation of a number of these vehicles for guided wire operation.

This story really ends at the end of the millennium. The last year of the old century, 1999, saw a record number of 249 bodies produced, more than half of which were double-deckers, but what of the future? The Company is entering the new millennium with confidence and the directors see the immediate future as a period of consolidation.

The order book is healthy and they have new designs to suit all types of chassis. The Lolyne body which has to date been mounted only on Dennis Trident chassis will be available for the Volvo B7 low floor double-deck chassis. The Myllennium single-deck body will continue to be available on DAF chassis and a modified version is to be introduced for the rebodying of underfloor-engined chassis. The Spryte body for low floor single-deck chassis will continue to be available but, with the decline of interest in step-entry single-deck chassis, the Flyte body is to be discontinued. However, with the Company's long standing reputation for 'building what the customer wants' no doubt, if the need arose, the design would be resurrected.

Thus, over 60 years since the Company began bus building in Blackburn, the aspirations and policies of Alfred Alcock and George Danson continue - with quality and customer satisfaction as important as ever.

The Dennis Arrow was soon superceded by the low-floor Dennis Trident for which East Lancashire Coachbuilders developed the Lolyne body. The first example went to Nottingham City Transport as No. 405, the first of an order for 12. The last of the batch, No. 416, is shown in the city centre in July 1999.

9 MANUFACTURE OF A BODY

This early photograph taken in the Whalley New Road works shows the framework of a trolleybus under construction. The curved supplementary framework towards the rear wheel arch confirms it to have been the lower saloon of one of the Hull double-deck Leyland trolleybuses delivered in 1939/40.

The manufacture of a bus body really commences with the submission of a tender. For East Lancashire Coachbuilders this was almost always to a municipal undertaking in response to a public advertisement. A specification would be received from the potential customer and the size and bulk of the specification would vary considerably from operator to operator. Generally, the larger the operator, the more bulky the specification.

In the early days the tenders would be prepared by George Danson, who was known to be meticulous in his record-keeping and after the order had been placed would mark his files accordingly. If the order had gone elsewhere this would be noted together with the value of the successful tender. After George Danson's time the tenders were prepared by his son Arthur Danson.

On receipt of an order the drawings would be prepared in the drawing office. This generally involved the modification of standard drawings to suit the reqirements of the customer. The order would be slotted into the the production programme and orders placed for bought-in materials and components. In the early days, and up to the time of the move to new premises in 1994, most of the items required would be manufactured in-house, the main bought-in parts being seat frames, opening-window mechanisms, door gear, lighting fittings and other electrical components.

The individual sections for the framework were manufactured in the fitting shop and then taken to the body shop where the framework for the body was assembled on vertical structures. The framework for the lower and upper saloons of double-deckers was made separately because of the height restriction of Brookhouse Mill. On completion of the various sections of the framework and chassis preparation the lower saloon framework was assembled on the chassis. The upper-saloon framework was assembled separately for mounting on the lower deck at a later stage. The framework was given anti-corrosion treatment by application of red lead or a similar coating.

Following the completion and erection of the framework, the fitting of the lower saloon and intermediate floors took place, followed by the fixing of internal and external panels including front and rear domes which had been manufactured in the works. The fitting of internal trim followed. In the days when polished timber finishes were used for window surrounds and bulkhead finishing, a bench would be set up inside the bus and the coachbuilder would cut and fit the timber sections before removing them for staining and varnishing by others. On completion of the staining and varnishing the timber trim would be refitted by the coachbuilder. Seat cushions and backs were manufactured in-house. The foreman upholsterer would mark out and cut the moquette or hide as applicable and machinists would then undertake the sewing. The covering would next be applied to the seating in the trim shop by a man with a mouthful of nails and with magnetic hammer in hand, in the way of all traditional upholsterers.

Internal and external painting would be carried out by brush and comprised seven coats. These were primer, two undercoats, 50/50 coat of undercoat and top coat, top coat, first coat of varnish, final coat of varnish. Other trades would work on the vehicle during painting except when the two coats of varnish were being applied. There was a departure from brush painting when the vehicles for Palestine were being built as they were specified to be finished in aluminium paint.

Above: **Whilst there was always variety in the chassis types to be seen in the factory the AEC Regal IV was rarer than most. Rochdale was East Lancashire's only customer for this model, in 1951, and it would have been amongst the first - if not the very first - underfloor engined chassis to be bodied by the Company.**

Below: **This example of lower saloon framework for a double-decker is thought to be for one of the bodies supplied to Aldershot and District in 1954. The Dennis Lance chassis stands on the one-time Blackburn tram track.**

This could not be applied successfully by brush at that time and spray painting was used. The work was carried out during the night when there were no other employees in the works. There was however a small spray painting area which was used for the painting of components including ceiling panels which were sprayed with primer and undercoat and then brush painted with top coat when in situ on the bus, following fitting of the aluminium alloy beading. In the days when polished timber beading was used on ceiling panels these were fitted after the panels had been painted.

The basic operation did not change greatly over the years. The main changes were the adoption of melamine plastic material for interior finishes, the introduction of underfloor-engined single-deckers and later the coming of rear-engined double-deckers and, later, single-deckers.

With the move to new premises at Whitebirk in 1994 there was a need to increase production and make the best use of space available in the works in order to keep up with customer demand and requirements. As a result of this situation the Company reviewed its design and building techniques. This led to the buying in of many of the components which had previously been manufactured in-house, thus enabling the workforce and the space in the works to be concentrated on the production of vehicles.

The main changes came with the introduction of computer aided design and the introduction of the Alusuisse system, basic details of which are given in Chapter 8. Initially this was used for single-deck bodies, but with its introduction for double-deck construction it was necessary to design new sections for intermediate cant, floor and upper deck cant rails. It was at this stage that the composite intermediate floor and top deck roof structures were introduced. This led to the speeding up of production and the whole process from welding of chassis-mounted brackets to fitting the exterior of the bus shell, intermediate floor, wheelboxes and staircase takes only three shifts of eight hours.

As the vehicle passes to the next stage of build, parts are then fitted to the vehicle to match the daily build slots, again saving skilled labour time. In sector 2 the fronts and rears are assembled and the whole of the exterior of the vehicle is completed up to paint stage. Whilst the exterior is being built the floor boarding and lagging is installed together with the East Lancashire Multi-Signal System interior electrical installation described in chapter 8. Following this the interior finishers take over.

Fibreglass components together with vacuum-formed moulded plastic components play an ever increasing role in vehicle build aesthetics, build tolerances and speed of build.

The painting process had to be speeded up and brush painting which took 24 hours per coat to dry

Left: **The burned-out remains of a Leyland Atlantean which should have been Southampton No. 123 stand amid the horrors of the fire at Easter 1970 as firemen continue the process of damping down. The chassis of this vehicle was salvaged and repaired before being exported to Australia where it received a single-deck body.**

Centre left: **Another view taken after the fire showing the damage to the roof and the remains of several vehicles in the foreground.**

Bottom left: **This view of the completed new building taken in 1972 shows three Bristol VRTs for Sheffield and two Coventry Daimler Fleetlines. The facade of the building was now a landmark in the town, proudly proclaiming the Company's name for all to see**

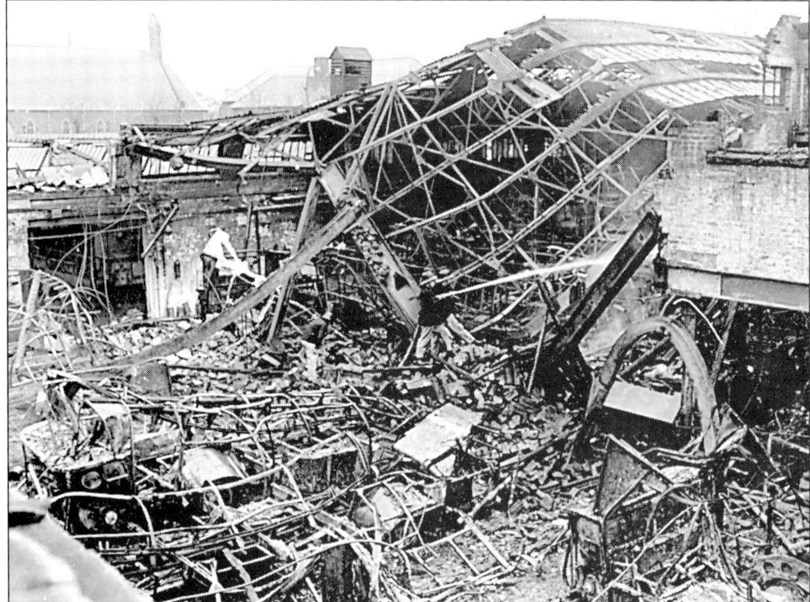

has been superceded by spray painting using two-pack paints which dry in the heated spray booth within 45 minutes. Prior to painting, the interior is completed including seating, handrails and cab area. If bonded glazing is specified this is also completed before painting. The vehicle is prepared for painting on day 13, depending on the customer's livery, and the painting process takes between one and two shifts. On day 15 the vehicle is lifted and all underbody work and associated underseal treatments are undertaken this being followed on day 16 by the glazing, exterior lighting and quality checks on the systems.

On day 17 the vehicle is water tested and road tested prior to certification and the pre-delivery inspection is carried out, normally during the evening. On day 18 the vehicle is finally cleaned, inspected and delivered to the customer.

Above: An internal view of the new building taken in 1981 shows Plymouth Leyland Atlantean No. 168 nearing completion with Plymouth 164 alongside and other bodies in various stages of construction. Also illustrated is the slide-along staging introduced by the Company. It is understood that when first introduced there was a reluctance by some sections of the workforce to use this staging until it was pointed out by the Health and Safety Executive that failure to use it could affect any subsequent claims which they might make in respect of an accident. The overhead radiant heating panels and the inspection pits are also evident.

Below: Another 1981 view of the new building showing Preston Leyland Atlantean No. 158 nearing completion and other vehicles under construction. The light, spacious working environment is clearly apparent.

Above: The new works at Whitebirk in September 1999. The view looks down the fitting shop towards the body shop. Single-deckers are under construction in the foreground and a double-decker nears completion in the distance.

Below: A single-decker on which interior fitting-out has just commenced. On the left, above the windows, electrical conduits for wiring can be seen. The use of angle rather than radius-type brackets indicates that the bus is to be provided with bonded glazing, as explained in the previous chapter.

Above: Alusuisse side-frames for single- and double-deck bodies ready for mounting on chassis.

Below: A Volvo B6LE for London Traveller. Painting has been completed and the bus is in the process of being glazed. The nearside windscreen is in place and the offside windscreen is awaited. The front dome and associated destination box is a one-piece fibreglass unit, a far cry from the days of panel beating in metal!

THE IMPRESSIVE FINISHED PRODUCT

Above: A Dennis Trident Lolyne for Preston Bus in the finishing section in the final stages of its construction.

Below: A Kingston upon Hull Scania N113DRB built in 1989 illustrates the previous generation of East Lancashire bodies. It was photographed in Queen's Gardens, Hull in May 1995.

10 THE CUSTOMER'S VIEW

The history of a Company such as East Lancashire Coachbuilders is much more than a history of vehicles produced, it is the story of people. Those on the inside producing the product and those all-important customers without whom there would be no Company. It has been a great pleasure for the author to talk to people on the inside, many of whom, such as George Alcock, Philip Hilton and John Bufton, have spent their entire working lives with the Company. One regret which the author has is never having met Arthur Danson for during the preparation of this book, the important role which he played, often as the initial and continuing customer contact, became evident.

The present Company Directors, publishers and author appreciate the willingness of customers and retired customers to contribute their viewpoint of the Company. Many of them express appreciation of Arthur Danson as their initial contact and much of his character becomes evident through their contributions.

GEOFFREY HILDITCH was unique in that after being a customer for many years, he later became a Director of East Lancashire Coachbuilders and he writes:- My first association with East Lancashire Coachbuilders began in 1954 when I was appointed Engineer to Halifax Passenger Transport. Amongst the 165 strong fleet were six Daimler CD650 double-deckers with East Lancashire bodies which were well-finished and unlike the chassis, with continuous flow hydraulic brakes, gave no trouble at all. Our bodyshop superintendent, Leslie Boulton, had previously been manager of East Lancashire (Bridlington) works and was continually sighing for more Blackburn products, having had more than his fill of Park Royal bodies with troublesome main pillars that formed 80% of the fleet, but management ignored his pleas and, due to the problems with the chassis, our East Lancashire bodies had short lives, to his everlasting regret.

I left Halifax in 1958 and after a short spell at Plymouth became General Manager at Great Yarmouth and from Spring 1960 started to attend

Geoffrey Hilditch's time at Leicester was to prove significant in many ways. His determination not to give in to Leyland when the Fleetline was withdrawn was directly responsible for the development of the Dennis Dominator and the subsequent and continuing relationship between Dennis and East Lancashire Coachbuilders as acknowledged on page 128. Leicester had a long association with East Lancashire, particularly with the Dennis Dominator. Number 91, seen below, was one of 13 supplied in 1988. It was in the city centre when photographed in July 1999 after the takeover of Leicester City Transport by First Bus. In addition to Dominators, Leicester had purchased Dennis single-deckers with East Lancashire bodies including No. 611, on a Dennis Falcon chassis supplied in 1991/92. Number 611 was also photographed in July 1999, in the city centre, operating to Highfields.

Above and Top: **In 1990 North Western, a member of the Drawlane Group, took eight Dennis Falcons with EL2000 bodies. All were later repainted for the Bee Line fleet. The rear view of 382 shows the Van Hool-type rear profile.**

Below: **North Western, as a member of the Drawlane Group, bought many East Lancashire bodies including Dennis Darts with EL 2000 bodies similar to No. 1240 shown in the 'City Plus' fleet operating in Liverpool in May 1999. It was one of a batch of 48 such vehicles delivered in 1995.**

conferences and similar gatherings. Some time later at one conference I enquired as to who that tall young man was who had started to appear at these events, to be told that he was Arthur Danson and he was representing East Lancashire Coachbuilders, but our paths never crossed and we did not even exchange a word. This lack of communication was to continue for rather too many years, in fact I do not think we even exchanged a nod of recognition. Then fate in the form of British Leyland took a hand, as recorded in Chapter 4.

My friendship with Arthur continued and then he told me that the Trafalgar House organisation was putting East Lancashire Coachbuilders up for sale. By this time, as a Director of the fledgling Drawlane concern it seemed to me that if we were to build up a sizeable fleet, a bus bodying plant would be more than useful. Our Chairman went with me to look and agreed it was a nice business and our bid was successful with the result that I became a Director of East Lancashire.

In this capacity I was able to promote the design and development of an improved single-deck body and a low height double-deck.

In this period it was fascinating to see East Lancashire from the inside and to strengthen the local management by electing one of the staff to the Board before I resigned

from the Group in 1989. My subsequent return to Leicester as Chairman saw more products from Blackburn enter the fleet. In the past ten years East Lancashire has changed hands again, moved to a new works, produced more new designs and continues to employ so many of its long serving highly skilled staff. During my time with the Company I thought it was a 'jobbing coachbuilder' and in this I am not being disparaging in any way. It could and did take on all sorts of work in addition to buses, from tramcars to prison vans and did not seem to have any difficulty in so doing.

Since my retirement I have missed my visits to Blackburn but obviously from orders now being received it continues to hold a high place in the confidence of its customers. I wish the Company and all who work in it every success in the future.

I end on a sad note for in 1989 when I told Arthur that I intended to resign from Drawlane, he told me that if I did go, he would soon follow and this he did but unfortunately his retirement was short for he passed away soon afterwards. To many managers in my day Arthur Danson not only represented East Lancashire Coachbuilders, but was also one of the most genuine and generous men in the industry, so in paying tribute to his memory, I stress how much I miss seeing him and hearing his ever cheerful voice.

Above: **Midland Red North No. 1711 was one of the Leyland Tigers with ECW coach bodies acquired from London and Country (South West) and fitted with new East Lancashire bodies in 1989 as described in the text. It is shown operating service 876 from Wolverhampton to Stafford.**

Above: **London and Country, another member of the Drawlane Group, purchased Volvo Citybuses and Dennis Dominators with this style of East Lancashire body. Volvo No. 614 (G614 BPH) dating from 1989, is shown at Kingston in March 1995.**

North Western purchased six Scania L113CRLs with East Lancashire Flyte bodies in 1996 and allocated all of them to Skelmersdale depot. Number 1038 was operating the Wigan to Skelmersdale service in May 1999 when it was photographed in Wigan Bus Station.

BOB DAVIES, former Director of Operations and Planning, West Yorks PTE:- It was in 1963 when I arrived in Eastbourne that I first became acquainted with East Lancashire Coachbuilders; until then I had never had dealings with the Company and did not know the owners. This soon changed as Eastbourne had a fleet of buses which, in the main, were bodied by East Lancashire.

Eastbourne's attractive livery complements the smooth lines of this AEC Regent V. Built in 1963 the vehicle gave some 17 year's service before withdrawal and was subsequently sold for preservation. It is one of the many East Lancashire vehicles which can be seen at rallies or in museums throughout the country and illustrates the elegance of the designs the Company produced for traditional front-engined chassis.

The first contact I made was with Alfred Alcock. After some discussion with Alf on the subject of specifications I was invited to have a few days at the works to see how specifications were written and then turned into bodies. I accepted this invitation and the visit proved of such value to me that what I learned stayed with me for the rest of my days in the transport industry.

During my 'course' I met many of the workforce including Arthur Danson, son of George, and George Alcock, son of Alf, and Philip Hilton who looked after me in the drawing office. During my short stay I picked up some basic knowledge of the business with regard to yearly outputs and staff employed, also the fact that the Company had a wide customer base, a policy which worked then and still works today. Changes in customer demand could be absorbed but if one large order changed, the order book could suffer. I recall being in Arthur Danson's office when he had a call from my old friend Albert Burrows at Liverpool for 200 bodies. Arthur had to say 'No' because he could not risk losing other customers of long standing, for a large order which may not have been repeated. In the event, Albert died not long after the enquiry and to my thinking it proved the point.

I have also been indebted on many occasions to Philip Hilton, who is now in his 40th year with the Company, having had a long experience in the role of apprentice vehicle builder working on the production line, was in the drawing office, who knows all about the intricacies of building bodies, and is now Deputy Managing Director.

I learned many things from East Lancashire. The customers trusted the Company and this was most apparent in 1970 when the fire stopped work on the production line. All documentation was lost, except for plans and drawings, the master copies of which were kept by George Alcock in a separate safe place, just in case disaster happened. All the customers sent copies of their current orders and it was said that East Lancashire files had never looked so good. We did try to rewrite the quoted price but to no avail. When the new building opened, every one of the East Lancashire customers, past and present, came along to see the Mayor of Blackburn drive out of the works in a newly built bus. A photograph of the customers was in the East Lancashire building for many years and it showed a loyalty in both directions, supplier and customer. During this period of upheaval, some customers helped East Lancashire in more specific ways. Building of bodies was carried out at Blackburn Transport where Laurie Oakes was Manager and Jim Chadwick arranged painting facilities at Accrington Transport.

East Lancashire always had a reputation for credibility, trust, value for money, cooperation and friendship; who could ask for more?

I have always thought that the 'East Lancashire Experience' was one of the most valuable lessons which I received during my service in the industry.

TOM HOLDEN, former Managing Director, Preston Bus:- Many thanks for your invitation to say a few words about my involvement with East Lancashire Coachbuilders and those legends of the bus industry, George Alcock and Arthur Danson, during periods of both good and bad for public transport.

My working life in the industry spanned 45 years experiencing rapid expansion, recession, stability and a return to growing demand for new vehicles, all of which in their own way placed vehicle manufacturers under increasing pressure to supply the goods to the required number and quality whilst predicting future industry trends.

East Lancashire Coachbuilders, ably led by Arthur and George, provided vehicles, not only to meet customers' needs but also offered flexible building arrangements to supply finished products which varied significantly according to location and the needs of General Managers and Chief Engineers.

Retaining a skilled labour force, increasing research and development facilities, forward bulk-ordering of materials and planning physical assets required to manufacture an unknown quantity of vehicles in an uncertain industry would have been difficult for most people, but apparently not to Arthur and George. They developed a sixth sense based upon their vast knowledge and experience of the industry which they used to the benefit of all who came into contact with them.

My recollections of East Lancashire Coachbuilders are those of a very friendly welcoming management and work force who worked hard to provide, with a smile, high quality technical standards to meet individual needs.

Above: Preston Corporation, having purchased two East Lancashire-bodied single-deckers in the early postwar period, returned to the Company for bodies on its second batch of Leyland Atlanteans in 1976. Thereafter regular orders followed, all being for dual-door bodies. Fleet No. 170 was supplied in 1982.

Preston No. 192 with Lolyne body on Dennis Trident chassis was returning from Tanterton when photographed in January 2000.

George Alcock, speaking to the Author in 1999, recalled the coach-seated Leyland Olympian London Liners with great affection, describing them as the finest vehicles ever built by East Lancashire during his many years with the Company.

BILL LEWIS, former General Manager, Southampton City Transport:- I first met Arthur Danson in the 1970s and he and East Lancashire supplied all our bodies until I retired in 1986. We became particularly close from 1973 onwards when I became General Manager at Southampton. He was my best friend in the industry and being larger than life he fitted in well with my extrovert personality! It was a very sad moment but a great privilege to be able to give the eulogy at his funeral in a packed church in Lytham. Many stories leap to mind about Arthur - little ones like the time he was setting fire to several glasses of Zambuca when he set his finger on fire and we had to douse it in the ice bucket; and big ones like his memorable trip to France with the Institute of Transport Southern Section.

The object of the trip was to visit the station, airport, oil terminal and bus depot as well as have a civic reception. However, the object of Arthur's party seemed also to call in at most of the bars in the vicinity to absorb the local ales.

At conferences Arthur and Pat were the perfect host and hostess and usually picked up many of the stray managers and councillors who had not received an invitation to dinner. His menus were the best and his hospitality legendary. At events in London he would be found after dinner escorting a party to one of the many clubs he knew. The scrapes that some of his guests got into cannot be outlined but Arthur usually managed to sort things out.

One of Arthur's problems was that all his customers required their vehicles before April to qualify for the bus grant. It was obviously impossible to please everyone so like all the manufacturing industry, untruths were told about expected delivery dates. These lies kept the customer happy until it was too late. All he could do was to share out the bad news. I noticed however that everytime he told me a white lie, he started to stammer and I made life difficult for him every time he stammered. At the end of the day I knew he was trying his best for all his customers.

After I retired we used to go for weekends together with Dina and Pat, usually in association with race meetings and each year we would go to Royal Ascot. It was on the first of these trips that I found out that Arthur was a member of the Guards Polo Club when we went to watch the polo. I roared thinking of Arthur's 20+ stone on a polo pony.

Arthur owned and ran greyhounds for many years and when Dina and I were going up North he would arrange for one or two of his dogs to run. Our most disastrous day was when we went to Preston dog track where Arthur had a 'cert' running. We all put large money on it and it duly won. Unfortunately one of the traps had failed to open and the race was declared void. When we went outside we found that three cars had been broken into and the radios taken (not Arthur's). It meant that I had to wait on my own for the police as I was the only one sober. Arthur was always the same, an outstanding gentleman, and I miss him.

East Lancashire's body styling had rather more elegance than some examples in the Southampton fleet when this photograph was taken in 1976.

THOMAS W W KNOWLES former Managing Director, Lancaster City Transport:- I was brought up in the Potteries where East Lancashire bodies were rare. PMT had none in their fleet when I joined them in 1960. So it was tempered with some rarity value when Roger Dixon and I acquired an ex-Southdown Leyland TD5 (FUF 228) which had been rebodied by East Lancashire in 1949. This was our first encounter with the organisation and we were quick to realise the quality of the postwar body which was built at a time when many bodybuilders were using unseasoned timber, but the East Lancashire body was built to last. Unfortunately, this early preservation attempt did not last and we reluctantly parted with the bus after it suffered from vandalism.

In 1971 I became Traffic Superintendent at Reading and this very professional undertaking had a number of East Lancashire and Neepsend bodies on AEC Reliance and Dennis Loline chassis. The Assistant Engineer, Ron Goodchild, was the liaison between operator and manufacturer and because of his high standards and expectations, it was very hard for a bodybuilder to satisfy him but East Lancashire achieved his requirements as proved by repeat orders. As the man operating the buses, I had nothing but praise for their quality even though, when I arrived, many were midway through their lives. I chose the Lolines to operate a new service to Turnham's Farm and particularly remember a rare drive of one. When I moved to Lancaster in 1973 in readiness for the local government reorganisation which amalgamated Lancaster City Transport with Morecambe and Heysham Borough Transport I was delighted to find that the majority of the Lancaster fleet had East Lancashire bodies. Recent deliveries carried Pennine bodies and it was pointed out to me that this change of policy had been forced on them by the fire at East Lancashire's works in 1970.

As General Manager I soon met many of the key suppliers to the industry and the face of East

Top: **Following deregulation Lancaster City Transport operated services from Morecambe to Preston and to Blackpool in competition with Ribble. Thomas W W Knowles writes of the consolation of having such excellent vehicles as the East Lancashire-bodied Leyland Atlaneans with which to operate these services. Number 221, with coach seating and dating from 1983, is shown at Poulton le Fylde operating the service to Blackpool in September 1987.**

Above: **Lancaster City Transport took a single example of this body on a Leyland Tiger chassis in 1986. Numbered 154 it was working from Lancaster to Combermere Road on service 224 when photographed at Heysham Towers in August 1993.**

Lancashire Coachbuilders was presented by the one and only Arthur Danson. There have been few more hospitable people in our industry and Arthur never put pressure on for Lancaster to return to East Lancashire, I suppose because he knew it would happen eventually, as it did in 1979 when the first three of a fleet of Leyland Atlanteans were delivered. Looking back at some of the events, the De Tably Arms, Crooklands, recognition of my marriage to Lindsey, exotic Conference Locations, Tom Kenny's farewell, repartee with Jim Chadwick (Hyndburn) at the dinner table and in the bar afterwards, and hospitality at Arthur and Pat's home are fondly remembered.

Whereas Arthur was the salesman, when it came to dealing with specifications George Alcock was the man. One particular feature of East Lancashire Coachbuilders was their flexibility in meeting operator's idiosyncrasies during vehicle build, and the gentle way in which alternatives were suggested if it was thought that the requirements were unrealistic. When it came to detail and reordering, the splendid Tony Cooper was always so cheerful and helpful; was there anyone else who knew so much about East Lancashire? I doubt it. He seemed to know who had ordered what over the years and was familiar with every customer's needs.

The support to operators did not end here, and in two booklets I produced at Lancaster, one for Lancaster's 75th Anniversary and the other entitled Morecambe Bay's Municipal Buses, East Lancashire supported the ventures with advertisements. Leyland also supported the publications and on the latter book used an East Lancashire official photograph of a Lancaster Atlantean, such was their regard for the bodybuilder.

A feature I remember was the way in which the Company operated as a family firm. On a prearranged arrival there would be a board in reception welcoming you by name. The bodies would be finished by different employees, each of whom had slight variations in the way they completed their tasks whilst a tour around the works accompanied by Arthur who had a kindly word for his staff usually sowed the seeds for ideas for the next order. On these tours one usually met a young Philip Hilton, now Deputy Managing Director, who to many is the present day face of East Lancashire.

I now look at changes in East Lancashire. Personnel have departed, premises have changed, but traditions still remain, the flexibility to meet operator's needs, design staff to the forefront of current thinking and the customer still comes first. Arthur Danson's name lives on with the golf competition sponsored by East Lancashire and played at the Annual Conference of the Association of Local Company Bus Managers.

East Lancashire Coachbuilders functioned for over 60 years in the old millennium; I hope it will carry on for at least that length of time in the new and that the many friends it has in the industry will continue to multiply.

The local municipal operator in Blackburn has been a regular user of East Lancashire bodywork over many years. Number 136 was one of a large number of similar bodies provided on Leyland Atlantean and Dennis Dominator chassis. It dates from 1980 and is shown in Blackburn town centre in July 1987.

When Hyndburn Borough was formed as part of local government reorganisation in 1974 it retained the former Accrington Corporation distinctive livery of dark blue and red for the bus fleet. Dennis Dominator 105 was photographed in Blackburn bus station in 1985 about to depart to Oswaldtwistle.

JOHN OWEN, Managing Director, Thamesdown Transport Ltd, Swindon:- My involvement with East Lancashire goes back to the mid sixties and is included in Chapter 3. I suppose the most vivid memory of my time at Southampton was what followed. The first East Lancashire bodied Atlanteans arrived in August 1967 and we built up a very standardised fleet and for a significant part of my 16 years there, every double-decker in service was East Lancashire-bodied and we also had some East Lancashire-bodied AEC Swift single-deckers. With only minor detail variations between batches, any bus could be allocated to any service - a dream situation for the Traffic Division for which I had overall responsibility. My recollection is of a good quality body which gave us very little trouble and having respect for Eric Bell, Chief Engineer in those days. I cannot imagine us buying over 240 bodies over a 20-year period had the product not been right.

Moving to Swindon in 1984 I inherited a fleet that was traditionally Northern Counties and this continued for several more years of new purchases. However in late 1985 we needed six second-hand double-deckers and bought 6 'V' and 'W' registered East Lancashire-bodied Dominators from East Staffordshire, which had been built to the George Hurst/Barry Greenhalgh specification common to the municipal operators in that area at that time. Most of these are still in service and their length of service in a secondary life is testimony to the product.

In 1990 we bought new from East Lancashire six 'Droop Nose' style bodies on Dominator chassis and these continue in all day service to-day having been joined by six almost identical examples bought from London and Country. All give excellent service with nothing in the way of body problems.

It is inevitable I suppose that bus industry managers will have varying views on any manufacturer and its various products, depending on their own individual experience. East Lancashire has had its ups and downs over the nearly 35 years that I have been involved with its products and inevitably this may have had some effect on the quality at various times. I can only speak as I have found and say that I have always considered the product and on-going support good. Whether I have been fortunate with the buses I have and the people I have dealt with I do not know, but East Lancashire has always been there when I needed them - including a couple of years ago to fit into the programme at nil notice the rebuilding of a double-decker bus decapitated in a collision with Swindon's infamous White House Bridge.

I have heard people say that East Lancashire never built two buses the same. Rather than being taken in a disparaging way, perhaps it should be used to illustrate that East Lancashire has always been flexible enough to build what the customer asks for, rather than what the manufacturer wants to build for him as part of a standardised design and production process. That tradition continues today with the seventeen special single-deckers for London Central for the Millennium Dome project.

Being a non-engineer, my personal contact with East Lancashire was always somewhat limited. George Alcock and Arthur Danson stood out as real characters even in an age in our industry when there were still some characters and I shall never forget the banter and rapport that existed between them and people like Bill Lewis for whom I worked at Southampton. East Lancashire has always had colourful characters and in a much blander industry these days, to some extent that still applies.

Thamesdown Transport, Swindon, became a customer of East Lancashire Coachbuilders in 1990 following the satisfactory purchase of six secondhand Dennis Dominators bought from East Staffordshire Transport. Five new Dominators were purchased in 1990 and one of them, No. 71, is shown in Swindon on 4th July 1998. Continuing satisfaction with the Dennis/East Lancashire combination led to Thamesdown purchasing further secondhand models, similar to 71, from London and Country.

TED REID, Former Managing Director, Bournemouth Transport Ltd:- My first experience, and it was an experience, of negotiating with the then Sales Director of East Lancashire was in 1985 when Arthur Danson visited Kingston upon Hull City Transport. We were looking to buy ten single-deck bodies for Scania chassis. The meeting started at 10.30am and by lunchtime an agreed specification was on the table. The talks continued through a sandwich lunch to try and establish a delivery date and price. By 3pm this had been achieved and in order to comply with standing orders we had to contact the Chairman for him to issue written confirmation and by 4.30pm Councillor Les Taylor had signed the order. A decision was taken to go and celebrate this event at a new hotel near the Humber Bridge. Between 5pm and 7pm several drinks were consumed and dinner was ordered. I remember leaving the hotel around 1am being unsure as to how many buses we had ordered.

Most municipal transport companies use East Lancashire because they would provide the specification that the operator wanted. To order from some of the larger companies meant you could have your buses at a certain date providing you accepted the specification of the latest big order that was going through for another company. Arthur Danson's claim to fame was that he would put a body on any four wheels you provided including a skateboard!

On one occasion, Arthur, a keen Blackburn Rovers supporter, had not seen a goal scored for two months. Early November saw them leave the field at half time, still not having scored a goal. As the players disappeared down the tunnel, someone set off a firework with a tremendous bang. One supporter was heard to say that a Blackburn player had shot himself. Arthur's reply was, 'Well, if it was one of the forwards he will have missed.'

Above: **Hull's East Lancashire-bodied Dennis Dominator No. 132, new in September 1987, was damaged by fire in July 1991. It was returned to the coachbuilder where it was rebodied as a 76-seater with dual doors for use on the shuttle from the North Sea Ferries terminal at King George Dock, a duty previously carried out by a dual-door Leyland Atlantean.**

Below; **Kingston upon Hull City Transport No. 149 was one of 20 Dennis Dominators purchased in 1988/89 and it is shown leaving the City's bus station for Bransholme Centre.**

Above: What a difference a livery makes. Eight single-deck Scania N113DRBs were supplied to Kingston upon Hull in 1989. Number 706, (left) painted in the original livery, was turning into Ferensway and Number 703, repainted by Stagecoach in an interim livery, was leaving Paragon coach station for the Bransholme housing estate. The pictures were taken in May 1995.

Above: Bournemouth became a regular user of East Lancashire bodywork in 1985. Number 263 was one of 14 Dennis Dominators supplied in 1990/91 with 'E' type bodies and it is shown at Alum Chine in 1991.

Above: Number 465 was one of ten Dennis Darts with EL2000 bodies supplied to Bournemouth in 1996. It is shown in the town en route to Boscombe Pier via Charminster.

Below: Bournemouth took delivery of nine Lolyne-bodied Dennis Tridents in 1999 and No. 270, the first of the batch, is seen here.

TONY DEPLEDGE, Managing Director, Blackpool Transport:- From our own perspective we can make comment about the work you have undertaken for us over many years and the fact that we are still happily running many products of your Company and, in particular, vehicles produced on the old site. You built the whole of our double-deck fleet over many years and you certainly figure among the companies we are happy to do business with. We welcome the survival of your Company through some very difficult trading times for bus manufacturers in the early years following deregulation. Our industry needs successful and innovative manufacturing companies and you have successfully developed yourselves and virtually reinvented your product range.

BILL GIBSON, Chief Engineer, Blackpool Transport:- Blackpool Transport Services and Blackpool Borough Transport has had a long and successful relationship with East Lancashire Coachbuiders. The most interesting project from an engineer's point of view was the engineering maintenance vehicle for our tramway. This involved detailed discussion, design and planning to our unique specification to provide a vehicle specific to our application. The experience of East Lancashire body design, and your willingness and ability to take our specification and turn it into reality was achieved in a remarkably short space of time. It also demonstrates your willingness to satisfy customer's detailed requirements. The vehicle has operated successfully for a number of years in our harsh environment and is testimony to the East Lancashire build quality.

Above: **Following the appointment of Derek Hyde as General Manager, Blackpool became a regular user of East Lancashire bodies, building up a large fleet of Leyland Atlanteans. Number 328 was one of ten supplied in 1979 and it is shown in June 1989 picking up passengers for Bispham.**

Above: **Blackpool was the only Lancashire municipal operator to purchase the 'E' type body, taking six on Leyland Olympian chassis in 1989. Number 373 was photographed in Cleveleys in April 1999.**

Below: **Tram No. 651 was an experimental car equipped by GEC Traction Ltd. It was fitted with the same style of East Lancashire body as Blackpool's other Centenary class trams and delivered in April 1985 on extended loan for operation on their system. Seen on the Promenade in September 1985 heading for the Pleasure Beach it was later taken over by Blackpool and renumbered 648.**

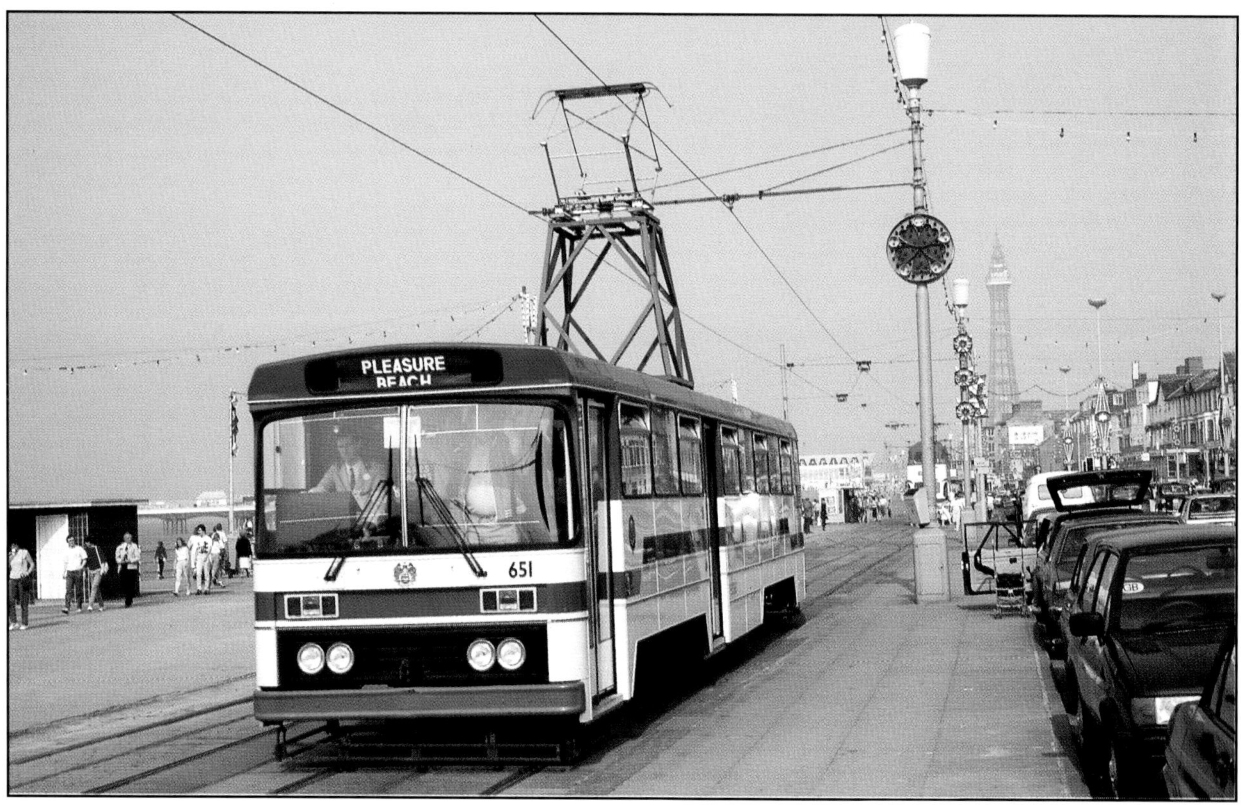

THE MALTESE OPPORTUNITY

In 1996/7 the then Maltese Government took the decision that the venerable fleet of old buses which provide transport on Malta, some dating back to World War 2, should be replaced with new accessible modern vehicles. The owner operators would be required to lodge an amount per new vehicle with the Government, which would then provide the balance as a subsidy. East Lancashire have an Agent on the island and he secured orders for two Spryte-bodied Dennis Darts for Leo Gretch, one of the largest operators with his base at Paramount Garage in Mosta, though in the event these were purchased outright. Subsequent changes of Government have resulted in the proposal being put on ice, partly perhaps because the island is more than ever dependent on tourism and the old buses have undoubted tourist appeal.

In the meantime the Sprytes go quietly about their business amongst the assorted selection of vintage machines, some of which are earlier-generation East Lancashire models. One of Leo's drivers, when asked what he thought of his new charge, dryly observed that it was a lot of bus to wash with a sponge and bucket between trips!

Malta's buses are well-known for being badged in most exotic fashion, many vehicles proclaiming to be of AEC, Leyland or Bedford make when they may in fact be by none of those one-time bus manufacturers. This example however is exactly what it says, a Dennis SLF carrying an East Lancashire Spryte body. It was photographed in Sliema on a typical spring day in 1999.

ALAN EATWELL, Group Engineering Director, Go Ahead Group:- The reduction in capital investment in the run-up to privatisation of the National Bus Company exposed many coachbuilders to a lean time from which some never recovered. East Lancashire however, having never enjoyed the patronage of NBC, continued with little regard. Our experience of dealing with East Lancashire Coachbuilders came on privatisation and is covered in Chapter 6.

Our introduction to East Lancashire was of course an introduction to Arthur Danson, George Alcock and 'young' Philip Hilton in the drawing office. No matter who actually owned the Company (Trafalgar House at the time) there was no doubt that the business was really theirs. A customer bought buses from Arthur, not from East Lancashire! While I doubt that Arthur's training in sales and marketing was any stronger than George's in design and engineering, between them they could deduce a customer's needs and interpret the specification into a substantial, reliable yet economical product. CAD facilities were preceded by FAG (packet that is) and whilst any attempts at cannibalisation in the event of accident damage might reveal that no two of those earlier vehicles were quite the same, the product has served us and our passengers very well.

The hiatus described in the privatisation of NBC while really leaving East Lancashire untouched, other than the coup of attracting a new ex NBC customer or two, was eventually repeated with inevitable run-up to changes in ownership of their traditional municipal customers and the depleted pattern of vehicle investment during this period. This coupled with the dilapidated condition of the Blackburn property, which when acquired almost 60 years previously had been a time-expired textile mill, could easily have led to ruin had it not been for the extreme efforts of the next generation of management and workforce under the leadership of Chris Clarke and Philip Hilton.

Relocation to a new property was a brave step and yet the risk and further investment in CAD (not the WD & HO Wills variety), the confidence of suppliers and support of customers has brought its deserved return and while I am sure there will always be room for another customer, no matter where he requires his fuel tank, seats, stairs, or wheels, it is pleasing to hear that Philip, (no longer young!) is embarrassed by lead times he sometimes has to quote, such is the throughput.

The industry's confidence in the future of East Lancashire was demonstrated by their winning the coveted order for the Millennium Dome vehicles from Go Ahead's London Central and they deserve the success through the next sixty years that they have earned in the past sixty five.

Brighton and Hove Bus and Coach Company became an enthusiastic user of East Lancashire bodywork following privatisation and in April 1997 took delivery of further East Lancashire-bodied Scanias comprising 17 Cityzen bodies on N113DRB chassis. All 17 are shown in a fine line-up shortly after delivery.

DERRICK DEAKIN, former Managing Director, Nottingham City Transport:- We always included East Lancashire as one of Nottingham's major suppliers and always retained an excellent working relationship with your Company.

This was the case with many of your customers, so much so that around the time buses were being deregulated, and it was thought by George Alcock and Arthur Danson that the company might encounter financial problems, a number of my colleagues and myself were willing to commit our own companies into injecting cash into East Lancashire should it become necessary. Fortunately, this action was not required and not only has the company gone from strength to strength, especially since you moved into your new premises, but evidence of your current build quality is here in Nottingham for all to see.

Right: Nottingham 511, a Volvo B6-50, was rebodied by East Lancashire in 1997 and is shown at Nottingham in May of that year displaying the special sign writing for '100 Years of Public Service 1897-1997'.

Below: Nottingham City Transport, having been a regular customer since the early seventies, continues to purchase from East Lancashire Coachbuilders. Number 470, shown in the City in August 1998, was one of 31 Pyoneer-bodied Volvo Olympians delivered in 1998/99.

Above: The end of an era. The last bus to leave the Whalley New Road Works in April 1994 was Nottingham City Transport No. 486 on a Volvo Olympian chassis with destination display suitably depicting 1934 - 1994.

Below: The beginning of a new era. The first bus to leave the new works at Whitebirk was Ipswich Transport Dennis Lance No. 162 in May 1994.

Right: In later years Hyndburn discontinued the dark blue and red livery in favour of this lighter colour scheme of silver, red and dark blue. Leyland Leopard No. 44 with dual-purpose seating dating from 1977 carried this livery when photographed entering Burnley bus station in April 1997.

Centre right: Burnley and Pendle Transport, the successor to Burnley Colne and Nelson, operated a fleet of Bristol VRT double-deckers bodied by either Eastern Coach Works or East Lancashire Coachbuilders. One of the latter, No. 154 delivered in 1976, is shown approaching Burnley bus station in July 1987.

Bottom left: Traditionally, municipal buses were not associated with rural scenes such as this but deregulation brought many changes. Burnley and Pendle took over operation of the Clitheroe to Slaidburn service in rural Lancashire. Number 31, an East Lancashire-bodied Leyland Leopard new in 1978, had just turned in Slaidburn for the return journey to Clitheroe when photographed in July 1990. Later vehicles of this type for Burnley and Pendle had BET style windscreens.

Bottom right: One of Plymouth's East Lancashire-bodied Atlanteans No.164 dating from 1981 heads for the city centre operating service 47 in February 1996.

Plymouth No.148, the first of 14 Leyland Atlanteans supplied in 1980/81, displays its 'Plymouth in Bloom' livery as it negotiates a roundabout in the City Centre in September 1983.

Cardiff had been a regular customer of East Lancashire Coachbuilders since early days and Leyland Olympian No. 564 was one of 36 delivered between 1981 and 1986. It is shown in Caerphilly in September 1996 heading for Tredegar.

Merseyside PTE became a customer of East Lancashire, having inherited orders placed by Liverpool City Transport. Number 1695, photographed at the corner of Sir Thomas Street, in Merseybus livery, was one of 40 on Leyland Atlantean chassis received in 1976.

Above left: Ipswich Transport, another of the Company's regular customers, bought 11 Dennis Falcons in 1988/89 numbered 114 to 124. The last of these is shown in service at Ipswich in July 1993.

Above right: The only Ailsa vehicles bodied by East Lancashire were 25 for Tayside transport in 1983/84. Number 74 was photographed in Dundee. The driver's door, made necessary by the front-mounted engine, is clearly visible.

Right: The Company also supplied bodies to the small municipal operators in South Wales including six with dual-purpose seating on Leyland Tiger chassis for Islwyn Borough Council in 1985/86. Number 46 was leaving Caerphilly for Cardiff in September 1996.

Below: Lincoln City Transport purchased four Volvo Citybuses with coach seating in April 1988 and the first of these, No. 67, is shown in the city in May 1988 with the magnificent cathedral forming an impressive backdrop. Yorkshire Traction later substituted normal registrations for the 'cherished' examples.

The Yorkshire Traction Group had a number of chassis rebodied including this Scania K112CRB *(above left)*, which received a Flyte body in 1997. On 11th September 1999 it was in Barnsley operating service 212 from there to Doncaster. In addition to purchasing Dennis Dart SLFs the Yorkshire Traction Group also purchased Spryte-bodied Volvo B6LEs as illustrated by No. 131 *(above right)* in the Yorkshire Traction fleet in Barnsley on the same date. It was one of eight received in January 1999. Although only two of the American built Spartan chassis were bodied in Britain, both by East Lancashire Coachbuilders and both going to Yorkshire Traction, the event was significant for the bodybuilder in that they were their first products incorporating Alusuisse construction on which the Company later standardised for both single- and double-deck bodies. Number 201 *(left)* carries the body designation 'Opus 2' at the front and side lettering 'SPARTAN CHASSIS made in the USA and EAST LANCS BODYWORK built in the UK'

Below: When the Yorkshire Traction Group took over the operations of Lincoln City Transport it transferred Lincoln's coach-seated Volvo Citybuses into the Yorkshire Traction fleet for use on express services. Number 901 was operating the X32 service from Leeds to Sheffield.

Above: The first Pyoneer bodies were supplied on Dennis Arrow chassis to the order of Capital Citybus in April and May 1997, a total of nine being provided of which one, No. 421, is illustrated. A tenth vehicle was supplied in November 1997 and a further 28 in 1998.

Below: In March 1998 the first two low-height Pyoneer bodies on Volvo Olympian chassis were supplied to Road Car, a member of the Yorkshire Traction Group, for operation on the Lincoln to Skegness service. Number 687 shows the lettering applied for the route branding.

Above left: Rebodying was a feature of the late eighties and early nineties and East Yorkshire turned to East Lancashire for the provision of new bodies on three Leyland Leopards in 1992. One of these, with registration number SIB 6615, was originally UGR 501R with a Plaxton coach body in the United fleet. It is shown in Pickering with the Scarborough and District fleetname operating service 128 between Helmsley and Scarborough in August 1995.

Centre left: Warrington had a long association with East Lancashire Coachbuilders going back to the war years. Number 97, a Dennis Dominator with the bus-seated version of the 'Droop Nose' body, was one of five delivered in 1989. It had just left the town's bus station en route to the Trafford Centre when photographed in September 1999.

Bottom left: The railway carriage supplied to Snowdon Mountain Railway is shown at Llanberis Station.

Top right: The East Lancashire 'European' body on Scania L113CRL chassis is illustrated by Arriva Fox County 2175, one of 14 delivered in 1996, shown in Leicester awaiting departure on service 50 to Narborough in July 1999.

Centre right: Northumbria Motor Services, now part of the Arriva Group took delivery of ten Scania L113CRLs with East Lancashire European bodies in 1995 and a further ten in 1996. Number 286, one of the earlier batch, arrives in Newcastle on service X24 from Blyth.

Bottom right: In 1994 the Company rebodied two Volvo B10M chassis for Western Buses, formerly Western Scottish. To date these are the only bodies to be finished in Stagecoach livery by East Lancashire Coachbuilders. Number V427 is shown prior to the application of fleetnames.

In 1998 Strathtay Scottish, the northern outpost of the Yorkshire Traction Group received four Volvo Olympians with Pyoneer bodies, one of which, No. 956, is shown here.

In 1996 Dunn Line of Nottingham bought three Dennis Dart SLFs with Spryte bodywork for operation of the Racecourse Park and Ride service in Nottingham. Number 31 was photographed in the city centre operating this service in July 1999.

Greenway PDZ 6262 numbered 3520 in the fleet of Arriva North East climbs up the A171 coast road into Saltburn in June 1999 having negotiated the double bend in the background and another one just before that, en route from Loftus to Middlesbrough. Saltburn Pier is in the background.

In 1997 two Dennis Dart SLFs with Spryte bodies were supplied to Paramount Garage, Mosta, Malta and one of them was photographed at Valletta bus station in May 1997.

East Lancashire Coachbuilders has become noted for its open-top double-deckers supplied on Volvo B10M chassis for tourist work in Paris. One of the first batch supplied to Guide Friday is shown here in Paris in May 1998.

Southern National placed its first order with East Lancashire Coachbuilders for two Spryte-bodied Dennis Dart SLFs which were delivered in February 1999. One of them was photographed at Colyton, Devon operating service 20 from Seaton to Taunton on 8th May 1999.

Number 774, from the Brighton & Hove batch of 17, was branded for service 5 when seen outside Marks and Spencers in Brighton on its way to Patcham in July 1997.

Above: An interesting export order was for the supply of three bodies on left-hand drive Dennis Lances to Poland for British Bus. The bodies were based on Duple Metsec frames and one of them was photographed before delivery.

Below: In 1998/99 an order was completed for thirty double-deckers on Dennis Trident three-axle chassis for export to Hong Kong. The order came from Duple Metsec and incorporated their frames. One of the buses is shown on a test run in Blackburn.

Left: By the time the second deliveries to Southern National were made, the undertaking had passed to First Group and this photograph shows John Horn, East Lancashire's Southern Area Sales Manager (on the left), handing over one of the six Dennis Dart SLFs to David Toy of First Group.

Below: A Dennis Dominator was bodied for the China Motor Bus Company, Hong Kong and delivered in 1979 after appearing at the 1978 Commercial Motor Show.

Above: **Mayne of Manchester Scania Cityzen No. 3 in Piccadilly, Manchester. This new style of body, of which the Cityzen was the first, incorporated an upper-deck frontal arrangement made entirely of glass.**

Right: **London Traveller R1 LTB is seen at Showbus, held each year at the Imperial War Museum at Duxford, in September 1999. It is a Dennis Arrow with Pyoneer body supplied in 1998.**

Above: Harris Bus took delivery of 35 Volvo Olympians in 1997 with Pyoneer bodies and this view taken at Gants Hill shows the arrangement of the rear.

Below: Another regular customer of East Lancashire Coachbuilders, Maynes of Manchester, bought five Lolyne-bodied Dennis Tridents in 1999. Number 28 was in Manchester Picadilly operating service 234 to Mossley when photographed.

Nottingham No.406 was numerically the second of the first batch of Lolyne-bodied Dennis Tridents to be delivered to this regular customer. It is shown in the city in June 1999.

London Traveller Volvo B6LE with Spryte body, V514 EFR, is shown at Showbus, Duxford in September 1999. Sister vehicle V515 EFR was in the demonstration park at the Coach and Bus Show.

Midland Red No. 1832, pictured at Tamworth in October 1999, is a Scania N113DRB with coach-seated East Lancashire 'E' type body supplied in 1995.

Blue Triangle DL 905, a Dennis Trident with Lolyne body was one of nine supplied to this operator in 1999. DL 901 from the same batch was in the demonstration park at the Coach and Bus Show.

Bluebird of Middleton near Manchester operate this Scania N113 with Cityzen body, one of those built for Scania stock. It is shown in Manchester in September 1999.

MAN demonstrator N222 LFR was new in October 1997 and was exhibited at the Coach and Bus Show in that year. It is shown in May 1999 acting as a demonstrator in South Yorkshire.

Dunn Line of Nottingham Volvo B10M with coach-seated double-deck body at Ripley in July 1999. This vehicle was an East Lancashire rebody.

A Lolyne-bodied Dennis Trident for Metrobus of Orpington.

A London Central gas-powered Myllennium appropriately working on service M1 between the Millennium Dome and North Greenwich station.

The Dennis contribution

JOHN SMITH, Chairman, Dennis Specialist Vehicles Ltd writes:-

In the Spring of 1974, Dennis decided to re-enter the bus business. This decision was based on the optimistic assumption by a bunch of youngsters in their thirties in Guildford that Leyland's 95% share of the UK bus market was unhealthy, unnatural and needed competition. Aided and abetted by some potential customers, led most notably by Geoffrey Hilditch, a chassis specification for a rear-engined double-decker was soon drawn up.

Our problem was - who would we find to body it? In our youthful optimism we, who are today's older and wiser (?) 50-year-olds, had overlooked the fact that Britain's bus body industry would perhaps not rush forward to welcome an upstart competitor to their existing bread-and-butter supplier.

So it took vision and courage for East Lancashire, in the form of Arthur Danson, to step forward and body our shiny new 'Dominator', "provided it doesn't differ too much dimensionally from a Daimler Fleetline chassis".

The compromise was achieved, and the product built, to the consternation and annoyance of the folk near Preston. The rest, as they say, is history. I can vouch, as one of those optimistic youngsters at the time, that had it not been for East Lancashire, Dennis would most definitely not be in existence to-day, let alone be market leader with 55% of the British bus market. So I salute and thank East Lancashire Coachbuilders on the approach of their 66th anniversary. All power to the Company's elbow and may it greet its second 66th anniversary in the same rude health as it greets its first.

The first 'Alexander lookalikes' were built for South Yorkshire PTE in 1984. They were numbered 2351 - 2365 of which 2358 was photographed when new. The split-level entrance step, developed by SYPTE, is clearly shown in this view. This style of body later became known as the 'E-type', avoiding confusion with the Alexander 'R-type'. The Dennis Dominator chassis was one of over 300 supplied to this operator.

11 COMPANY OWNERSHIP AND PERSONALITIES

The origin and growth of the Company has largely been covered in the text and it will be apparent that it operated very much as if it were a family firm under the direction of Alfred Alcock and George Danson as partners. This was not actually the case of course and the Register of Shareholders records that when Alcock and Danson came into the firm in 1938 their holdings represented 40% and 10% respectively to Walter Smith's 49% and Lilian Smith's 1%. This changed in 1943 when Lilian Smith resigned.

Walter Smith's role continued, as Company Secretary, until his death in 1958. However, day to day running had always been firmly in the hands of Messrs Alcock and Danson who operated a very strict regime, and in the manner of the times, they kept themselves apart from the employees. They operated a very successful and profitable company.

One common factor of all the changes of ownership which have taken place is that, in each case, those personnel who were in office were allowed to continue without interference from the new owners.

The founders' sons, George Alcock and Arthur Danson both followed their fathers into the business, George in August 1951 and Arthur around the same time.

The directors remained unchanged from 1943 until the death of Walter Smith on 15th January 1958 when his shares passed to Martins Bank Ltd, as has been explained at the end of Chapter 3. At this time Walter Smith had owned two fifths of the shares, Alfred Alcock owned two fifths and George Danson one fifth.

On the death of Walter Smith the Danson family were interested in buying more shares but would not pay the current rate and the family of Walter Smith were not prepared to sell them at a reduced price and, as a result of this lack of agreement, Martins Bank Ltd sold these shares to Bishopsgate Nominees Ltd, 15 Bishopsgate, London EC2 in January 1963.

Following earlier informal conversations between Alfred Alcock and Joseph Edward Owston, the Managing Director of Cravens Ltd, Alcock and Danson apparently considered that perhaps the time was right to sell out if the opportunity presented itself.

Accordingly they then also sold their shares to Bishopsgate Nominees Ltd and in September 1963 three additonal directors were appointed, to the East Lancashire Board, all three living in Sheffield and being employed by Cravens.

As previously recorded they were Joseph Edward Owston, the Managing Director of Cravens, Edward Thomas White, an Engineer and Henry Booker, a Chartered Accountant. Mr Booker had been with the John Brown Group of Companies since 1951, Secretary of Cravens Homalloy (Sheffield) from 1953 to 1961 and a director of this firm from 1961. In addition, from 1963 he was Director and General Manager of Cravens Homalloy (Preston) Ltd and also from the same date, Director and General Manager of Transport and Commercial Aluminium Ltd.

As has been seen in January 1964 Bishopsgate Nominees Ltd subsequently sold all the shares to Cravens Ltd, Darnall, Sheffield 9. The name Cravens Ltd was changed to Cravens Industries Ltd in February 1964 and the shares were accordingly transferred. The agreement for the sale of East Lancashire Coachbuilders to Cravens included a two year contract for Alfred Alcock, a five year contract for George Danson and directorships for George Alcock and Arthur Danson.

Shown below is part of a draft letter sent from Cravens to Alfred Alcock in December 1962 during the course of the discussions between the two companies which led to the take over of East Lancashire by Cravens.

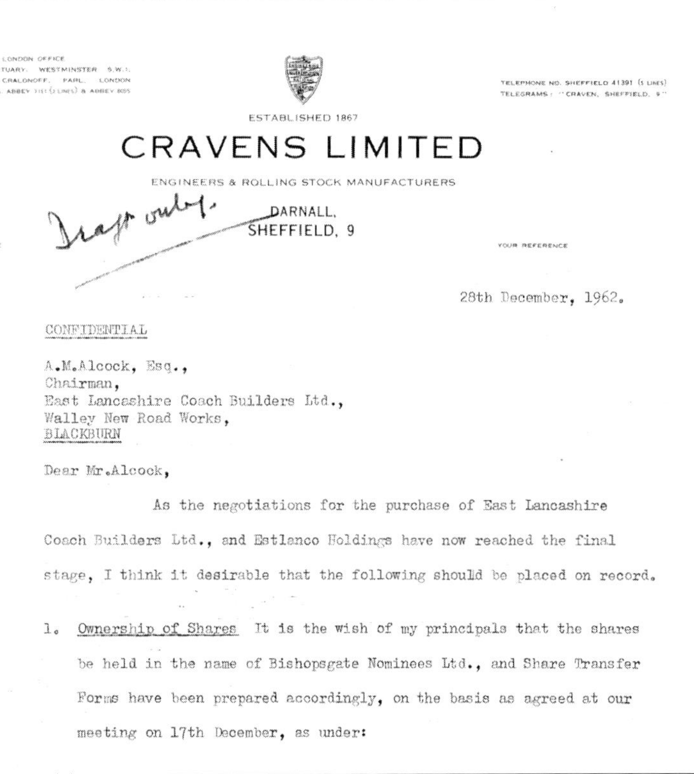

LONDON OFFICE

TELEPHONE NO. SHEFFIELD 41391 (5 LINES)
TELEGRAMS: "CRAVEN, SHEFFIELD, 9"

ESTABLISHED 1867

CRAVENS LIMITED

ENGINEERS & ROLLING STOCK MANUFACTURERS

Draft only.

DARNALL,
SHEFFIELD, 9

YOUR REFERENCE

28th December, 1962.

CONFIDENTIAL

A.M.Alcock, Esq.,
Chairman,
East Lancashire Coach Builders Ltd.,
Walley New Road Works,
BLACKBURN

Dear Mr.Alcock,

As the negotiations for the purchase of East Lancashire Coach Builders Ltd., and Estlanco Holdings have now reached the final stage, I think it desirable that the following should be placed on record.

1. Ownership of Shares It is the wish of my principals that the shares be held in the name of Bishopsgate Nominees Ltd., and Share Transfer Forms have been prepared accordingly, on the basis as agreed at our meeting on 17th December, as under:

Ownership by Cravens Industries Ltd continued until 29th March 1968 when Cravens and its East Lancashire subsidiary passed to John Brown and Company Ltd, of Carlisle Street, Sheffield 4.

In June 1981 John Brown and Company Ltd became John Brown plc, Head Office, 20 Eastbourne Terrace, London W2 6LE. Subsequently an attempt to sell East Lancashire Coachbuilders in 1983 was unsuccessful.

John Brown plc became part of the Trafalgar House Group in June 1987 and later that year a decision was made by them to sell East Lancashire Coachbuilders, and another company in the group, Craven Tasker Ltd. A press release was made in September of that year to announce the forthcoming sale and this was worded as shown.

Preliminary offers had to be made by 31st October with revised offers being accepted no later than 13th November.

Several companies showed interest including Northern Counties Motor and Engineering Company, Walter Alexander Ltd, Marshall of Cambridge and Drawlane. Some of the other companies who expressed interest are thought to have been interested in Craven Tasker and others possibly just curious. The Company was eventually sold to the Drawlane Group in January 1988.

It says much for Trafalgar House that they were prepared to follow the advice of the Company Directors with regard to choice of buyer. The Directors spelled out the implications for the Company's workforce if, for example, Northern Counties or Alexander might have purchased the Blackburn Company. Both would, almost certainly, have wished to close the factory to take out some of the competition and remove excess production capacity from the industry.

At this time, Geoffrey Hilditch, who had been a regular East Lancashire customer for many years, was Engineering Director of the Drawlane Group and it was at his instigation that Drawlane became interested. He visited the works with his chairman and they agreed that it would be useful to have a coachbuilding subsidiary within their Group.

In January 1988 Hilditch became a Director of East Lancashire Coachbuilders along with Peter Raymond McEnhill and Stanley Lawrence McArdle. They were joined in April 1989 by Adam Francis Mills. Geoffrey Hilditch resigned in December 1989, Stanley McArdle in February 1992 and Peter McEnhill and Adam Mills in November 1992.

Prior to the retirement of Geoffrey Hilditch from Drawlane, and his resignation as mentioned above, Philip Hilton was appointed a Director of East Lancashire. Dawson Williams now joined the Drawlane Group and became Group Operations Director, and, from July 1990 a Director of East Lancashire Coachbuilders. He had in his possession the name 'British Bus' and when he found himself at the helm of Drawlane, he changed

PRESS RELEASE

CRAVEN TASKER LTD AND EAST LANCASHIRE COACHBUILDERS TO BE SOLD BY JOHN BROWN PLC

John Brown plc, a member of the Trafalgar House Group of Companies, is offering for sale its interests in the road transport industry represented by Craven Tasker Ltd and East Lancashire Coachbuilders Ltd.

The road transport industry is not a major business area for the Trafalgar House Group and it has therefore been decided that it would be in the best interests of Craven Tasker and East Lancashire Coachbuilders to seek purchasers who are committed to the road transport industry where the businesses will be better able to develop their full potential.

Both businesses are prospering with substantially larger order books and improved profitability compared to a year ago.

Note for Editors

Craven Tasker
Craven Tasker with its headquarters in Sheffield, is one of the leading companies in the UK trailer industry. The company's products have an excellent reputation and the "Task" brand name has a high profile and is well regarded.

East Lancashire Coachbuilders
East Lancashire Coachbuilders (ELC) based in Blackburn, Lancashire, has a first class reputation in the bus body building industry. The company designs and builds a wide range of special single and double deck, midi and mini bus bodies for operators throughout the UK.

For Further Information
Klienwort Benson Ltd have been retained as advisors to John Brown plc for this disposal. Requests for further information or expressions of interest should in the first instance be referred to:- Mr P J Martin, Corporate Finance Department, PO Box 560 20 Fenchurch Street, London EC3P 3DB.

October 1987

the name to British Bus in August 1993, believing that this reflected more truly the nature of the Group.

East Lancashire Coachbuilders was then part of British Bus until January 1994 when it was sold along with other group companies that were not bus operators.

The new owners were Dazzle Investments, Aral Holdings, Emerald Holdings, and Hermon Investments, all of 19/21 Broad Street, Jersey, Channel Islands. Dazzle Investments took two fifths of the shares and the others one fifth each. However in August 1996 the others passed their shares to Dazzle Investments owned entirely by Dawson Williams.

In September 1997 Dawson Williams ceased to be a Director of East Lancashire Coachbuilders and from then took no part in the day to day operation of the Company. Dazzle Investments is administered by the Royal Bank of Canada.

The Directors at the time of writing in January 2000 are:- Philip Hilton - appointed 12th December 1989; Christopher William Clarke - appointed 2nd January 1992 and Michael Kevin Kilroy - appointed 4th June 1998 - Finance Director.

A further development took place with effect from 1st November 1999 when the Company took a 51% shareholding in the local company S & T Coachpainters whose Directors were Mr and Mrs Thomas Orrel. The company was renamed S & T Coachbuilders and moved to new premises in Appleby Street, Blackburn. This acquisition enabled repair and refurbishment work to be undertaken at the new premises and allowed the main works to concentrate on new bodies.

PERSONALITIES

In a book such as this it is not possible to mention everyone who has been involved in the background research, nor all those whose contribution to the firm's current success is rightly due.

We have seen that Walter Smith was the true founder, being involved from the formation of the company in 1934. Little is known of his original fellow Directors but Walter was well-known to the employees right up to his death.

As already recorded Alfred Alcock had joined the Company on 9th May 1938 and retired on 31st December 1966. George Danson joined on 9th May 1938, and retired in September 1984.

They are said to have had little in common on personal matters and never socialised together. Indeed there was known to be intense rivalry between them, so much so that after Alfred Alcock had worked until he was in his seventies and attended board meetings for three or four years after that, George Danson was determined to outdo him and work even longer, despite the fact that by then, Alfred had died. It was only the intervention of the then owners of the Company, John Brown Engineering, which led to his retirement.

The founders' sons, George Alcock and Arthur Danson both followed their fathers into the business, George straight from school and Arthur after a short period of employment with Blackburn Corporation Transport. We will now look at their careers and a few of the later significant members.

Below left: **Walter Smith's role continued, as Company Secretary, until his death in 1958 and he would regularly walk through the works wearing his familiar black homburg hat. He is seen here in the year before his death with Works Manager Tom Kenny during the tilt-testing of one of the single-decker Colombo trolleybuses. It is said that he was a very cautious man and as the vehicle began to tilt would nervously scratch the back of his head, causing his homburg to jump up and down. He looks somewhat ill at ease in this picture!**

Below: **George Danson, on the left, is shown during the tilt-testing of Bradford trolleybus No. 693 in 1955.**

GEORGE ALCOCK

George Alcock, son of Alfred Alcock, was born on 25th October 1935 at Enfield Street, Wigan. This was of course the address of Massey Brothers and later the address of Northern Counties after they moved from Wigan Lane to the new premises. He joined East Lancashire Coachbuilders straight from school in 1951 but his recollections of the Company go back to 1941 and subsequent years when he would visit the works and also accompany his father to the Commercial Motor Shows at Earls Court, being granted time off school for this purpose.

He spent his first twelve months with the Company in the drawing office and during this time won second prize in a drawing competition organised by the Institute of Carriage Builders. In connection with this award he recalls going to Charles Roe's works at Leeds and meeting Mr J W Shirley, then Managing Director of Park Royal Vehicles in London - to whom Roe were responsible as members of the ACV Group - and a well-known figure in bus body building. His spell in the drawing office was followed by three years in the sheet metal department and a further twelve months in the drawing office before being called up for national service in 1956.

On release from the Forces he returned to the drawing office as a draughtsman, working under the then Chief Draughtsman, Len Barradell. He recalls that his father Alfred was very much a conceptual draughtsman and that it was left to others to translate his ideas into working drawings which could be used on the shop floor.

In the early days full-size drawings were produced on 8ft x 4ft drawing boards with tee squares over 6ft in length with the result that if a draughtsman needed to draw a long parallel line he had to enlist the help of a colleague to hold the other end of the tee square. Later, drawings to a scale of half full size were used. George later became Chief Draughtsman and, along with Arthur Danson, was made a Director of the Company in 1964, when the Company was taken over by Cravens.

He recalls having a good relationship with the directors from Cravens and claims that he and Arthur Danson were looked after better by Cravens than by their fathers. The Cravens Directors always referred to George and Arthur as 'the boys.' He remembers going to Sheffield for an interview at the Master Cutler's Hall in connection with his appointment as a Director and being interviewed by Sir Eric Mensford and a professor. The professor questioned him about the use of glues and bonding in coachbuilding but George dismissed the idea as being impracticable. He sees it as somewhat ironic that in the later years of his career he became known as George Bond because of his promotion of bonding.

He became Joint Managing Director with Arthur Danson in 1985. In this position he was mainly responsible for design and production whilst

George Alcock, on the left of this picture, and Arthur Danson stand proudly in front of the first tramcar to be built by East Lancashire Coachbuilders. Blackpool No. 641 is seen on the tracks at Blackpool on 14th June 1984. Arthur had been involved with trams of an earlier generation at Blackburn of course whilst apprenticed to the Corporation.

Arthur Danson was mainly responsible for sales and administration although both did have their own customers. George Alcock took early retirement from the Company in 1991 and is now involved in running a successful hotel with one of his sons. George's recollections of the founders, the family ties and the growth of the business have helped enormously in the preparation of this book and his other son, Alistair, maintains the family link as the Company's Purchasing Manager.

ARTHUR DANSON

Born on 11th May 1931 Arthur Danson was encouraged by his father to seek outside experience before joining the Company. He joined Blackburn Corporation Transport, as an apprentice, and was there until buses replaced the trams. His career at East Lancashire Coachbuilders began in the fitting shop assembling metal frames, followed by the usual pattern of time spent in different departments learning the business. By 1960 he was assistant to Alf Bramley, the Works Manager, but was later moved to sales, becoming Sales Manager by 1965. Appointed a Director when Cravens took over he was appointed Joint Managing Director in 1985 with the other founder's son, as mentioned above. In later years he became very much the face of East Lancashire Coachbuilders to many of its customers, a big man whose capacity to entertain his clients was legendary. Behind the scenes he was a very shrewd manager and a great asset to the Company. In 1990 he took early retirement, maintaining his interest in breeding, training and racing greyhounds which was matched by his enthusiasm for crown green bowls. Philip Hilton remembers with affection the grounding in those aspects of the Company's business which he received at Arthur's hands, in addition to his training from George in the Drawing Office. He speaks of his intense personal sorrow and sense of loss when Arthur died at the age of 64 in September 1995 after a short illness.

PHILIP HILTON

Philip Hilton was born in 1945 in the village of Billington, near Whalley in the Ribble Valley. His father was a tackler and his mother a weaver in one of two cotton mills in the village, where most of the village inhabitants were employed. His journey towards East Lancashire Coachbuilders really started when, at about 13 years of age, he was standing outside a fish and chip shop in Whalley and was approached by Colonel Green, owner of the mill where his parents worked. Having satisfied himself, 'You're Hilton's boy aren't you?' the Colonel then asked Philip 'When are you starting?' (at the mill). Philip did not want to work in the mill and went home and told his father of his meeting with Colonel Green. His father's response was, 'If you can find yourself a job, you won't need to go in the mill. If you don't, you go in the mill!' Philip really wanted to be an electrician but despite various applications and interviews was unsuccessful.

One Saturday morning whilst going into Blackburn by bus with his mother to shop, his mother recalled that a family friend, John Bufton, worked at East Lancashire Coachbuilders and decided that they should get off the bus and see him with regard to the possiblity of a job. As a result of this Philip started as an apprentice coachbuilder and recalls that his first day there almost put him off. A St Helens Leyland double-decker had been in an accident with a crane jib as a result of which two children had been killed. The vehicle had come in for repair and he was given the job of removing the damaged parts in preparation for rebuilding, not a pleasant task for a 14-year-old for he had, due to an oversight, commenced two weeks before his 15th birthday, so keen was he not to go in the mill!

By the time he was eighteen he had passed a number of examinations at technical college and taken a liking to technical drawing. Arising from this, he pestered George Alcock about going to work in the drawing office for even at that age he was ambitious and saw such a move as the first step up the ladder of promotion. Eventually he was allowed to work in the drawing office on Saturday mornings. His mother bought him a new red sweater in preparation for his work in the drawing office but a few days after his first morning there, he was informed that Mr Alcock had stated that if he wished to return to the drawing office the following Saturday, he would have to wear a collar and tie. After about three months he was offered a position as a junior draughtsman. He progressed in the drawing office and became Chief Designer in 1985 when George Alcock became Joint Managing Director with Arthur Danson.

Philip Hilton is seen here, centre, with members of the Delaine-Smith family on the occasion of the handover of their Leyland Olympian N3 OCT in 1995.

In 1986 he left the drawing office to look after production, assisting the Works Manager, John Bufton. Arthur Danson recommended him as a Director in 1989 and, following the retirement of Arthur in 1990, he became Deputy Managing Director to George Alcock. At the end of 1991 George Alcock retired and Chris Clarke was appointed Chief Executive and Managing Director. Philip continued in the position of Deputy Managing Director, a position which he still holds at the time of writing.

JOHN BUFTON

It was Easter 1941 when John Bufton joined the Company as a 14-year-old apprentice coachbuilder. He spent most of his time in the finishing department and recalls working alone at a bench within a bus, making and fitting the internal timber finishers which were in use at that time. After cutting them to size many hours would be spent in sanding them - no electric sanders in those days, and they had to be perfect. They would then go for staining and varnishing by a Mr Clarke and after drying would be fitted by John to the bus.

His weekly wage when he started was four shillings (20 pence) per week but he was able to supplement this. During the war firewatchers were required to be on duty at night in all factories. A firewatcher from outside the Company, normally a retired policeman, would come in and keep guard overnight. His presence would be supplemented by two Company employees who would sleep on mattresses on canteen tables, ready to be called upon in the event of an emergency. For this they would be paid four shillings per night. Some of the men did not like doing this, preferring to be at home with their families, and John Bufton and another apprentice would deputise for them, unofficially of course. For this they received the four shillings due to the men plus another four shillings which the men gave them because they were so pleased to avoid the duty themselves. They would do this up to three times per week and so earn about six times their weekly wage. On one occasion they went to the cinema and on return found that the local police had been in to check that there was someone on duty. The official firewatcher told them that they were asleep and should not be disturbed!

In March 1945 John was called up for Army service, joining the Grenadier Guards, later telling the tale that when he joined up, Hitler gave in. He enjoyed his time in the army, being in no hurry to return to civvy street, but eventually returned to rejoin East Lancashire Coachbuilders in 1948 to complete his apprenticeship.

He continued with the Company as a coachbuilder and took a leading role in trade union activities becoming local President of the National Union of Vehicle Builders and taking on the role of wage negotiator for the Company. He was very good at this, so much so that it has been alleged that the Directors, recognising his skills, decided it would be better to have him on their side. In 1964 he was made General Foreman thus leapfrogging over others who were already departmental foremen. In due course he went to see Arthur Danson to complain about his wages and to ask for a rise. Arthur gave him many reasons as to why he could not give him a rise but obviously, behind this facade, there was a deep respect for John and his ability and he was made Assistant Works Manager to Alf Bramley. During Alf Bramley's illness John was acting Works Manager and took over from him on his retirement. John continued in this position until his own retirement in February 1992 after 51 years' service. His reminiscences have been invaluable in preparing this book.

CHRISTOPHER CLARKE

Chris Clarke was born in 1944 and after leaving school joined the Rootes Group as a management pupil, later becoming a development engineer in the Truck Division. A career change took him to a senior management position with Shell International Petroleum and after some years he moved to Shell International Chemicals as Head of Commercial Affairs Worldwide. After being head-hunted he joined the Stirling Winthorp Group responsible for the well-known business Roncraft. After 10 years and becoming bored with white pills and varnishes he decided, in 1989, to return to engineering and worked as a consulting engineer with the Drawlane Group where he was given the task of looking at the ageing Leyland National vehicle with a view to refurbishment to extend its life. This materialised as the Greenway project in which East Lancashire Coachbuilders was to play a major role.

It was during his involvement with this project that he moved to East Lancashire Coachbuilders in January 1992 to take on the position of Chief Executive, following the early retirement of George Alcock. Here he continued to mastermind the Greenway project and headed the team of directors, supported wholeheartedly by Dawson Williams, in the Company's move to new premises. Once settled in the new works, Chris organised changes to the product range and was heavily involved in the introduction of Alusuisse and composite construction. At the time of writing he continues as Chairman and Chief Executive of East Lancashire Coachbuilders.

Chris Clarke at his desk.

Relaxation and Retirement

Continuity has been a factor of the Company personnel throughout its existence with many long serving employees, some spending their entire working life with East Lancashire and many being followed by sons into the Company.

Some long serving members of staff are:- Jim Martindale, Foreman, 45 years; John Hargreaves, Skilled Sheet Metal Worker, 41 years; Jim Boothman, Foreman, 40 years; David Huntingdon, Foreman, 37 years; John Tattersall, Foreman, 30 years; Brian Oldfield, Design, 30 years.

Above: **Arthur Danson in later life was a staunch Blackburn Rovers supporter, but we have no record of him playing for the works team, seen here in 1956/57. John Bufton, however, ever the sportsman, was very much at home as captain and is seen here third from right, tall and upright as befits one who had been in the Guards.**

Below: **Some of Arthur's many contacts in the industry came to join him for a farewell lunch following his retirement. It was held at the Mitton Fold Farm Hotel. The event had been kept secret from Arthur who was under the impression that he was merely being taken to lunch with Philip Hilton and Geoffrey Hilditch.**

FAMILY TREE

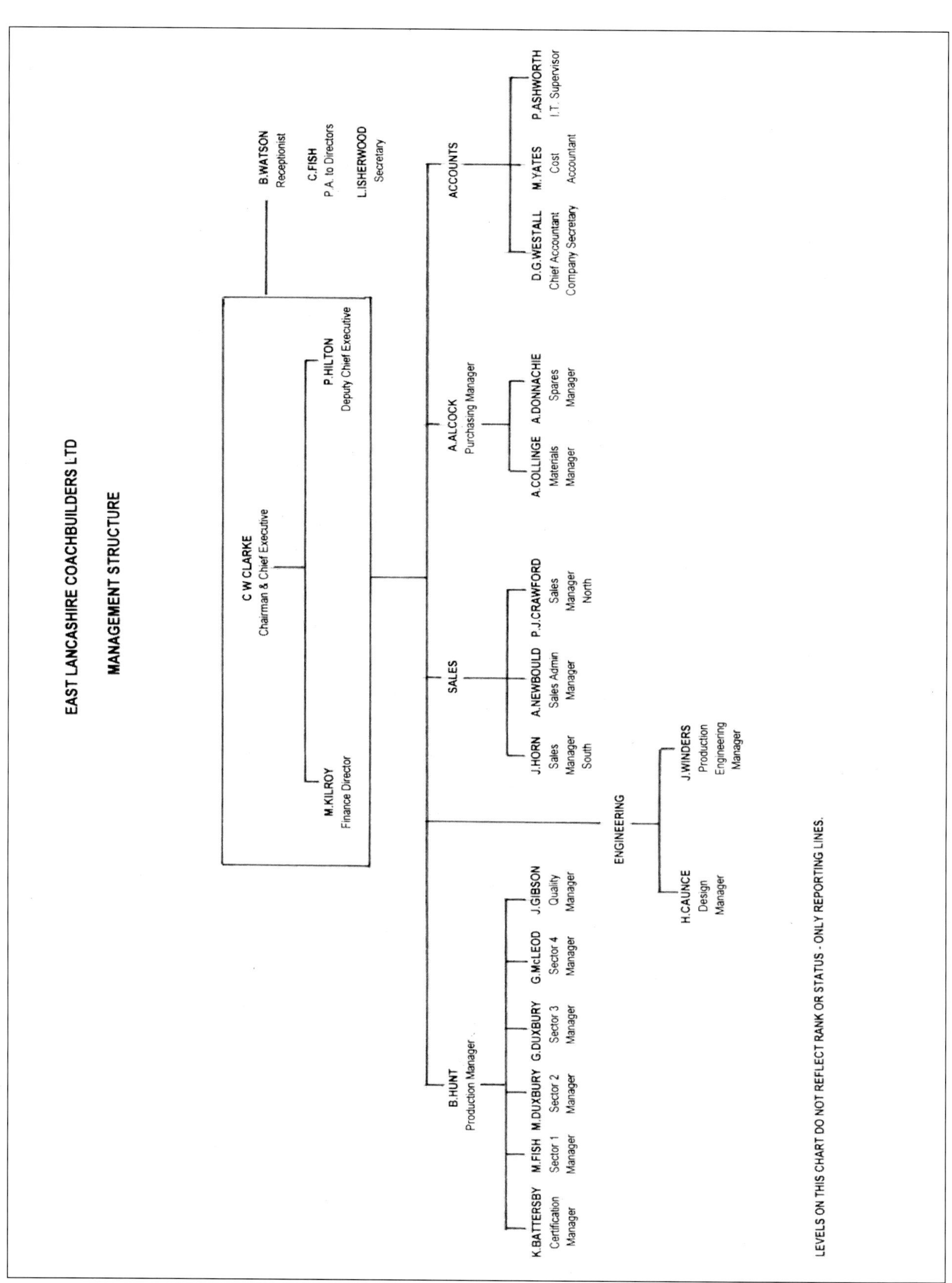

EAST LANCASHIRE COACHBUILDERS LTD
MANAGEMENT STRUCTURE
C W CLARKE
Chairman & Chief Executive
P.HILTON
Deputy Chief Executive
M.KILROY
Finance Director
B.WATSON
Receptionist
C.FISH
P.A. to Directors
L.ISHERWOOD
Secretary
ACCOUNTS
D.G.WESTALL
Chief Accountant
Company Secretary
M.YATES
Cost
Accountant
P.ASHWORTH
I.T. Supervisor
A.ALCOCK
Purchasing Manager
A.COLLINGE
Materials
Manager
A.DONNACHIE
Spares
Manager
SALES
J.HORN
Sales
Manager
South
A.NEWBOULD
Sales Admin
Manager
P.J.CRAWFORD
Sales
Manager
North
ENGINEERING
H.CAUNCE
Design
Manager
J.WINDERS
Production
Engineering
Manager
B.HUNT
Production Manager
K.BATTERSBY
Certification
Manager
M.FISH
Sector 1
Manager
M.DUXBURY
Sector 2
Manager
G.DUXBURY
Sector 3
Manager
G.McLEOD
Sector 4
Manager
J.GIBSON
Quality
Manager
LEVELS ON THIS CHART DO NOT REFLECT RANK OR STATUS - ONLY REPORTING LINES.

A1 1919 EXAMINATION PAPER

City and Guilds of London Institute.

DEPARTMENT OF TECHNOLOGY.

TECHNOLOGICAL EXAMINATIONS, 1919.

47.—Road-Carriage Building.

Final Examination.

Written Paper.

Thursday, May 1st, 7 *to* 10.

INSTRUCTIONS.

The number of the question must be placed before the answer in the worked paper.

The maximum number of marks obtainable is affixed to each question.

The use of scale rules and drawing instruments is allowed. Drawing paper is supplied. No curves or patterns are allowed.

Three hours allowed for this paper.

Ten questions only to be attempted.

Candidates must have already forwarded to the Institute the required specimens of their work.

Candidates must also take the Final Drawing Examination to be held on Saturday, May 3rd, from 2.30 to 6.30 p.m.

1. You are required to build a copy of a Continental built body which has the following dimensions:—Dash to front pillar 1,155 mm., width of front pillar 57 mm., width of doorway 609 mm., rear door shut to back of body 1,676 mm., height of doorway 1,250 mm., depth of quarter 702 mm. To what corresponding dimensions in inches would you set out the full size drawing for the bodymaker? (*25 marks.*)

2. In making up a scale design of a three-quarter landaulette for despatch to a customer, what points would you particularly endeavour to convey, and what views would you show, assuming that you had six working hours in which to prepare the design? What room would you allow from the front casing board to the rear seat for extra seats facing forwards? (*20.*)

3. Describe briefly the different methods adopted for the seasoning of timber and the time required for each process. (*20.*)

4. How would you ascertain the usable contents of a log of timber in the round? What are the cubical contents of a London standard of timber? (*20.*)

5. If it were not possible to set out the working drawing of a body to full size, to what scale would you draw it, and why? (*15.*)

6. What sectional size would you make the bottom side in the centre of the doorway of a body to open or close entirely? What style and size of doorplate (if any) would you use in such a case? Illustrate by a freehand sketch. (*20.*)

7. Give the specific gravity of steel, ash, pine, Honduras mahogany, and aluminium. What is the break weight of ash (English)? (*15.*)

8. A limousine landaulette has become damaged through another vehicle striking the rear corner of the frame with sufficient force to knock the chassis frame out of alignment. How would you test the body to ascertain if it is also moved out of square? What other damage would you expect from such an accident? (*25.*)

9. What metal, and what gauge or section would be best for (*a*) a set of domed wings, (*b*) the rear corners of a rotund panelled body, (*c*) a folding luggage grid to carry $1\frac{1}{2}$ cwt., (*d*) a pair of solid front canopy supports, (*e*) a set of platform step stays? (*20.*)

10. Estimate the cost of labour and material for each of the items set out in question 9, with labour at the rate of 1*s.* 3*d.* per hour. (*30.*)

11. Describe the process of marking and cutting out, fitting and fixing a complete head-leather for (*a*) a canoe landau, or (*b*) a single landaulette with round corners. Estimate the approximate cost in each case. (*35.*)

12. Give the quantities of material required for completely trimming a two-seated body with a hood and folding dicky seat, all in leather. (*30.*)

13. Whence and how are the following derived:—(*a*) Lamp black, (*b*) ivory black, (*c*) umber? How are white lead and varnish respectively made, and how would you test them for quality? (*25.*)

14. What is meant by the following terms:—(*a*) Establishment or over-head charges, (*b*) visor screen, (*c*) baghide, (*d*) guide coat, (*e*) glazing colour, (*f*) seaming lace and pasting lace, (*g*) torsional stress, (*h*) shearing stress? (*30.*)

15. In machining the framework for 12 closed bodies to the same design, what work would you carry out on the vertical spindle? (*25.*)

Candidates will be required to sit for the Drawing Examination to be held on Saturday, May 3rd, from 2.30 to 6.30 p.m. At this examination the question will deal with a double brougham, or alternatively a cabriolet.

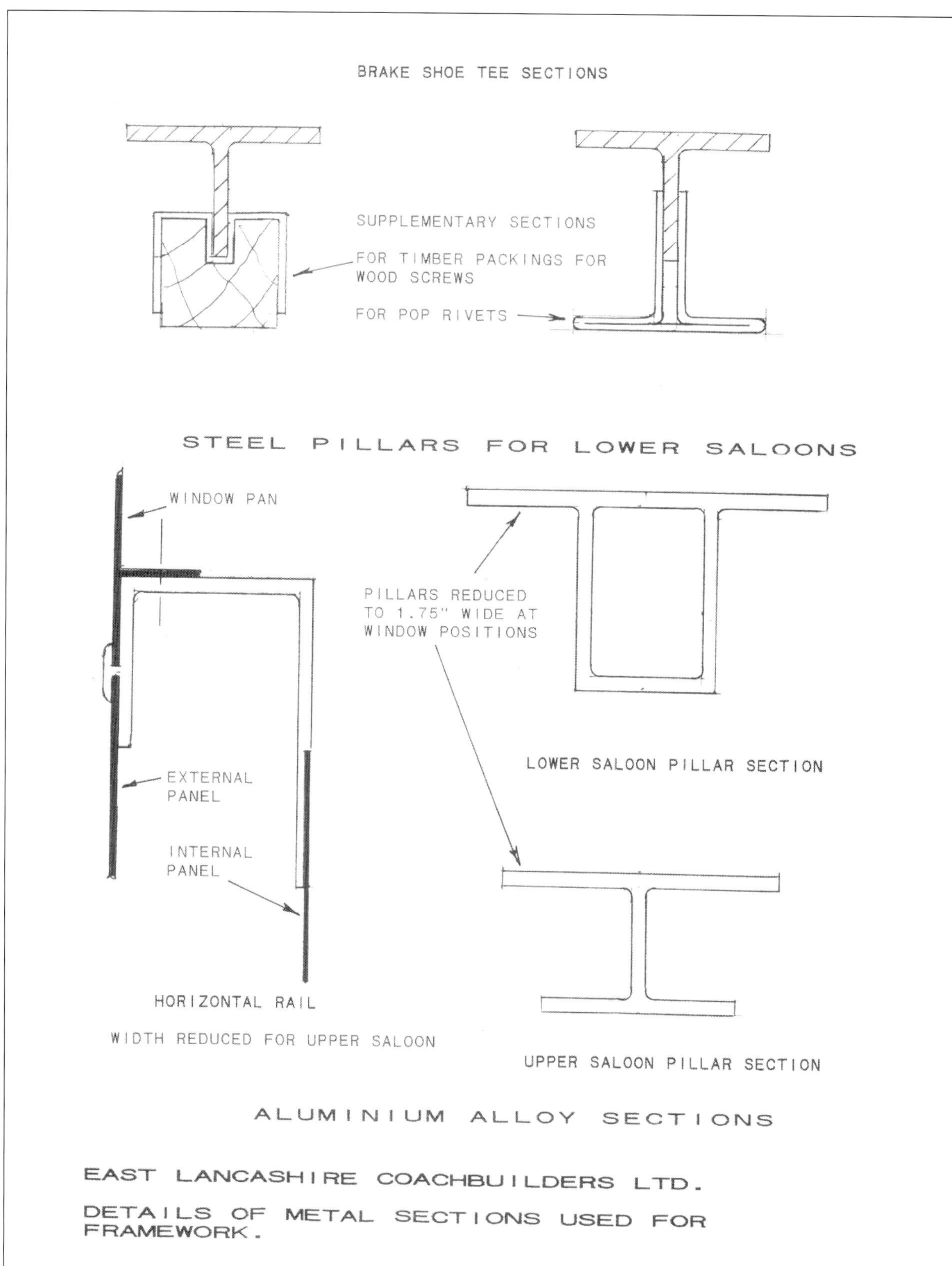
BRAKE SHOE TEE SECTIONS
SUPPLEMENTARY SECTIONS
FOR TIMBER PACKINGS FOR WOOD SCREWS
FOR POP RIVETS
STEEL PILLARS FOR LOWER SALOONS
WINDOW PAN
PILLARS REDUCED TO 1.75" WIDE AT WINDOW POSITIONS
EXTERNAL PANEL
INTERNAL PANEL
LOWER SALOON PILLAR SECTION
HORIZONTAL RAIL
WIDTH REDUCED FOR UPPER SALOON
UPPER SALOON PILLAR SECTION
ALUMINIUM ALLOY SECTIONS
EAST LANCASHIRE COACHBUILDERS LTD.
DETAILS OF METAL SECTIONS USED FOR FRAMEWORK.

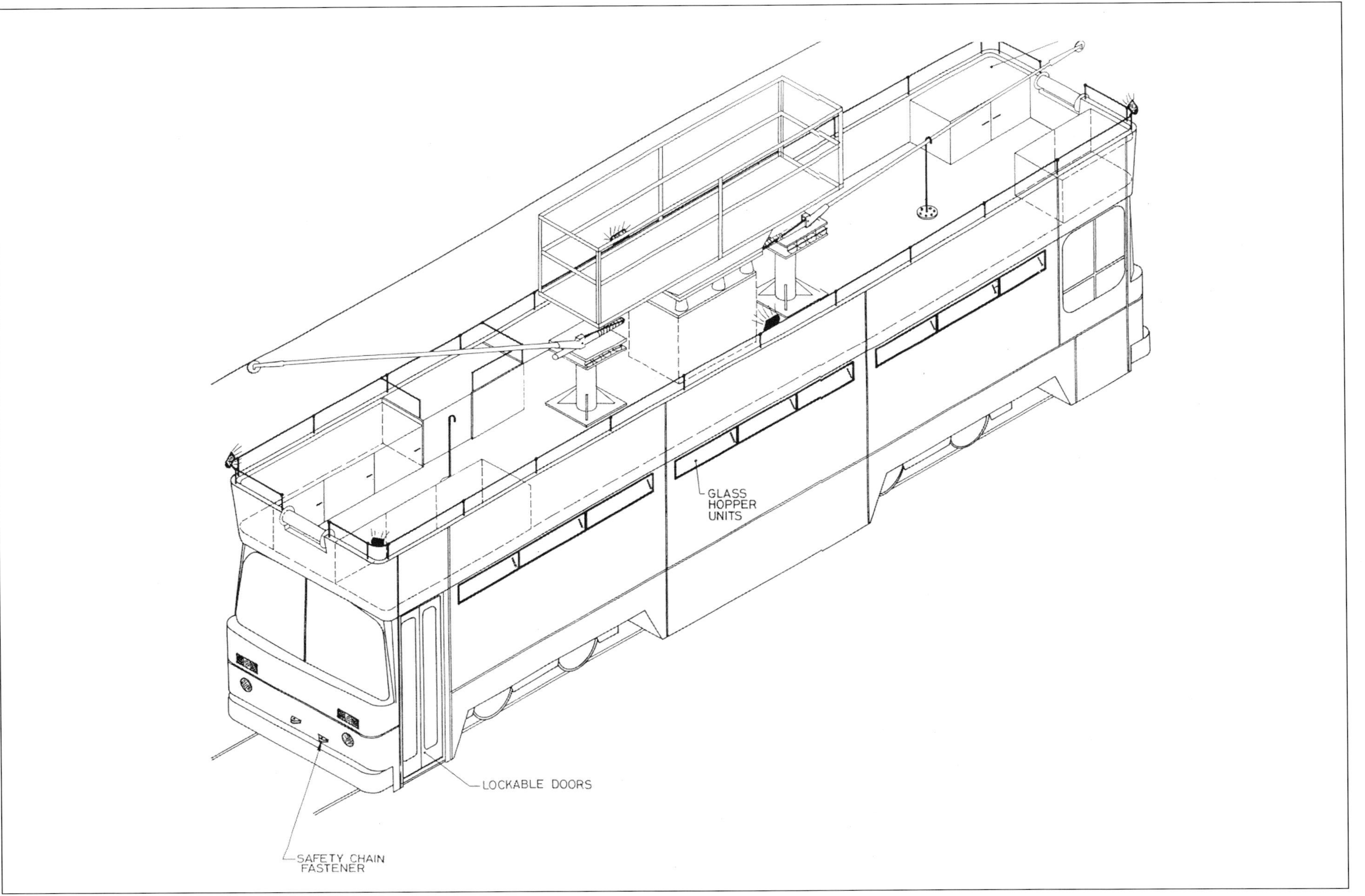
GLASS HOPPER UNITS
LOCKABLE DOORS
SAFETY CHAIN FASTENER

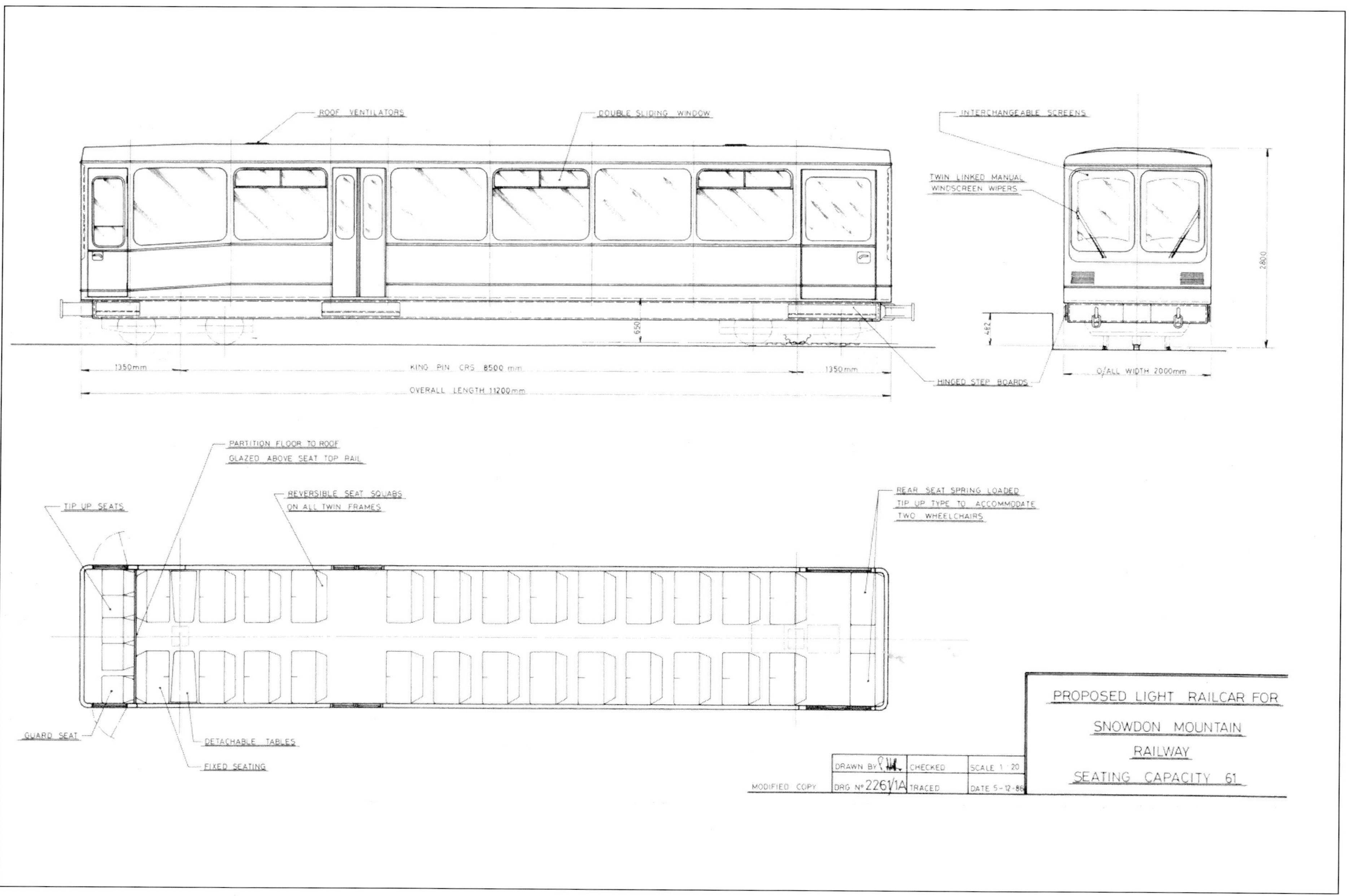
ROOF VENTILATORS
DOUBLE SLIDING WINDOW
INTERCHANGEABLE SCREENS
TWIN LINKED MANUAL
WINDSCREEN WIPERS
2800
650
482
1350mm
KING PIN CRS 8500 mm
1350mm
OVERALL LENGTH 11200mm
HINGED STEP BOARDS
O/ALL WIDTH 2000mm
PARTITION FLOOR TO ROOF
GLAZED ABOVE SEAT TOP RAIL
REVERSIBLE SEAT SQUABS
ON ALL TWIN FRAMES
TIP UP SEATS
REAR SEAT SPRING LOADED
TIP UP TYPE TO ACCOMMODATE
TWO WHEELCHAIRS
GUARD SEAT
DETACHABLE TABLES
FIXED SEATING
PROPOSED LIGHT RAILCAR FOR
SNOWDON MOUNTAIN
RAILWAY
SEATING CAPACITY 61
DRAWN BY
CHECKED
SCALE 1:20
MODIFIED COPY
DRG No 2261/1A
TRACED
DATE 5-12-86

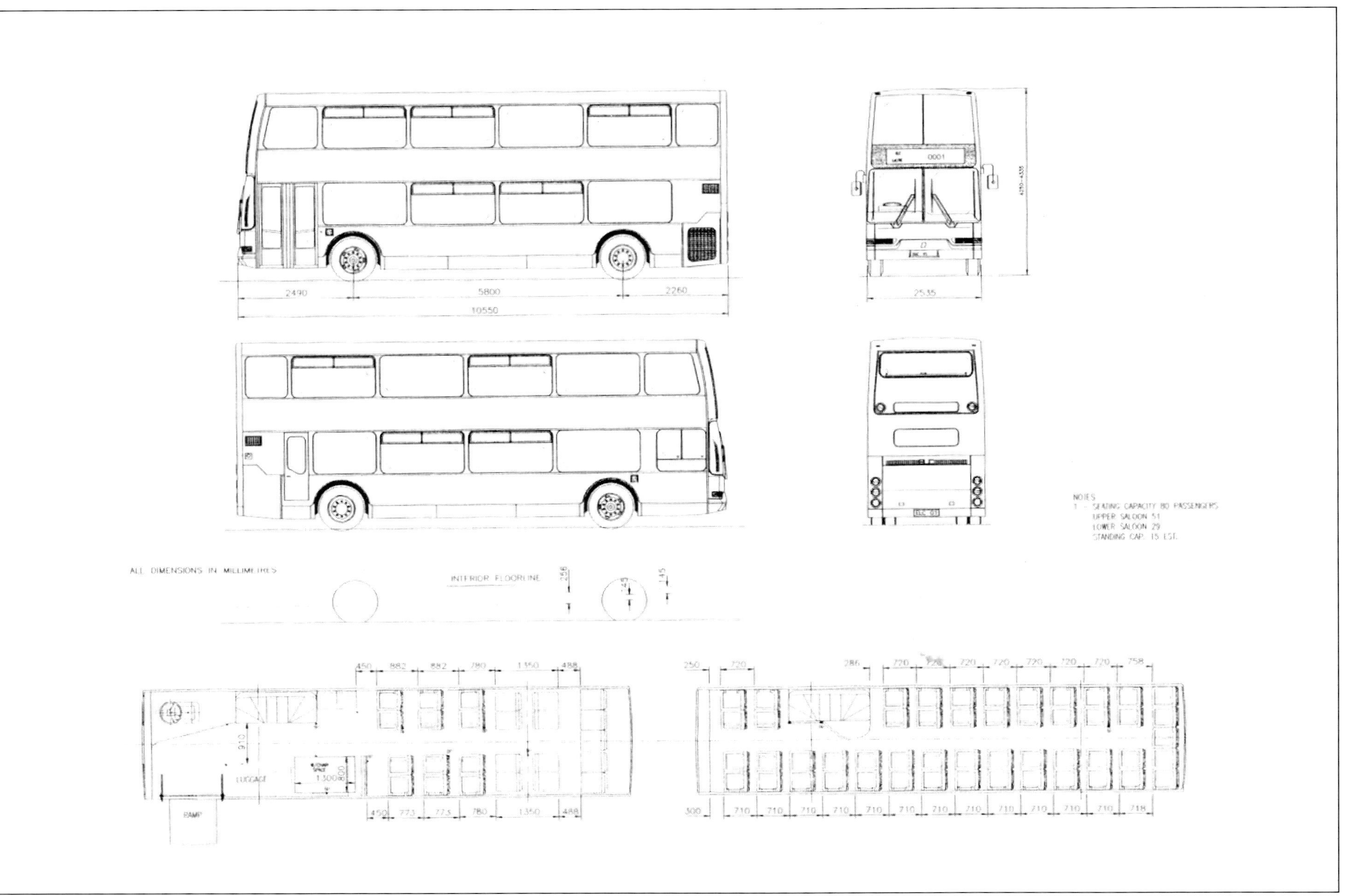
2490
5800
2260
10550
2535
NOTES
1 - SEATING CAPACITY 80 PASSENGERS
UPPER SALOON 51
LOWER SALOON 29
STANDING CAP. 15 LST.
ALL DIMENSIONS IN MILLIMETRES
INTERIOR FLOORLINE
LUGGAGE
RAMP

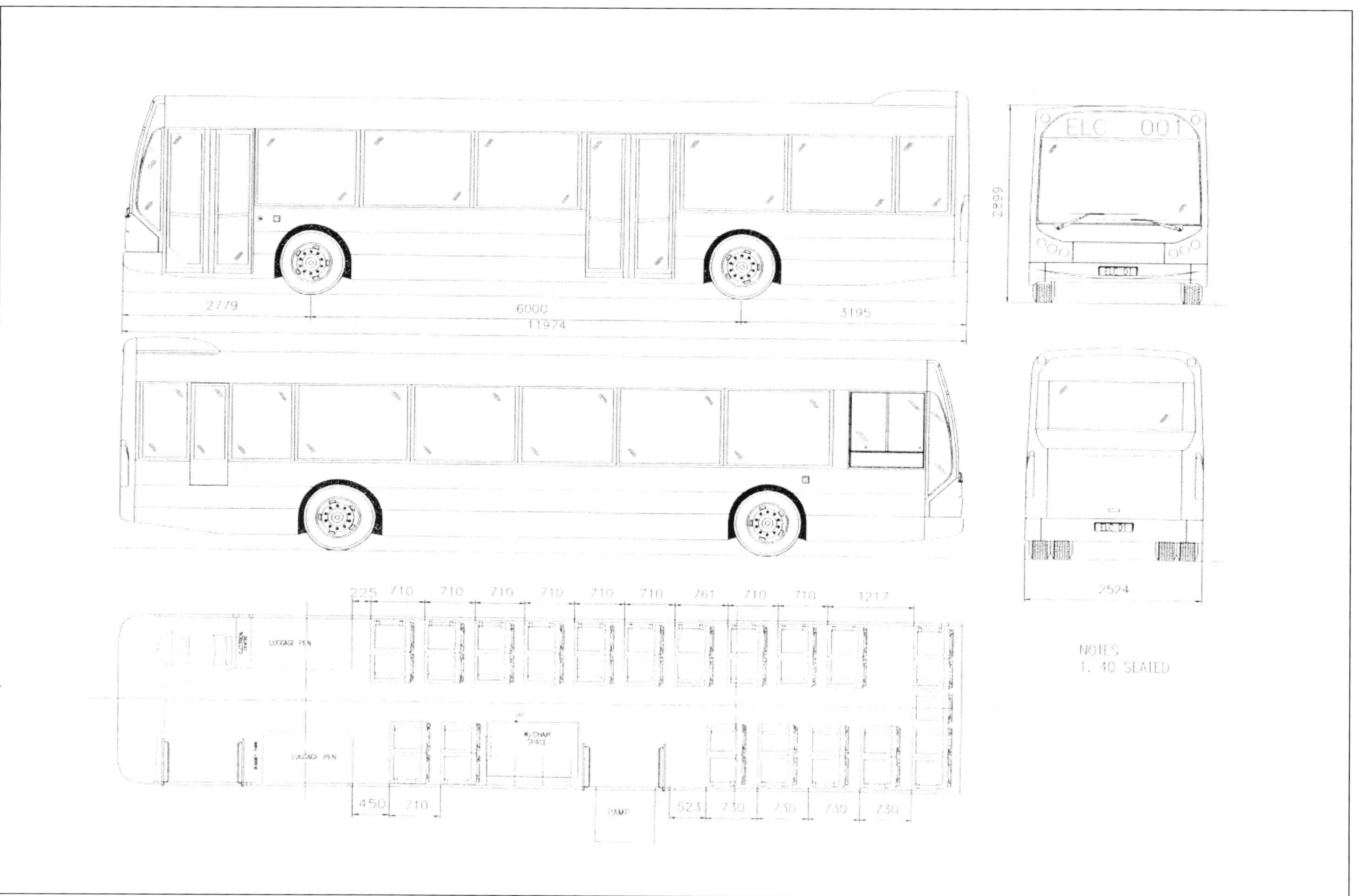

ELC 001
2779
6000
3195
11974
2899
2524
225
710
761
1217
LUGGAGE PEN
W/CHAIR SPACE
450
523
730
RAMP
NOTES
1. 40 SEATED

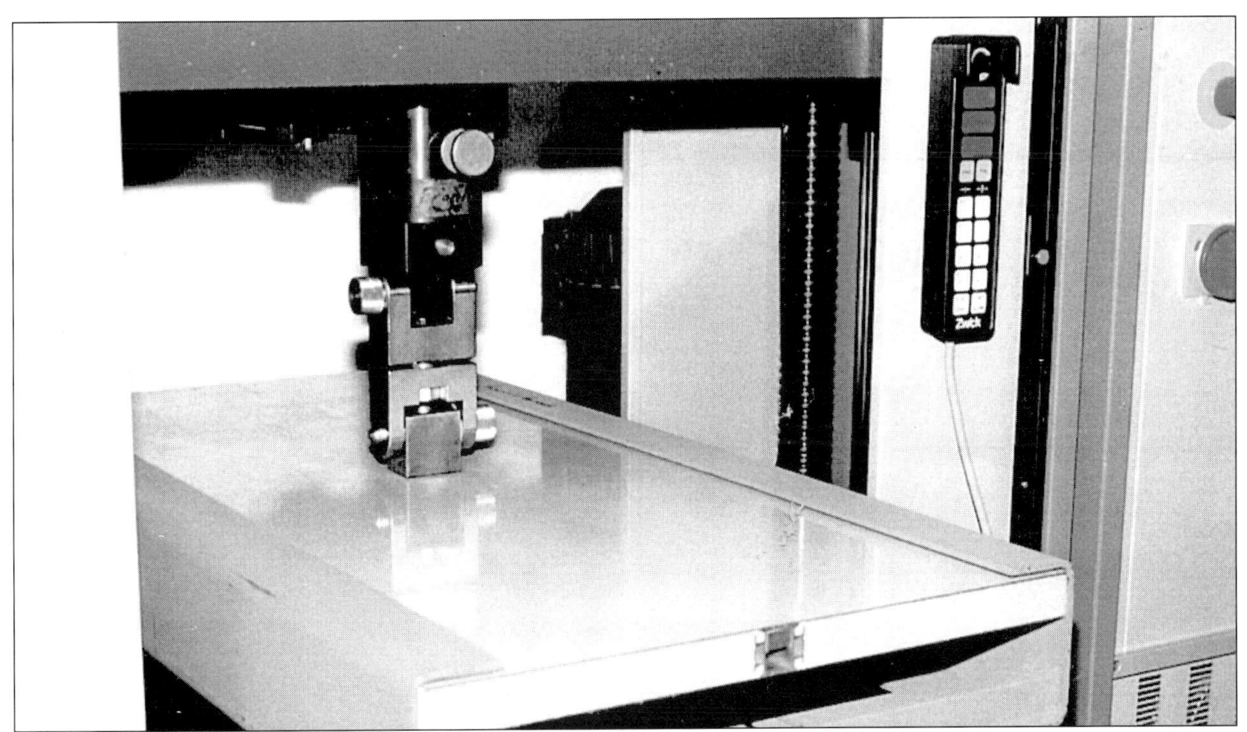

Two detailed views of the intermediate floor pull-out force test applied to Alusuisse components. The lower picture shows an unscathed Alusuisse composite test specimen alongside a plywood and steel example which has rather alarmingly failed the test.

A3 PATENTS

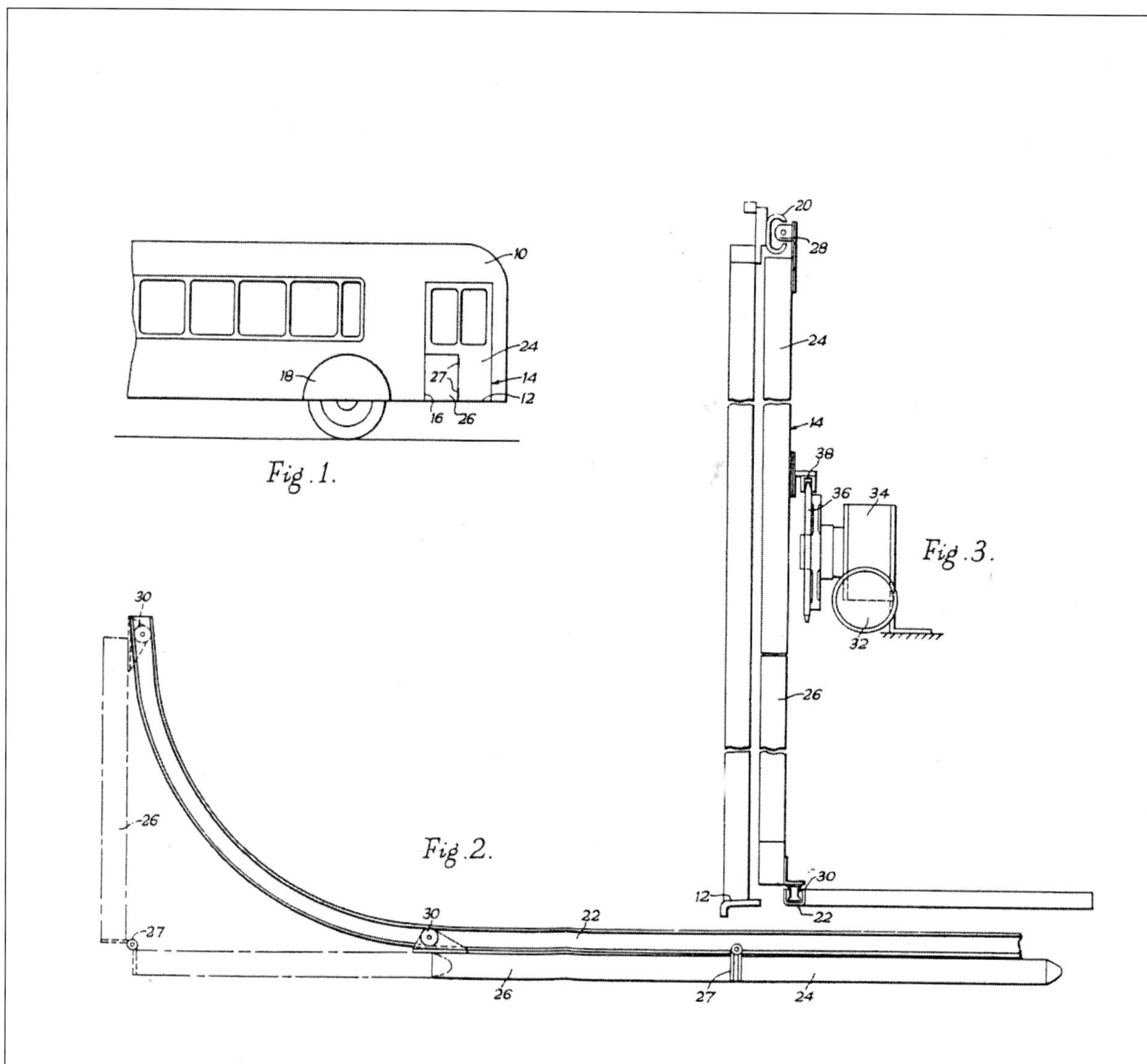

KEY.

10. BODY	26. HINGED FLAP
12. PLATFORM	27. HINGES
14. DOOR	28. ROLLER BEARING - UPPER
16. REAR BULKHEAD	30. ROLLER BEARING - LOWER
18. WHEEL ARCH	32. REVERSIBLE ELECTRIC MOTOR
20. UPPER TRACK	34. REDUCTION GEAR BOX
22. LOWER TRACK	36. SPROCKET
24. DOOR - MAIN PORTION	38. CHAIN

EAST LANCASHIRE COACHBUILDERS LTD.

ARRANGEMENT OF 'EASTLANCO' DOOR
PATENT NO. 813272

KEY
10. DOOR SECTION
12. DOOR SECTION
14. BRACKET
16. BAR
18. CHAIN
24. DOOR STOP
28. SHAFT
30. LARGE SPROCKET WHEEL
32. SMALL SPROCKET WHEEL

DOOR SECTION 10 MOVES AT TWICE THE SPEED OF DOOR SECTION 12 SO THAT BOTH REACH OPEN AND CLOSED POSITIONS SIMULTANEOUSLY.

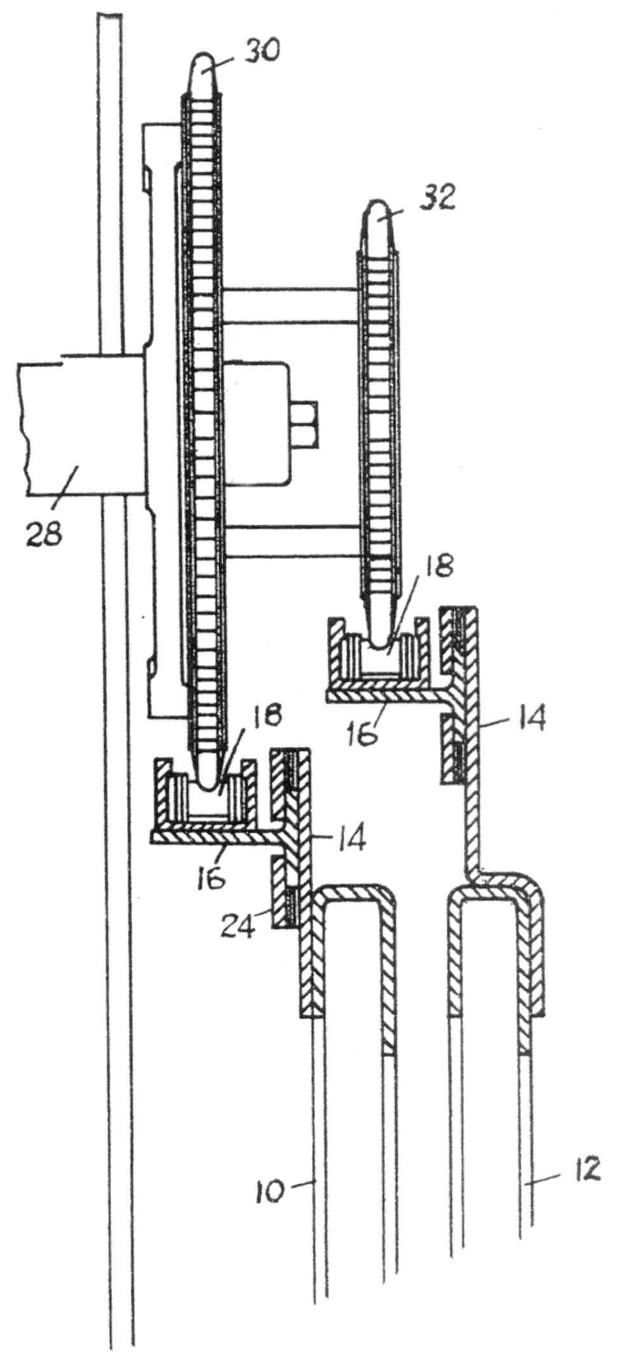

EAST LANCASHIRE COACHBUILDERS LTD.

ARRANGEMENT OF 'SOUTHLANCO' DOOR
PATENT NO. 771672

A4 WORKS LAYOUTS

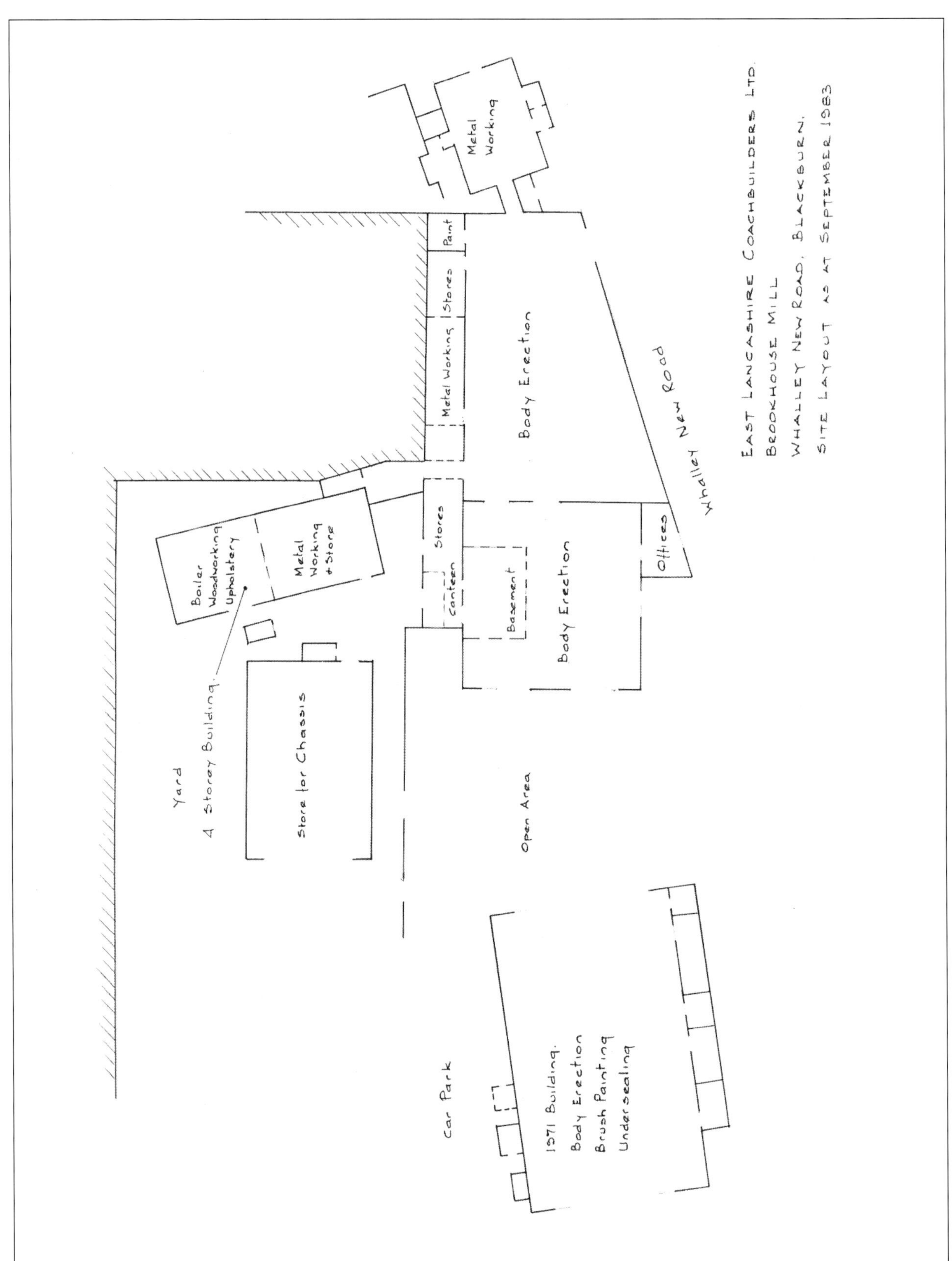

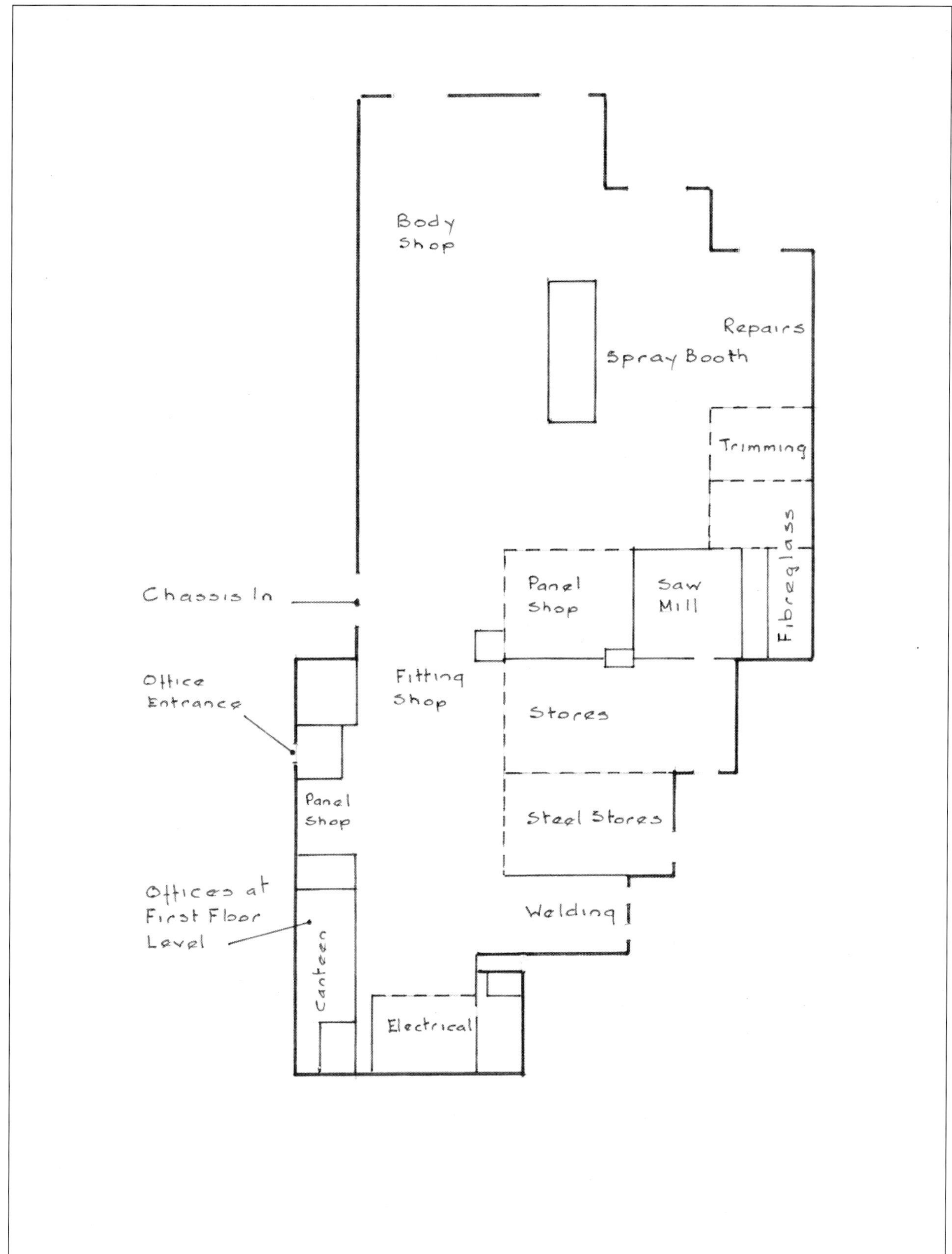

EAST LANCASHIRE COACHBUILDERS LTD.

WHITEBIRK INDUSTRIAL ESTATE, BLACKBURN.

SKETCH LAYOUT OF WORKS.

A5 BODY AND CUSTOMER LIST

A 4-digit body numbering system was used in the early days but no records of numbers allocated prior to 1944 have been found. The earliest number available is 2807 allocated to Cardiff Corporation rebodied Leyland TD2 No. 54, KG 1147, completed in 1944. The highest number in this series, used for a bus, was 2978 allocated to the rebuilding of Plymouth Corporation Leyland TD5c No. 208 in June 1945. However the number 2980 appears to have been allocated to a railcar cab for Walker Brothers and the numbers 2981- 89 to crane cabs also for Walker Brothers.

A new 4-digit series commenced at the end of 1945 with the number 4001, some records showing this allocated to St Helens Corporation Leyland TD7c rebuilt after fire damage, whilst other records show No. 4003 allocated to this vehicle. After this point records become more reliable and this series continued up to number 7258 allocated to Ipswich Corporation AEC Swift No. 93 in July 1973. Body numbers are not available for bodies built at Neepsend, apart from those for which the frames were supplied from Blackburn.

A new system was introduced from October 1973, the first recipients being three Leyland Atlanteans for Caerphilly Urban District Council. This comprised blocks of numbers known as 'Series' commencing at Series 24 allocated to the Caerphilly vehicles and going through to Series 101 allocated to five Leyland Atlanteans for Lancaster City Transport delivered between December 1979 and November 1980. The body number comprised the series number plus a supplementary number, for example 24.01, 24.02, etc. Generally a series would be allocated to a single customer but there were occasions when small orders would be grouped together under one series.

A variation on the 'Series' system was introduced in July 1980 on a batch of ten bodies on Leyland Atlantean chassis for Nottingham City Transport. This introduced a letter prefix to the series number commencing with 'A' and although series A1 was allocated to the Nottingham vehicles, there were veicles delivered to Plymouth commencing in December 1979 and these were covered by Series A2.

On reaching A99 in May 1990 with two Volvo B10Ms for Burnley and Pendle, a new series commencing at B01 was introduced for 8 Scania N113DRBs supplied to Kingston upon Hull City Transport in September 1990. The 'B' series then continued to B99 allocated to five Dennis Darts for Derby City Transport supplied in July 1994 and a single Dennis Dart for Silcox of Pembroke Dock delivered in August 1994.

This series then recommenced at B110 with two rebodies for Blue Bus of Horwich in December 1994 and has continued to the time of writing with Series 323 allocated to an order for Lolyne bodies on Dennis Trident chassis for Go Ahead North East. From Series 242 upwards, allocated in February 1998 to 13 Dennis Darts for Capital Citybus, the prefix letter was changed to 'C' but in recent times the prefix letter has been discontinued. There are a number of gaps in the Series numbers brought about by the allocation of series numbers at enquiry stage, some of the enquiries not materialising into orders.

Author's Note

In this list minor differences in chassis specifications and seating arrangements within batches of vehicles have been ignored in the interests of containing the list within manageable proportions.

Further, there were inconsistencies among the various sets of records which were consulted during the list's preparation.

Below: **A rare view of the interior of the Neepsend Works in about 1965 taken from a Company publicity brochure includes, on the far left, three Dennis Loline chassis, probably for Luton Corporation for whom a batch of six was being built at that time. At centre and right are Leyland Atlanteans, the unpainted example being for Sheffield and in the bottom right corner is the front of an AEC Reliance, one of a batch of ten for Chesterfield Corporation. An interesting feature of the work in hand is what looks like a Plaxton-bodied 41-seat coach apparently being repaired.**

EAST LANCASHIRE COACHBUILDERS LIMITED.

BODY AND CUSTOMER LIST 1938 to 1999.

YEAR	CHAS	MOD.	SEATING	NO.	CUSTOMER & FLEET NOS.	NOTES.
1938	Ld.	TD5	H28/26R	10	Bolton 143-52	
1938	Ld.	TD5	L24/24R	2	Leigh 70-71	
1938	AEC	Rt.	H28/26R	2	Chester 29-30	
1938-40	Ld.	TD1	L27/24R	19	Cumberland Nc.& 148-51	Rbd.
1939	AEC	Rt.	H30/26R	2	Blackburn 54-55	
1939	Ld.	TD5.	L27/26R	2	Cumberland 145-46	
1939	Bl.	L5G	B32C	9	Rotherham 104-12	
1939	Gy.	BTX	B38C	4	Rotherham 19-22	
1939	AEC	664T	B38C	4	Rotherham 23-26	
1939/40	Ld.	TB7	H28/26R	20	Hull 47-66	
1940	AEC	Rt.	H30/26R	7	Cardiff 192-198	
1940	Bl.	L5G	B32C	9	Rotherham 157-65	
1940	Ld.	TB5	B32C	4	Darlington 64-67	
1940/1	Sm.	MS2C	B39C	8	Rotherham 70-77	
1941	Ld.	TD7	H29/23R	4	Barrow 15-18	
1941	Ld.	TD7	L27/26R	5	Cumberland 164-68	
1941/2	Bl.	L5G	B32C	4	Rotherham 100-103	
1942	AEC	Rt.	L27/26R	2	Brown,Tunstall 32-33	Rby.
1942	Bl.	L5G	B32R	1	Aberdare 31	
1942	Bl.	L5G	B35F	2	Caledonian M275-76	
1942	Ld.	TD2,4,5	H30/26R	5	Birkenhead Nc.	Rby.
1942	Ld.	TD4c	H30/26R	1	Birkenhead 214	Rbd.
1942	Ld.	TD7	H30/26R	2	Western SMT	
1942	Ld.	TD7	H30/26R	1	Lancaster 41	
1942	Ld.	TD7	L27/26R	2	Lanc.United 260-61	
1942	Ld.	TD7	L26/22R	2	Aldershot L1-2	
1942	Ld.	TD7	L27/26R	1	Wigan 122	
1942	AEC	Rt.	H24/24R	1	Lancaster 23	Rbd.
1942	Ld.	TD7	H30/26R	1	Warrington 91	
1942	Ld.	TD7	H29/23R	1	Barrow 79	
1942	Ld.	TD1	H30/26R	1	Eastbourne 75	Rby.
1942	Ld.	TD1	L24/24R	1	Plymouth 131	Rby.
1942	AEC	Rt.	H30/26R	1	Cardiff 199	
1942	Kr.	E4S	B32C	2	Darlington 1,11	
1942	Ld.	TD7	L27/26R	3	Ribble 2388-90	
1942	Sm.	MS2C	B39C	8	Rotherham 82-89	
1942	Sm.	MF2A	B32R	1	Teeside 14	
1943	AEC	Rt.	L30/26R	3	Eastern National Nc.	Rby.
1943	Ld.	TD4c	H30/26R	1	Birkenhead 198	Rby.
1943	Ld.	TS3,4	B32R	7	Barrow Nc.	Rby.
1943	AEC	Rt.	H30/26R	3	Grimsby 60-62	Rby.
1943	AEC	Rt.	H33/28F	1	Maynes,Manchester	Rby.
1943	Ran.	D6	L24/26R	1	St.Helens 119	Rby.
1944	AEC	Rt.	H30/26R	9	Cardiff 1-8,10	Rby.
1944	Ld.	TS2	B31F	1	East.National 3217	Rby.
1944	Ld.	TD1	L30/26R	1	East.National 2847	Rby.
1944	AEC	Rt.	L30/26R	6	East.National Nc.	Rby.
1944	Ld.	TD1	H30/26R	1	Eastbourne 64	Rby.
1944	AEC	Rt.	H30/26R	3	Venture 43,60-61	Rby.
1944	AEC	Rt.	L27/24R	6	Oxford Nc.	Rby.
1944	Cy.	Con.	H30/26R	5	Northampton Nc.	Rby.
1944	Ld.	TD4,5	L24/24R	2	Plymouth 155,202	Rbd.
1944	AEC	Rt.	H30/26R	7	Bradford Nc.	Rby.
1943	Bl.	JO5G	B32C	1	Rotherham 123	Rbd.
1944-6	Ld.	TD2	H30/26R	10	Cardiff 53-62	Rby.
1944-5	AEC	Rt.	H30/26R	7	Cardiff 192-98	Rbd.
1945-7	Ld.	TBD2	L24/26R	16	St.Helens 121-36	Rby.
1944-7	Bl.	JO5G	B32C	5	Rotherham Nc.	Rbd.
1945	Gy.	BTX	B39/40C	2	Rotherham 50,64	Rbd.
1945	AEC	Rt.	H30/28F	3	Mayne,Manchester	Rby.
1944	Dr.	COG5	H30/26R	1	Aberdare 10	Rby.
1945	Ld.	TD7	L27/26R	1	Leigh 72	Rby.
1944-5	Ld.	TD5c	L24/24R	5	Plymouth Nc.	Rbd.
1945	Cy.	Con.	H30/26R	2	Northampton 63-64	Rby.
1944-5	Ld.	TD2	H26/26R	10	Southdown Nc.	Rby.
1944-5	Ds.	Lance	L22/26R	10	Aldershot Nc.	Rby.
1945	Ld.	TD3,4	H30/26R	7	Bolton Nc.	Rby.
1945	Ld.	TD5c	L24/24R	4	Plymouth 208,12,29,34	Rbd.
1945	Ld.	TD7c	L27/26R	1	St.Helens 71	Rbd.
1945	AEC	Rt.	H29/25R	2	Burnley C&N 50,51	Rby.
1946-9	Bl.	K6A	H30/26R	2	Cardiff 80,84	Rbd.AD
1946	Ld.	TS7	L27/26R	2	Leigh	Rby.
1946-8	Ld.	TD3,4,5	H26/26R	26	Southdown Nc.	Rby.
1945-6	Ld.	LPTB70	H40/30R	13	London Transport Nc.	Rby.
1946	Ld.	TD5c	L24/24R	1	Plymouth 206	Rbd.
1947-8	AEC	Rt.	H30/26R	13	Leeds Nc.	Rbd.Bri.
1946	Ld.	TD3	L27/26R	1	St.Helens 59	Rby.
1946-7	Ld.	LPTB70	H40/30R	6	London Transport Nc.	Rby.
1947-8	AEC	664T	H40/30R	3	London Transport Nc.	Rby.
1948	AEC	Ch'less	H40/30R	3	London Transport Nc.	Rby.
1948	AEC	Rt.	H30/26R	1	Hull 197	Rbd.Bri.
1948	Gy.	Arab 1	H30/26R	1	Hull 208	Rbd.Bri.
1947-8	Ld.	TBD2	L24/26R	4	St.Helens 101-104	Rby.
1946-7	Ld.	PD1	H28/24R	6	Eastbourne 13-18	
1946	Bl.	K5G,6B	H30/26R	4	Rotherham 170-73	
1947	AEC	Rl.	B32R	5	Cardiff 143-47	Rbd.AD.
1948	Sm.	MF2	L24/26R	1	St.Helens 165	Rbd.
1947	Bl.	K6A	L27/26R	3	St.Helens 44-46	
1947	Ld.	OPD1A	H30/26R	7	Madrid	
1947	Ld.	PD1	L27/26R	3	Leigh 37-39	
1947	Ld.	PD1	H29/26R	4	Burnley C&N 163-66	
1949	Ld.	PD2/3	H31/26R	4	Burnley C&N 189-92	
1947-9	AEC	Rt.	H30/26R	45	Cardiff Nc.	Rbd.Bru.
1949	Ld.	PS1	B35R	2	Preston 74,75	Bri.
1949	Ld.	PS1	B34R	2	Rawtenstall 53,54	Bri.
1948	Ld.	PD2/1	H30/26R	2	Rawtenstall 14,15	
1948	AEC	Rt.	H33/26R	7	Rochdale 201-207	
1948-50	BUT	9641T	H38/29D	49	Cardiff Nc.	25 Bru.
1947-8	AEC	Rt.	H30/26R	15	Cardiff 95-113	AD
1947	AEC	Rt.	L27/26R	4	Cardiff do.	
1948	Gy.	Arab 2	H30/26R	1	County Motors 65	Rbd.
1947	Ld.	PD1	L27/26R	3	St.Helens 41-43	
1948-9	AEC	Rt.	L27/26R	14	St.Helens 27-40	
1950-1	Sm.	F4	H29/26R	8	St.Helens 174-81	Bri.
1950-1	BUT	9611T	H30/26R	8	St.Helens 182-89	
1947	Ld.	PD1A	L27/26R	2	Warrington 100-101	Bru.
1947	Bl.	K6G	H30/26R	2	Warrington 14-15	
1948	BUT	9641T	H38/29D	1	Cardiff 226	
1946-8	Ds.	Lance	L22/26R	13	Aldershot	
1948	Ld.	PD2/1	H30/26R	3	Rawtenstall 11-13	
1949	Ld.	PD1A	H30/26R	8	Accrington 115-22	4Bru.
1948	Ld.	PD2/1	H28/24R	4	Eastbourne 25-7,40	Bru.
1950	Bl.	L6B,5G	B32C	8	Rotherham 112-19	Bri.
1950	Bl.	KS6B	H30/26R	12	Rotherham 100-11	Bri.
1949	Ds.	Lance	L25/26R	6	Aldershot D729-34	5 Bri.
1949-50	Ld.	TD4,5	H28/26R	25	Southdown Nc.	Rby.
1948	Ld.	OPD2/1	H--/--R	10	Golden Arrow,Capetown	
1949	Ld.	LOPS2	H--/--R	1	CNETC Palestine	
1949	AEC	Rt.3	L27/26R	3	Leigh 4-6	
1948	Bl.	K6B	H30/26R	6	Rotherham 173-78	
1948	AEC	Rt.3	H28/24R	4	Eastbourne 28-31	Bru.
1948-9	Bl.	KW6G	H33/26R	20	Cardiff 114-33	Bru.
1950	AEC	Rl.	B35F	6	Llanelly & Dist. Nc.	Bru.
1949	Bl.	L6B	B32C	6	Rotherham 179-84	Bru.
1949	Fn.	PVD6	H30/26R	5	Warrington 38-42	
1949	Ld.	TD4,5	H28/24R	2	Widnes 42,46	Rby.
1949	AEC	Rt.	H30/27F	2	Mayne,Manchester	Rby.

1949	BUT	9611T	H30/26R	6	Darlington 68-73	
1949	Bl.	K6G	H30/26R	10	Warrington Nc.	Bru.
1949	AEC	Rt.3	L27/26R	2	West Monmouthshire 28,29	Bru.
1949	AEC	Rt.3	L27/26R	2	Gelligaer 9,18	Bru.
1950	Ld.	PD2/3	H30/26R	10	Newport 27-36	Bru.
1949	BUT	9641T	B38D	5	Cardiff 238-42	
1949	Cy.	DD42/5	H28/24R	8	Eastbourne 32-39	
1950	Guy	Arab 2	H30/26R	3	Burnley C&N 21-23	Rby.Bri.
1950	Sm.	F4	H30/26R	7	Teeside 1-7	Bri.
1950	Ld.	TS8	B34F	1	Gelligaer	Rbd.Bru.
1949	AEC	Rt.3	L27/26R	2	Green,Haverfordwest	Bru.
1949	Ds.	Lance	L25/26R	3	Aldershot 702-3,735	Bri.
1949	AEC	Rt.3	H33/26R	2	Mayne,Manchester	
1949	AEC	Rt.3	H30/26R	2	Swan,Swansea 36-37	Bru.
1949	Bl.	K6B	H30/26R	6	Rotherham 197-202	Bri.
1949	Ld.	PD2/3	H31/26R	4	Burnley C&N 193-96	
1949	Dr.	CTE6	B38C	8	Rotherham Nc.	
1949-50	Bl.	K6G	H30/26R	17	Warrington 52,56-71	Bru.
1949-50	Ds.	Lance	L25/26R	21	Aldershot Nc.	
1949-50	Dr.	CTE6	B38C	8	Rotherham Nc.	Bri.
1950	AEC	Rt.3	H33/26R	20	Cardiff 1-20	Bru.
1949	Dr.	CVD6DD	H30/26R	10	SHMD Board 46-55	
1950	AEC	Rt.3	H30/26R	12	Huddersfield 158-69	
1951	AEC	Rl.3	B35R	4	Nottingham 700-703	
1950	AEC	Rl.3	DP30R	1	Eastbourne 11	
1950	Ld.	TD4,5	H28/26R	9	Southdown Nc.	Rby.
1950	Dr.	CTE6	B38C	10	Rotherham 91-4, 1-6	Bri.
1950	Dr.	CVD6DD	H30/26R	4	Swan,Swansea 38-41	Bru.
1950	Dr.	CVD6DD	L27/26R	2	West Monmouthshire 14,27	Bru.
1950-1	Guy	Arab 3	H31/26R	16	Burnley C&N 197-210	
1950	Guy	Arab 2	H30/26R	6	Burnley C&N 24-29	Rby.
1951	Bl.	L5G	B32C	1	Rotherham 123	Bri.
1950	Guy	Arab 3	B31R	3	Darlington 75-77	
1950	Ld.	PS2/1	B35R	2	Rawtenstall 55-56	
1950-1	Ld.	PD2/3	CL27/22RD	20	Ribble 1231-50	
1950-1	Ds.	Lance	L25/26R	10	Aldershot 163-72	
1951	Ld.	LOPS2	H--/--R	2	Palestine diverted to	Cuba
1950-1	Dr.	CTE6	B38C	18	Rotherham 7-24	Bri.
1950	Guy	Arab 2	L27/26R	1	West Monmouthshire 21	Rby.Bru.
1952	Guy	Arab 1	H30/26R	1	Coventry 309	Rbd.Bri.
1952	Dr.	CWA6	H30/26R	1	Coventry 342	Rbd.Bri.
1952	Dr.	CWA6	H30/26R	3	Coventry 376,8,80	Rbd.Bond
1951	AEC	Rt.3	H30/26R	8	Eastbourne 41-48	
1951	AEC	Rl.3	B35R	2	Bedwas & Machan 6,7	Bru.
1951	AEC	Rt.3	H31/28R	5	Rochdale 233-37	
1951	AEC	Rt.3	H30/28R	6	Huddersfield 170-75	
1951	AEC	Regal 4	B42D	7	Rochdale 301-307	
1951	Dr.	CD650	H30/26R	6	Halifax 349-54	
1951	Bl.	K6B	H30/26R	6	Rotherham 179-84	Rby.
1951	Bl.	L5G	B32C	3	Rotherham 120-22	Bri.
1952-3	Bl.	L5G	B35/37R	9	Rotherham 147-55	Rby.
1952	Ld.	PSU1/13	B44F	5	Cardiff 134-38	Bru./EL
1951	Guy	Arab 2	H30/26R	1	Rawtenstall 37	Rby.
1952	AEC	Rt.3	L27/26R	7	Leigh 40-46	
1952-3	An.	CX19	H30/26R	30	Glasgow BR1-30	Rby.Bri.
1953	Bl.	L5G	B37R	1	Rotherham 143	Rby.RCT
1952	Ld.	PSU1/13	B40R	10	Southdown 1500-09	
1952-3	AEC	Rt.3	H33/26R	40	Bradford 66-105	
1952	Guy	Arab 3	H33/26R	15	Birkenhead 226-40	
1952	Bl.	K6B	H30/26R	3	Rotherham 112-14	Rby.
1952	AEC	Rt.3	L27/28R	6	Huddersfield 226-31	
1953	Ld.	PD2/12	H31/28R	4	Rawtenstall 20,24-26	
1953	BUT	RETB1	B27D	10	Glasgow TBS2-11	
1953	Guy	Arab LUF	B41R	1	Aldershot 186	
1953	Ld.	PSU1/13	B40C	30	Southdown 1510-39	
1953	Guy	Arab 4	H32/26R	5	Accrington 129-33	

1953	Ld.	PSU1/9	B44F	1	Green,Haverfordwest	
1953	BUT	9641T	H40/32R	12	Huddersfield 607-18	
1953	Ld.	PD2/12	H31/26R	6	Burnley C&N 71-76	
1953	Ld.	PS2/14	B39R	3	Burnley C&N 36-38	
1954	Ds.	Lance	L28/28R	20	Aldershot 203-22	
1954	Guy	Arab 2	L28/28R	6	Aldershot G21-26	Rby.
1954	BUT	9611T	H30/26R	15	Colombo,Ceylon 21-35	
1954	Dr.	CWA6	H31/28R	1	Widnes 60	Rby.
1954	Ld.	PD2/12	H30/28R	1	Haslingden 5	
1954	Guy	Arab 4	H32/26R	4	Accrington 134-37	
1954	Dr.	CWA6	H30/28R	30	Glasgow DR1-30	Rby.
1954	Ld.	PS2/14	B39R	8	Burnley C&N 39-46	
1954	LD.	PD2/22	H30/28R	9	St.Helens E83-91	
1955	Sm.	MS2	H40/32R	6	Huddersfield 553-58	Rby.
1954-5	Guy	Arab 2	H32/26R	6	Blackburn 59-64	Rby.
1954	AEC	Rt.3	L30/28R	8	Huddersfield 232-39	
1955	AEC	Rt.3	L27/28RD	1	Bamber Bridge 4	
1954	Dr.	CWA6	L29/28R	1	Widnes 59	Rby.
1955	Ld.	PSU1/14	B43F	1	Bolton 9	
1954	Ld.	PD2/22	H30/28R	3	Warrington 105-107	
1954-5	Dr.	CWA6	H30/28R	3	Widnes 49,51,53	Rby.
1955	BUT	9641T	H40/42R	13	Cardiff 275-87	
1955	BUT	9641T	B40R	1	Cardiff 243	
1955-6	Sm.	MS2	H40/32R	6	Huddersfield Nc.	Rby.
1955	AEC	Rt.3	L30/28R	10	Huddersfield Nc.	
1955	Ld.	PS2/14	B39R	3	Burnley C&N 47-49	
1955	Ld.	PD2/12	H32/28R	6	Burnley C&N 219-24	
1956	Guy	Arab LUF	B43R	3	Accrington 14-16	
1955	Ld.	PD2/20	H33/28R	9	St.Helens F101-9	
1955	Ld.	PD2/22	H30/26R	1	Darwen 16	
1955	Ld.	PD2/12	H31/28R	1	Haslingden 12	
1955	Ld.	PD2/12	H31/26R	5	Birkenhead 362-66	
1955	Ld.	PD2/20	H31/28R	6	Rawtenstall 60-65	
1956-7	BUT	9641T	H40/32R	12	Huddersfield 619-30	
1956	Guy	Arab 2	H32/26R	2	Blackburn 65-66	Rby.
1955	Sm.	MF2	H35/28R	10	Bradford 693-702	Rby.
1956	AEC	661T	H35/28R	10	Bradford Nc.	Rby.
1956	Kr.	W	H35/28RD	10	Bradford 775-84	Rby.
1957	Sm.	MS2	H40/32R	6	Huddersfield Nc.	Rby.
1955	Ld.	PD2/20	L30/28R	5	Leigh 47-51	
1956	Dr.	CVG6DD	H35/28R	10	Cardiff 301-10	
1956	Fn.	PVD6	H32/26R	5	Warrington 108-12	
1956	Guy	Arab 4	H31/28R	5	Birkenhead 382-86	
1956	AEC	Rt.5	H30/26R	7	Eastbourne 49-55	
1957	Ld.	PS2/14	B39F	6	Burnley C&N 39,42-46	Rbd.
1956	Guy	Arab 4	H35/28R	9	Cardiff 316-24	
1956	Dr.	CVG6DD	H35/28R	1	Cardiff 311	
1956-7	Ld.	PD2/12	H31/28RD	24	Southdown 789-812	
1957	Guy	Arab 4	H32/26R	10	Blackburn 140-49	
1956	Ld.	PD2/12	H32/28R	7	Burnley C&N 225-31	
1956	Ld.	PD2/20	H33/28R	6	St.Helens 118-22,125	
1957	Guy	Arab 4	H32/26R	4	Accrington 138-41	
1957	Ld.	PD2/20	L30/28R	3	Leigh 52-54	
1956	Ld.	PD2/24	L27/28R	2	King Alfred,Winchester	
1957	Sm.	MF2B	B34D	6	Colombo,Ceylon 56-61	35ft.
1957	Sm.	MF2B	B26D	20	Colombo,Ceylon 36-55	30ft.
1957	Ld.	PD2/20	H33/28R	4	St.Helens G123-27	
1957	Guy	Arab 4	H35/28R	6	Cardiff 325-30	
1957	Dr.	CVG6DD	H35/28R	4	Cardiff 312-15	
1957	Ld.	PS2/1	B35F	1	Haslingden 3	Rbd.
1958	Ld.	PS2/14	B39F	2	Burnley C&N 40-41	Rbd.
1957	Ld.	PD2/12	H31/28R	2	Widnes 26-27	
1957	Ld.	PD2/12	H31/28R	1	Haslingden 13	
1957	Ld.	PD2/41	H35/28R	4	Lancaster Nc.	
1956	Bl.	L5G	B37R	1	Rotherham 159	Rby.RCT
1957	Dr.	CVG6DD	H35/28RD	10	Bolton 85-94	

1957	AEC	Rt.5	H31/28R	1	Darwen 17	
1957	Kr.	W	H35/28RD	10	Bradford 715-24	Rby.
1957-8	AEC	661T	H35/28RD	10	Bradford 587-96	Rby.
1958	Cy.	Reliance	B43F	3	Darwen 18-20	
1957	Dr.	CVG6DD	H35/28R	12	Cardiff 331-42	
1957	Guy	Arab 4	H32/26R	4	Accrington 142-45	
1957-8	Ld.	PD2/30	L30/26R	5	Leigh 55-59	
1958	Guy	Arab 4	H35/26R	12	Cardiff 343-54	
1958	Ds.	Loline	H37/31RD	1	Aldershot 336	
1958	Guy	Arab 4	H32/26R	8	Blackburn 150-57	
1959	Ld.	PS2/14	B39F	4	Burnley C&N 34,47-49	Rbd.
1958	Ds.	Loline	H37/31RD	33	Aldershot 337-69	
1958	Ds.	Loline	H37/31RD	1	Hutchings & Cornelius	
1958	Ld.	PD3/5	H41/33R	10	Bolton 113-22	
1958	Ld.	PD3/4	H41/32R	5	Merthyr Tydfil 101-105	
1958-9	Kr.	W	H39/32F	9	Bradford 785-93	Rby.
1958	Ld.	PSUC1/1	B43F	1	Rawtenstall 58	
1958	Ld.	PSUC1/3	B43F	3	Lancaster 175-77	
1958	AEC	Rt.5	H33/28R	8	St.Helens J156-63	
1958	Guy	Arab 4	H32/26R	2	Accrington 146-47	
1958	Ld.	PD2/31	H32/28R	2	Accrington 148-49	
1959	Ld.	PD2/31	H31/28RD	3	Darwen 24-26	
1959	AEC	Reliance	B44F	6	Huddersfield 13-18	
1958	Ds.	Loline	H41/31R	2	Leigh 60-61	
1960	Ld.	PS2/14	B35F	9	Burnley C&N 8-11,30-3/5	Rbd.
1959	Ds.	Loline	H41/31R	2	Leigh 62-63	
1959	Ld.	PD2/40	H35/28R	2	Widnes 28-29	
1959	Ld.	PD3/4	H41/32F	5	Bolton 128-32	
1960	Dr.	CVG6.30	H41/32F	8	Bolton 143-50	
1959	Ld.	PD3/6	H41/32F	2	Burnley C&N 232-33	
1959	Dr.	CVG6DD	H35/28R	6	Cardiff 355-60	
1959	Ld.	PSU1/1	B43F	6	Burnley C&N 21-26	
1959	Kr.	W	H37/28F	9	Bradford Nc.	Rby.
1959	Ld.	PSUC1/3	B43F	2	Lancaster 389-90	
1960	Ld.	PSUC1/1	B43F	1	Rawtenstall 59	
1959	Guy	Arab 4	H32/26R	4	Accrington 150-53	
1959	Sm.	S7	H40/32R	10	Huddersfield 631-40	
1959-60	Kr.	W	H37/29F	18	Bradford Nc.	Rby.
1959	Guy	Arab 4	H37/28R	2	Huddersfield 190-91	
1960	AEC	Rt.5	H37/28R	2	Huddersfield 192-93	
1959	AEC	Rt.5	H41/32F	1	St.Helens K199	
1960	Ld.	PSUC1/2	DP43F	2	Leigh 1,2	
1960	Ds.	Loline 2	H39/32F	15	North Western 812-26	
1960	Ld.	PD3/1	H41/31R	4	Leicester 205-8	
1960	Ld.	PD3/4	H41/32R	8	Merthyr Tydfil 106-13	
1960-1	Ld.	PS1	B35F	2	Burnley C&N 12,14	Rbd.
1960	Ld.	Pd2/40	H31/28R	1	Haslingden 14	
1960	Ld.	PD2/30	L27/28R	5	Luton 158-62	
1960	Ld.	PD2/31	H35/28R	2	Accrington 154-55	
1961	Guy	Wulfrun.	H37/29R	2	Accrington 156-57	
1960	Ds.	Loline 2	H35/28R	2	Luton 163-64	
1960	AEC	Rt.5	H37/28R	4	Ipswich 37-40	
1960	Ld.	PD2/30	H36/28R	4	St.Helens K175-78	
1961-2	Guy	Wulfrun.	H42/30F	2	Wolverhampton 70-71	
1960	AEC	Rt.5	H35/28R	2	West Bridgford 34-35	
1961	Ld.	PD3/4	H41/32F	11	Bolton 151-61	
1960	AEC	Rt.5	L30/28RD	5	Oxford L196-200	
1961	Ld.	PD3/6	H41/32F	4	Burnley C&N 234-37	
1961	Ld.	PD2/40	H37/28R	15	Birkenhead 46-60	
1961	Ld.	PD2/40	H35/28R	2	Widnes 30-31	
1961	AEC	Rt.5	H39/31F	2	Huddersfield 194-95	
1961	Ds.	Loline 2	H35/28F	5	Oxford 301-305	
1961	AEC	Rt.5	H37/28R	4	Ipswich 41-44	
1961	Guy	Wulfrun.	H44/33F	1	West Wales 42	
1961	Ld.	PD2/24	H35/28R	1	Ramsbottom 1	
1961-2	Sm.	MS2	H40/32R	8	Huddersfield Nc.	Rby.

1961-2	Ld.	L1	B42D	3	Lancaster 101-103	
1961	Guy	Arab 4	H35/28R	12	Blackburn 158-69	
1961	AEC	Rt.5	H33/28R	5	Eastbourne 56-60	
1961	Ld.	L1	B44F	1	Todmorden 12	
1961	Ld.	PD2A/30	H36/28R	5	St.Helens L8-12	
1961	AEC	Rt.5	H35/28R	10	Cardiff 372-81	
1961	Ld.	PD3/4	H41/32R	8	Merthyr Tydfil 114-21	
1962	AEC	Rt.5	H37/28R	4	Ipswich 45-48	
1961	Do.	Loline 3	H41/31R	2	Leigh 64-65	
1961	Ld.	PD2/40	H37/28R	2	Widnes 32-33	
1961-2	Ld.	PD2A/30	H32/28R	10	Stockport 353-62	
1962	Ld.	PD3A/2	FH41/32F	9	Bolton 168-76	
1962	Ld.	PD2/30	H35/28R	1	Ramsbottom 2	
1962	Ld.	L1	B44F	2	Todmorden 16,31	
1962	AEC	Rt.5	H37/28R	2	West Bridgford 36,38	
1962	Ld.	L2	DP41F	1	Bolton 22	
1962	Ld.	PD3A/1	H38/32R	2	Accrington 158-59	
1962	Ld.	PSUC1/13	B43F	2	Accrington 17-18	
1962	Ld.	PD2/40	H37/28R	8	Warrington 82-89	
1962	Ds.	Loline 3	H38/30F	8	Reading 29-36	
1962	BUT	9611T	H37/29F	5	Bradford 831-35	Rby.
1962	Ld.	PD2A/30	H36/28R	7	St.Helens L26-32	
1962	AEC	Rt.5	H32/28R	5	Eastbourne 61-65	
1962	Ld.	PD3A/1	L34/32R	2	Leigh 3,37	
1962	Ld.	PD3A/1	H41/33R	6	Leicester 250-55	
1962-3	Ld.	PD2/24	H35/28R	12	Blackburn 21-32	
1962-3	Sm.	F4	H37/28F	7	Bradford 841-47	Rby.
1962	AEC	Rt.5	H35/28R	10	Cardiff 382-91	
1963	Ld.	PD2A/30	H37/28R	10	Cardiff 392-401	
1962-3	Ld.	PD2/40	H37/28R	4	Widnes 34-7	
1963	Ld.	PSUC1/11	B43F	6	Burnley C&N 50-55	
1963	AEC	Rt.5	H37/28R	7	Ipswich 49-55	
1963	AEC	Rt.5	H37/28R	7	Ipswich 56-62	Neep.
1963	Ld.	PDR1/1	H45/33F	8	Bolton 185-92	
1963	Ld.	L1	B42D	6	Barrow 68-73	
1963	Ld.	PD3A/1	H38/32R	6	Cardiff 402-407	
1963	Ld.	PD2/37	H37/28F	3	Lancaster 201-203	
1963	Ld.	PD2A/30	H35/28F	1	Ramsbottom 3	
1963	Ld.	PD3A/1	H38/32R	1	Accrington 160	
1963	AEC	Rt.5	H32/28R	5	Eastbourne 66-70	
1963	Ld.	PD2A/30	H32/28R	10	Stockport 1-10	
1963	An.	LR7	H35/30F	10	Luton 165-74	
1963	An.	LR7	H35/30F	6	Luton 175-80	Neep.
1963	Ld.	PSUC1/13	B43F	2	Accrington 19-20	
1963	Ld.	PSUC1/11	B43F	4	Burnley C&N 56-59	
1963	Dr.	CRG6LX	H45/32F	9	Warrington 18-26	
1963	AEC	Renown	H41/31R	4	Leigh 25-28	
1963	AEC	Rt.5	H37/29R	15	Southampton 343-57	
1963	Ld.	L1	B44F	2	Todmorden 28,37	
1963-4	AEC	Rt.5	H35/28R	12	Cardiff 408-19	6 Neep.
1964	Ld.	PD3A/1	H41/33R	15	Leicester 81-95	
1964	AEC	Rt.5	H37/28R	2	West Bridgford 39,40	
1963	Ld.	PD3A/2	H38/32R	2	Accrington 161-62	
1964	AEC	Reliance	B42D	1	Rochdale 21	
1964	Guy	Arab 5	H38/32R	3	Accrington 163-65	
1964	Ld.	L2	B43D	2	Bolton 16-17	
1964	Ld.	PSU3/4R	B49D	2	Bolton 14-15	
1964	Ld.	PDR1/1	H45/33F	12	Bolton 200-11	5 Neep.
1964	Ds.	Loline 3	H38/30F	10	Reading 37-46	
1964	Ld.	PD2A/24	H35/28R	12	Blackburn 33-44	
1964	Ld.	PD3/4	H41/32F	4	Merthyr Tydfil 132-35	
1964	Ld.	L1	B44F	2	Rawtenstall 50-51	
1964-5	Ld.	PDR1/2	H44/33F	20	Sheffield 341-60	Neep.
1964-5	Guy	Arab 5	H37/28R	17	Cardiff 420-36	Neep.
1964-5	AEC	Rt.5	H37/29R	15	Southampton 358-72	Neep.
1964	Ld.	PD3/4	H41/32F	4	Rawtenstall 30-33	

1965-6	Ld.	PD3A/1	H41/32F	2	Ramsbottom 4-5	
1964	Ld.	PD3A/1	H41/31F	2	Darwen 27-28	
1965	Ld.	PDR1/1	H45/33F	7	Bolton 212-18	
1964	Ld.	PD2/40	H36/28R	15	Stockport 11-25	
1964-5	Ld.	PD2/40	H37/28R	7	Warrington 11-17	
1964	AEC	Reliance	B43D	2	Rochdale 22-23	
1964	Dr.	CVG6	H39/31F	6	Huddersfield 435-40	
1964	AEC	Renown	H41/31F	5	Leigh Nc.	
1965	AEC	Reliance	B42D	12	Chesterfield 31-42	Neep.
1965	Ld.	PD2A/30	H34/28R	2	Lowestoft 9-10	
1964-5	Ld.	PSUC1/11	B43F	10	Burnley C&N 60-69	
1965	Ld.	PD3A/1	H41/33R	10	Leicester 66-75	
1964	Ld.	PD2/40	H37/28R	3	Widnes 38-40	
1965	Ld.	PSUC1/13	B43F	4	Accrington 21-24	
1965	AEC	Renown	H44/31F	2	West Bridgford 41-42	
1965	Ld.	PD2/37	H37/28F	3	Lancaster 204-6	
1965	Dr.	CRG6LX	H43/31F	6	Bury 132-37	
1964-5	Ld.	L1	B45F	3	Merthyr Tydfil 136-38	
1964-5	Ld.	L1	B44F	2	Haslingden 17,18	
1965	Ld.	PD2/40sp.	H34/30F	12	Warrington 41-52	7'6"wide
1965	Dr.	CRG6	H45/32F	2	Warrington 27-28	
1965	Ld.	PD3/4	H41/32F	4	Rawtenstall 34-37	
1965	Ld.	PD3A/1	H41/31F	3	Darwen 29-31	
1965	Ld.	PD3/4	H41/32F	3	Merthyr Tydfil 139-41	
1965	Ld.	PD2A/27	H37/27F	5	Burnley C&N 248-52	
1965-6	Ld.	PDR1/1	H45/33F	15	Bolton 227-41	
1965	AEC	Renown	H44/31F	3	Leicester 188-90	
1965	AEC	Renown	H41/31F	4	Leigh Nc.	
1965	Ld.	PD2A/30	H36/28R	5	St.Helens L41-45	
1965	Ld.	PD2/40	H36/28R	15	Stockport 26-40	
1966	Ld.	PDR1/1	H43/34F	5	Oldham 131-35	
1966	Ld.	PD2/27	H37/28R	3	Widnes 41-43	
1965-6	AEC	Renown	H43/31R	10	Leicester 36-45	
1966	Ld.	PD2A/30	H32/28R	10	Eastbourne 71-80	
1966	Ld.	PD3/4	H41/32F	4	Rawtenstall 38-41	
1966	Ld.	PD3/4	H41/32F	5	Merthyr Tydfil 142-46	
1966	Ld.	PD3/4	H41/32F	1	Haslingden 1	
1966	Dr.	CVG6	H41/29F	16	Huddersfield 457-72	8 Neep.
1966	Ld.	PD2A/27	H37/28F	3	Darwen 32-34	
1966	Ld.	PSUC1/11	DP41F	1	Darwen 23	
1966-7	AEC	Rt.5	H40/30R	20	Southampton 373-92	8 Neep.
1966	Dr.	CRG6LX	H45/31F	9	Coventry Nc.	
1966	Ld.	PDR1/1	H45/33F	15	Bolton 242-56	
1967	Ld.	PD2A/27	H37/27F	6	Burnley C&N 258-63	
1967	Ld.	PD3A/2	H41/31F	4	Accrington 166-69	
1967	Ld.	PD2/37	H37/28F	4	Bury 187-90	
1966-7	Ds.	Loline 3	H38/30F	8	Reading 76-83	
1967	Ld.	PSUC1/13	B45F	8	Blackburn 11-18	
1966-7	AEC	Renown	H41/31F	5	Leigh Nc.	
1967	Ld.	PD2/40	H36/28R	30	Stockport 41-70	15 Neep.
1967	Ld.	PSUC1/11	B43F	4	Burnley C&N 70-73	
1967	Dr.	SRG6LX	B41D+19	3	Bury 89-91	
1967	Ld.	PSRC1/1	B43F	2	Ashton U Lyne 55-56	
1967	Ld.	PSRC1/1	B41D	1	Warrington 90	
1967	Ld.	PD2A/27	H37/28R	6	St.Helens 50-55	
1967	Dr.	CRG6LX	H45/32F	3	Warrington 29-31	
1967	Ld.	PD3/4	H41/32F	2	Ramsbottom 6-7	
1967	Ld.	PD3/14	H41/32F	1	Haslingden 2	
1967	Ld.	PD2A/30	H32/28R	5	Eastbourne 81-85	
1967	Dr.	SRC6-36	B45D	1	Eastbourne 86	
1967	AEC	Swift	B46F	3	West Bridgford 43-45	
1967	Ld.	PDR1/1	H45/33F	15	Bolton 257-71	
1967	Ld.	PD2A/27	H37/28F	3	Darwen 36-38	
1967	Ld.	PD3/12	H41/33R	10	Leicester 16-25	
1967	Ld.	PSU4/1	B42D	3	Widnes 44-46	
1967	Ld.	PSRC1/1	B41D	3	Warrington 91-93	

1967-8	Ld.	PSU4/2R	B42D	10	Merthyr Tydfil 147-56	
1968	Ld.	PD3/14	H38/32R	15	Stockport 71-85	
1968	Ld.	PSU4/1R	B43D	5	Stockport 404-408	
1967-8	Ld.	PSUR1/1R	B53F	3	Lancaster 104-106	
1967	Ld.	PD3/4	H41/32F	2	Ramsbottom 8-9	
1967	Ld.	PD3/4	H41/32R	3	Southend 345-47	
1968	Ld.	PSU3/1R	B51D	4	Southend 215-18	
1968	Ld.	PSU4/2R	B44F	3	Rossendale 52-54	
1968	Ld.	PSU4/2R	B45F	5	Leigh 20-24	
1968	Ld.	PD2/47	H37/28F	3	Darwen 39-41	
1968	Ld.	PSUR1/1R	B45D	3	Eastbourne 87-89	
1968	Ld.	PSU3A/2R	B51D	5	Barrow 60-64	
1968	Ld.	PSU4/1R	B42D	2	Widnes 47-48	
1968	Ld.	PSU4/2R	B44F	2	Rossendale 55-56	
1969	Ld.	PD3/4	H41/32F	1	Ramsbottom 10	
1969	Ld.	PD3/4	H41/32F	1	Ramsbottom 11	Selnec
1968	Dr.	CRG6LX	H45/31F	6	Bury 138-43	
1968	Ld.	PSUR1/1R	B53F	3	Lancaster 107-109	
1968	Dr.	SRC6-36	B45D	2	Eastbourne 90-91	
1968	Ld.	PDR1A/1	H45/31F	10	Blackburn 45-54	
1968	Ld.	PDR1A/1	H45/31F	20	Southampton 101-20	
1968	Ld.	PSU4/2R	B43F	6	Merthyr Tydfil 157-62	
1968	Ld.	PSU3A/2R	B51D	6	Merthyr Tydfil 163-68	
1968	Bl.	RELL6L	B41D	2	Warrington 94-95	
1968	Bl.	RESL6G	B47F	3	Accrington 25-27	
1968	Ld.	PDR1A/1	H45/33F	15	Bolton 272-86	
1969	Ld.	PD3/14	H38/32R	6	Stockport 86-91	
1969	Ld.	PD3/14	H38/32F	6	Stockport 92-97	
1969	Dr.	SRG6LX	B41D+19	6	Bury 92-97	
1969	Ld.	PDR1A/1	H45/27D	3	Bury 1-3	
1969	Dr.	CRG6LX	H45/27D	18	Coventry 41-58	
1969	Ld.	PSUC1A/13	B45F	12	Blackburn 55-66	
1969	Ld.	PSU3A/2R	B51F	3	Lancaster 110-112	
1969	Ld.	PD2/47	H37/28F	3	Darwen 42-44	
1969	Ld.	PDR1A/1	H45/33F	3	Accrington 170-72	
1969	Ld.	PSU3A/2R	B51D	5	Barrow 45-49	
1969	AEC	Swift	B47D	4	Southampton 7-10	
1969	Ld.	PSU4A/2R	B43F	5	Merthyr Tydfil 169-73	
1969	Bl.	RESL6G	B47F	2	Accrington 28-29	
1969	Ld.	PSU4A/2R	B42D	2	Widnes 49-50	
1969	Ld.	PDR2/1	H47/32F	12	Manchester 1131-42	Selnec
1970	Ld.	PDR2/1	H47/26D	12	Manchester 1143-54	Selnec
1969-70	Ld.	PDR1A/1	H43/29D	15	Bolton 287-301	Selnec
1969-70	Ld.	PDR1A/1	H45/31F	16	Southampton 121-36	
1969	Bl.	RESL6L	B46F	5	Burnley C&N 89-93	
1970	Bl.	VRTLH6G	H49/31D	24	Liverpool 2026-49	M'side
1970	Dr.	CRG6LX	H43/29F	6	Warrington 32-37	
1970	Ld.	PSU3A/2R	B51F	3	Lancaster 113-15	
1970	Dr.	CRG6LX	H45/28D	7	Selnec 6344-50	Bury
1971	Dr.	CRG6LX	H45/27D	18	Coventry 77-94	
1970-1	Ld.	PSUR1A/1R	B43D	10	Eastbourne 1-10	
1971	Bl.	RESL6L	B42D+18	2	Widnes 51-52	
1971	Ld.	PDR1A/1	H45/33F	3	Accrington 173-75	
1971	Ld.	PDR1A/1	H45/31F	25	Southampton 137-61	
1971	Ld.	PDR1A/1	H45/31F	8	Blackburn 73-80	
1971	Dr.	SRG6LX	B49D	5	Barrow 1-5	
1971	Ld.	PSU4A/2R	B46F	5	Rossendale 60-65	
1971	Ld.	PSU3A/2R	B51F	6	Merthyr Tydfil 174-79	
1971	Bl.	VRTLH6G	H49/31D	35	Liverpool 2051-85	M'side
1971	Ld.	PDR1A/1	H45/33F	4	Accrington 176-79	
1971	Bl.	RESL6L	B42D+20	3	Widnes 53-55	
1971	Bl.	RESL6L	B47F	2	Darwen 1-2	
1971-2	Ld.	PDR2/1	H49/37F	15	Selnec 6802-16	Bolton
1972	Ld.	PDR1A/1	H45/31F	7	Eastbourne 11-17	
1972	Sn.	RU	B45F	6	Blackburn 67-72	
1972	Ld.	PSU3B/2R	B51F	6	Merthyr Tydfil 180-85	

1972	Bl.	RESL6L	B40D	5	Warrington 61-65	
1972	Bl.	RESL6L	DP40F	2	Warrington 1-2	
1972	Dr.	CRG6LX	H44/30F	1	Coventry 76	Rby.
1972	Dr.	CRG6LX	H44/30F	28	Coventry 95-122	
1972	Bl.	RES6L	DP42F	4	Accrington 30-33	
1972	Ld.	PSU4B/2R	B46F+19	5	Rossendale 66-70	
1972	Ld.	AN68/1R	H45/33F	2	Accrington 180-81	
1972	Ld.	AN68/1R	H45/31F	12	Blackburn 81-92	
1972	Ld.	AN68/1R	H45/31F	10	Southampton 162-71	
1972	Bl.	RESL6L	B47F	2	Darwen 3-4	
1973	Ld.	AN68/1R	H43/32F	50	Merseyside 1396-45	
1972-3	Bl.	RESL6L	B42D	3	Widnes 2-4	
1972	Bl.	VRTSL6G	H43/30F	18	Sheffield 267-84	
1972	Ld.	AN68/1R	H43/31F	1	Fishwick 17	
1973	Ld.	PSU4B/2R	B45F	5	Rossendale 1-5	
1973	Ld.	AN68/1R	H43/30F	14	Sheffield 307-20	
1973	Dr.	CRG6LX	H44/30F	20	Coventry 123-42	
1973	Ld.	PSU3B/2R	B51F	2	Bedwas & Machan 10-11	
1973	Dr.	CRG6LX	H43/29F	6	Warrington 100-105	
1973	AEC	Swift	B40D	5	Ipswich 89-93	
1973	Ld.	AN68/1R	H45/33F	3	Caerphilly 39-41	
1973-4	Ld.	AN68/1R	H47/30D	46	Nottingham 540-85	
1974	Ld.	AN68/1R	H45/31F	15	Southampton 172-86	
1974	Dr.	CRG6	H44/30F	20	West Midlands 4447-66	
1974-5	Bl.	VRTSL6G	H43/32F	50	Merseyside 2096-45	
1974	Ld.	AN68/1R	H43/31F	2	Fishwick 18-19	
1973	Sn.	RU	B42F	4	Accrington 34-37	
1974	Sn.	RU	C39F	1	Hyndburn 38	
1973	Bl.	RELL6L	B48D	3	Widnes 5-7	
1973	Bl.	RESL6L	B47F	3	Darwen 5-7	
1975	Ld.	PSU3B/4R	C49F	2	Halton 8-9	
1975	AEC	Swift	B43F	3	Grimsby Cleeth's 48-50	
1974	Bl.	RESL6G	B46F	5	Burnley & Pendle 146-50	
1974	Bl.	RESL6L	B46F	5	Rossendale 6-10	
1975	Bl.	RESL6L	B41D	4	Warrington 66-69	
1974	Bl.	RESL6G	B42F	2	Hyndburn 39-40	
1975	Bl.	RELL6L	DP47D	4	Halton 10-13	
1974-5	Ld.	AN68/1R	H47/31D	34	Nottingham 586-619	
1975-6	Ld.	AN68/1R	H45/33F	11	Hyndburn 182-92	
1975	Ld.	AN68/1R	H45/31f	12	Blackburn 93-104	
1975	Ld.	AN68/1R	H43/32F	8	Eastbourne 18-25	
1975	Ld.	AN68/1R	H45/33F	2	Rhymney Valley 21-22	
1975	Ld.	AN68/1R	H47/35F	1	Hale-Trent Cakes C4	
1975	Ld.	AN68/1R	H44/29D	10	Brighton 53-62	
1976	Ld.	AN68/1R	H47/31D	17	Nottingham 620-36	
1976	Ld.	PDR1/2	H47/31D	1	Nottingham 500	Rby.
1975	Ld.	AN68/R	H45/31F	15	Southampton 187-201	
1975	Bl.	RESL6L	B47F	4	Merthyr Tydfil 199-202	
1975	Bl.	RESL6L	DP42F	2	Rossendale 11-12	
1975	Bl.	RESL6L	B45F	2	Rossendale 13-14	
1975	Bl.	RESL6G	B42F	2	Hyndburn 41-42	
1975	Bl.	RESL6G	B41D	4	Warrington 70-73	
1976	Ld.	PSU3C/2R	B51F	3	Rhymney Valley 6-8	
1976	Ld.	PSU4C/2R	B45F	2	Rhymney Valley 50-51	
1977-8	Ld.	PSU4E/2R	B43F	6	Hyndburn 43-48	
1979	Ld.	B43	B-F	1	Leyland (Experimental)	
1978-80	Ld.	PSU4E/4R	B47F	14	Burnley & Pendle 30-43	
1979	Ld.	PSU3E/2R	B51F	3	Rhymney Valley 16-18	
1979	Ld.	PSU4E/2R	B45F	3	Rhymney Valley 65,67,68	
1980	Ld.	PSU3E/2R	DP47F	3	Rhymney Valley 76-78	
1976	Ld.	AN68A/1R	H43/32F	40	Merseyside 1686-1725	
1976	Ld.	AN68A/2R	H50/32D	10	Preston 111-20	
1976	Ld.	AN68A/1R	H45/31F	12	Blackburn 105-16	
1976	Ld.	AN68A/1R	H43/32F	1	Fishwick 22	
1976-7	Ld.	AN68A/1R	H43/32F	2	South Yorkshire 322-23	
1977	Ld.	AN68A/1R	H43/32F	3	Rossendale 15-17	

1976	Bl.	VRTSL6G	H43/32F	14	Burnley & Pendle 151-64
1976-7	Ld.	AN68A/1R	H44/29D	10	Brighton 63-72
1977	Ld.	AN68A/2R	H50/36F	10	Blackpool 301-10
1976-7	Ld.	FE30ALR	H45/29D	15	South Yorkshire 1561-75
1977	Ld.	AN68A/1R	H45/31F	18	Southampton 202-19
1976-7	Ld.	AN68A/1R	H43/32F	40	Merseyside 1726-65
1977-8	Ld.	AN68A/2R	H50/32D	10	Preston 121-30
1977-8	Ld.	AN68A/1R	H45/31F	8	Blackburn 117-24
1977-8	Ld.	FE30AGR	H43/33F	40	West Midlands 6721-60
1977-8	Ds.	Dominator	H43/33F	7	Leicester 233-39
1977	Ld.	AN68A/1R	H45/33F	2	Warrington 74-83
1977-8	Ld.	AN68A/1R	H45/31F	8	Warrington do.
1978	Ld.	AN68A/1R	H43/31F	15	Brighton 1-15
1978	Ld.	AN68A/2R	H50/36F	10	Blackpool 311-20
1978	Ld.	AN68A/1R	H45/29D	15	South Yorkshire 1576-90
1978	Ld.	AN68A/1R	H45/31F	12	Southampton 220-31
1977	Ds.	Dominator	H45/32F	1	South Yorkshire 522
1978	Ds.	Dominator	H45/28D	1	South Yorkshire 521
1978	Fn.	04B016G	H45/29D	1	South yorkshire 511
1978-9	Ld.	AN68A/1R	H43/32F	6	Rossendale 18-23
1979	Ds.	Dominator	H43/31F	2	Blackburn 131-32
1979	Ld.	AN68A/1R	H43/31F	6	Blackburn 125-30
1978	Ld.	AN68A/1R	H43/31F	3	East Staffordshire 22-29
1978-9	Ds.	Dominator	H43/31F	5	East Staffordshire do.
1978	Ds.	Dominator	H43/31F	1	Cardiff 51
1978	Ds.	Dominator	H43/33F	17	Leicester 188-204
1978	Ld.	AN68A/1R	H45/31F	7	Warrington 5-11
1978-9	Ld.	AN68A/2R	H47/35F	10	Eastbourne 26-35
1979	Ld.	AN68A/2R	H50/36F	10	Blackpool 321-30
1978-9	Ld.	AN68A/1R	H45/33F	4	Hyndburn 193-97
1979	Ds.	Dominator	H45/33F	1	Hyndburn do.
1979	Ld.	AN68A/1R	H45/31F	15	Southampton 232-46
1978-9	Ld.	AN68A/1R	H47/33D	25	Nottingham 637-61
1979	Ds.	Dominator	H62/42F	1	China Motor Bus DD1
1979	Ld.	AN68A/2R	H50/32D	10	Preston 131-40
1980	Ld.	AN68A/1R	H43/31F	10	Blackburn 133-42
1979-80	Ld.	AN68A/1R	H45/33F	22	Merseyside 1821-42
1979-80	Ds.	Dominator	H43/33F	22	Leicester Nc.
1980	Ld.	AN68A/1R	H45/31F	6	Warrington 12-17
1979	Bl.	VRTSL6G	H45/32F	4	Lincoln 31-34
1980	Ld.	AN68A/2R	H50/36F	10	Blackpool 331-40
1980	Ds.	Dominator	H45/29D	2	South Yorkshire 523-24
1979	Ds.	Dominator	H47/29D	1	Tayside 279
1979	Ds.	Dominator	H45/32F	1	A1 - Hunter
1979	Ds.	Dominator	H45/32F	1	A1 - McKinnon
1980	Ds.	Dominator	H46/32F	1	A1 - Hunter
1980	Ds.	Dominator	H46/32F	1	AA - Dodds
1980	Ld.	AN68A/1R.	H45/31F	15	Southampton 247-61
1979	Ds.	Dominator	B43D	6	Hartlepool 8-13
1979	Ds.	Dominator	B46F	2	Barrow 18-19
1979-80	Ld.	AN68A/2R	H45/33F	5	Lancaster 207-11
1980	Ld.	AN68A/1R	H47/33D	10	Nottingham 401-10
1979	Ld.	AN68A/1R	H43/31F	2	Plymouth 136-47
1979-80	Ld.	AN68A/1R	H43/28D	10	Plymouth do.
1980	Ds.	Dominator	H43/32F	5	East Staffordshire 30-34
1980-2	Ds.	Dominator	H43/33F	34	Leicester 251-64, 40-59
1980-1	Ld.	AN68B/1R	H45/31F	5	Warrington 18-21
1981	Ld.	AN68C/1R	H45/31F	1	Warrington 23
1980-1	Bl.	VRTLL6G	H50/36F	7	Lincoln 35-41
1982	Ld.	ONLXB/2R	H49/35F	1	Lincoln 42
1982	Ld.	ONLXB/2R	H50/35F	3	Lincoln 43-45
1981	Ld.	AN68C/2R	H50/36F	10	Blackpool 341-50
1980	Ld.	AN68B/1R	H43/32F	3	Rossendale 24-26
1982	Ld.	AN68C/1R	H43/32F	2	Rossendale 27-28
1982	Sca.	BR112DH	H46/32F	1	Scania(GB)
1981-2	Ld.	AN68C/1R	H45/31F	15	Southampton 262-76

1980	Sca.	BR112DH	H46/32F	1	Nottingham 400	
1980	Sca.	BR112DH	H49/37F	1	Gibson,Barlestone 265	
1980	Ld.	AN68A/1R	H46/27D	10	Portsmouth 345-54	
1980	Ld.	AN68B/1R	H43/31F	2	Eastbourne 36-37	
1981	Ds.	Dominator	H47/35F	2	Eastbourne 40-41	
1981	Ds.	Dominator	H43/31F	2	Eastbourne 38-39	
1980-1	Ld.	AN68B/1R	H43/28D	14	Plymouth 148-61	
1980	Ld.	AN68B/1R	H45/33F	2	Hyndburn 198-99	
1981	Ld.	AN68C/1R	H43/31F	5	Blackburn 143-47	
1981	Ds.	Dominator	H43/31F	5	Blackburn 1-5	
1981	Ld.	AN68C/1R	H45/33F	5	Warrington 24-28	
1980-1	Ld.	AN68C/1R	H46/27D	5	Ipswich 36-40	
1985	Ld.	ONLXB/1R	CH43/27D	1	Ipswich 45	
1985	Ds.	Dominator	CH43/27D	1	Ipswich 82	
1981	Ds.	Dominator	H50/32D	5	Tayside 280-84	
1981	Ld.	PSU4E/2R	DP43F	1	Hyndburn 49	
1981	Ds.	Dominator	H43/31F	2	Brighton 16-17	
1981	Ds.	Dominator	H45/33F	2	Hyndburn 101-102	
1981	Ds.	Dominator	H45/31F	1	A1 - Duff	
1982	Ds.	Dominator	H46/32F	1	AA - Dodds	
1982	Ds.	Falcon V	H45/37F	1	Hestair Dennis	
1981	Bl.	VRTSL6G	H44/32F	3	Rhymney Valley 84-86	
1981-2	Ld.	AN68C/1R	H47/33D	20	Nottingham 446-65	
1981	Ld.	AN68B/2R	H50/32D	15	Preston 151-65	
1981	Ds.	Dominator	H43/32F	5	East Staffordshire 35-39	
1982	Ds.	Dominator	H50/29D	1	Singapore Bus Service	
1982	Bl.	LHS6L	B28F	2	Rossendale 50-51	
1982	Ld.	AN68C/1R	H43/31F	17	Blackburn 6-22	
1983	Ld.	AN68D/1R	H43/31F	7	Blackburn 23-29	
1981	Ld.	AN68C/2R	H50/36F	6	Lancaster 201-206	
1982-4	Ld.	AN68D/2R	H50/36F	5	Lancaster 200,212-15	
1983-4	Ld.	AN68D/2R	CH45/32F	3	Lancaster 221-23	
1981-2	Bl.	VRTSL6G	H44/28D	6	Northampton 71-76	
1981	Ld.	AN68C/1R	H43/31F	10	Plymouth 162-71	
1982	Ld.	ONLXB/1R	H43/31F	3	Plymouth 172-74	
1981-4	Ld.	ONLXB/1R	H43/31F	19	Cardiff 501-19	
1984-6	Ld.	ONLXB/1R	CH43/27F	17	Cardiff 551-67	
1982	Ld.	AN68D/2R	H49/36F	4	Blackpool 351-54	
1982	Ds.	Dominator	H43/31F	5	Eastbourne 42-46	
1982-3	Ld.	AN68D/2R	H50/32D	12	Preston 166-77	
1983	Ld.	AN68D/2R	CH45/29F	2	Preston 1-2	
1982-3	Ds.	Dominator	H45/33F	6	Hyndburn 103-108	
1981-2	Ld.	PSU4G/2R	B45F	5	Rhymney Vall.81-3,7,8	
1981-3	Ld.	PSU3G/2R	B51F	5	Rhymney Vall.79-80,89-91	
1983	Ld.	PSU3B/4R	B52F	2	Halton 8-9	Rby.
1982-3	Ds.	Dominator	H51/37F	8	Warrington 41-48	
1982-3	Ld.	ONLXB/2R	H51/37F	4	Warrington 84-87	
1985	Ld.	ONLXB/2R	CH47/31F	2	Warrington 1-2	
1983-5	Ds.	Falcon H	B44D	7	Ipswich 100-106	
1983-4	Vo.	B55-10	H51/33D	25	Tayside 61-85	
1984	Vo.	B10M-56	H51/34D	3	Tayside 86-88	
1984	Vo.	B10M-56	CH45/33F	2	Tayside 89-90	
1983	Ds.	Falcon H	B52F	4	Chesterfield 40-43	
1983	Ld.	AN68D/2R	H49/36F	8	Blackpool 355-62	
1984	Bla	Tram	ST55D	1	Blackpool 641	
1984	Ld.	AN68D/2R	CH49/25F	2	Blackpool 363-64	
1982-3	Ds.	Dominator	H43/33F	11	Leicester 60-70	
1982-3	Ds.	Falcon V	H51/37D	2	Nottingham 396-97	
1983	Vo.	B10M-56	H49/37D	2	Nottingham 398-99	
1983	Vo.	B10M-56	H47/36F	1	Volvo	
1984	Vo.	B10M-56	H--/--D	1	Singapore Bus Service	
1984	Ld.	TRBTL/1R	DP43F	1	Rhymney Valley 71	
1983-4	Ld.	TRBTL/2R	DP47F	5	Rhymney Val.72-73.25-27	
1983	Ds.	Dominator	H43/33F	8	Leicester 71-78	
1984-5	Ds.	Falcon H	DP43F	2	Hyndburn 50-51	
1984	Vo.	B10M-56	H45/31F	5	Derby 129-33	

1984	Ld.	ONLXB/1R	H45/27F	5	Derby 206-210	
1985	Vo.	B7M	B53F	1	Raisbeck,Morpeth	
1984	Ld.	ONLXB/1R	H47/25D	6	Northampton 77-82	
1984	Ds.	Lancet	B47F	3	Taff-Ely 35-37	
1984	Ds.	Dominator	H46/30F	1	Southampton 277	
1984	Ld.	ONTL11/1R	H47/29F	1	Southampton 278	
1984	Ld.	ONLXB/1R	H46/30F	1	Southampton 279	
1984	Ld.	ONLXB/1R	H45/31F	1	Southampton 280	
1984	Ds.	Dominator	H46/33F	15	South Yorkshire 2351-65	
1984	Ds.	Dominator	H46/33F	3	Leicester 84-86	
1984	Vo.	B10M-50	CH43/35F	2	Plymouth 175-76	
1984-5	Ds.	Dominator	H43/33F	5	Leicester 79-83	
1985	GEC	Tram	ST53D	1	Blackpool 651	
1986-8	Bla.	Tram	ST52D	6	Blackpool 642-47	
1985	Vo.	B10M-50	H51/35D	7	Nottingham 301-307	
1985-6	Ds.	Dominator	H45/30F	12	Hull 120-31	
1986	Ds.	Dominator	CH43/28F	3	Hull 111-13	
1987-8	Ds.	Dominator	H45/31F	20	Hull 132-51	
1989	Ds.	Dominator	H47/33F	6	Hull 152-57	
1989	Sca.	N113DRB	H51/37F	8	Hull 801-808	
1985	Ld.	ONTL11/2R	CH47/31F	3	Rhymney Valley 28-30	
1985	Ld.	ONLXCT/2R	CH47/23F	2	Eastbourne 1-2	
1985	Ds.	Dominator	H43/32F	2	Brighton 18-19	
1985	Ds.	Dominator	CH45/28F	2	Brighton 20-21	
1985	Vo.	B10M-50	CH45/35F	1	Wright,Wrexham	
1985	Ld.	ONLXCT/2R	CH47/29F	3	Lincoln 46-48	
1986	Vo.	B10M-50	CH43/33F	5	Bournemouth 200-204	
1985-6	Ld.	TRCTL/2R	DP47F	6	Islwyn 41-46	
1986-7	Sca.	N112DR	H47/33F	2	A1 - Brown	
1986	Sca.	N112DR	H43/33F	8	Newport 27-34	
1986-7	Ld.	ONLXB/1R	CH43/27F	4	Southampton 285,86,89,90	
1986	Ds.	Dominator	H45/31F	4	Southampton 281-84	
1986	Ld.	ONLXCT/2R	CH47/29F	2	Southampton 287-88	
1986	Sca.	N112DRB	H46/33F	4	Leicester 110-13	
1986	Ds.	Dominator	H46/33F	4	Leicester 100-103	
1986	Ld.	ONTL11/2R	CH45/31F	2	London Coaches LC1-2	
1986	Vo.	B10M-50	CH45/31F	2	Northampton 1-2	
1986	De.	S56	B21F	3	Ipswich 200-202	
1986	De.	S56	DP24F	4	Eastbourne 71-74	
1986-8	Ld.	Cub		2	Lancs.Police	P.Carr.
1987	De.	G08	DP25F	6	Islwyn 47-52	
1986	De.	S56	B25F	4	Maidstone 233-36	
1987	De.	S56	DP24F	2	Taff-Ely 38-39	
1986	De.	S56	B/DP22F	5	Barrow 82-86	
1987	De	S56	B29F	2	Kettlewell,Retford 37-38	
1987	De.	S56	DP24F	8	Newport 4-9,63-64	
1987	De.	S56	B29F	4	Cynon Valley	
1986-7	Sca.	K92CRB	B51F	2	Kettlewell	
1987	Sca.	K92CRB	B59F	1	Jones,Login	
1986	Ld.	TRBTL11/2	B59F	1	Lancaster 154	
1987	Sca.	K92CRB	H55/37F	2	Maidstone	
1987	Sca.	K92CRB	B62F	1	Maidstone	
1987	Ld.	ONTL11/2R	CH47/31F	1	Rossendale 88	
1987	Sca.	N112CRB	DP33F	2	BCP London W1	
1987-8	Sca.	K112CRB	DP37F	11	British Airways CC425-35	
1987	Vo.	B10M-56	CH45/33F	2	Great Yarmouth 40-41	
1987	Sca.	N112CRB	B51F	2	AA Dodds,Troon	
1987-8	Sca.	K92CRB	CH45/30F	2	Grey Green N16 107-108	
1988	Sca.	N112DRB	H46/29F	6	Grey Green N16 109-14	
1988	Ld.	Swift	B39F	1	Lancs.Police F807 SFV	
1988	Rly.	Carriage	61 seats	1	Snowdon Mountain Railway	
1988	Ds.	Dominator	H46/33F	13	Leicester 87-99	
1989	Ds.	Dominator	H46/33F	13	Leicester 140-52	
1988	Vo.	B10M-50	H47/38D	15	Nottingham 315-29	
1988-9	Ld.	LDT11/1R	H47/41F	5	Nottingham 387-91	
1989	Ld.	LDT11/1R	CH43/37F	5	Nottingham 382-86	

1988	Vo.	B10M-50	CH49/31F	4	Lincoln 64-67	
1988	Sca.	N112DRB	H47/31F	10	Brighton & Hove 701-10	
1989-90	Sca.	N113DRB	H47/31F	20	Brighton & hove 711-30	
1988	Sca.	N112CRB	DP49F	6	Hull 701-706	
1988-9	Ds.	Falcon HC	B44D	11	Ipswich 114-24	
1988	Ds.	Dominator	CH49/27F	2	Warrington C'lines C6-7	
1988-9	Ds.	Dominator	H51/37F	9	Warrington 96-99,1-4	
1988	Ds.	Dominator	CH49/27F	1	London & Country SW 601	
1989	Ds.	Dominator	H45/31F	7	London & Country SW 602-8	
1989	Ds.	Dominator	H49/35F	1	London & Country SW 609	
1989	Ds.	Dominator	H45/31F	4	North Western 636-39	
1989	Ds.	Dominator	CH43/25F	6	North Western 630-35	
1989	Ld.	ONLXB/1RZ	H45/29F	4	Midland Red North 1916-19	
1989	Vo.	B10M-50	H49/39F	13	London & C'ntry SW 610-22	
1989-90	Vo.	B10M-50	H49/39	14	North Western Nc.	
1988	Ds.	Dominator	H45/26D	1	Ipswich 81	
1989	Ds.	Dominator	H45/31F	8	Southampton 291-98	
1989	Ld.	TRBTL11/2	DP49F	1	Rossendale 92	
1989	Ld.	TBRTL11/2	B51F	3	Rossendale 93-95	
1989	Ld.	ONCL10/1R	H45/31F	6	Blackpool 368-73	
1989-90	Ld.	TRCTL11/1	DP49F	6	Midland Red North 1710-	Rby.
1989-90	Ld.	TRCTL11/1	B51F	5	Midland Red North -1720	Rby.
1991	Ld.	TRCTL11/2	B61F	10	Midland Red North Nc.	Rby.
1992	Ld.	TRCTL11/2	B55F	5	Midland Red North Nc.	Rby.
1993	Ld.	TRCTL11/2	B61F	1	Midland Red North 1740	Rby.
1990	Ds.	Falcon	B48F	10	London & C'try SW 301-10	
1990	Ds.	Falcon	B48F	8	North Western 381-88	
1990	Ds.	Dominator	H47/29F	8	North Western Nc.	
1990	Ds.	Dominator	H47/29F	6	Midland Red North 1801-6	
1990	Vo.	B10M-55	B51F	2	Burnley & Pendle 67-68	
1990	Sca.	N113DRB	H47/37F	8	Hull 809-16	
1990	Ds.	Dominator	H43/33F	5	Thamesdown 69-73	
1990	Vo.	B10M-55	B41F	13	Cowie,N16 913-25	
1990-1	Ds.	Dominator	H47/33F	14	Bournemouth 251-65	-260
1991-2	Ds.	Falcon	B48F	9	Leicester 611-19	
1990-1	Vo.	B10M-50	H45/31D	36	London & C'try SW 648-84	
1991	Ds.	Dart	B35F	1	Midland Red North 501	
1991	Ds.	Dart	B42F	1	Midland Red North 701	
1991	Ds.	Dominator	H45/33F	4	Grimsby Cleethorpse 82-5	
1991	Vo.	B58-56	DP49F	1	Crowther,Morley	Rby.
1991	Ld.	AN68/1R	B35F	5	Southampton 350-54	Rby.
1991	Vo.	B10M-50	CH48/30F	2	Plymouth 177-78	
1991	Vo.	B10M-55	DP51F	5	Blackburn 201-205	
1991-2	Vo.	B10M-61	B55F	3	Buffalo,Flitwick 45-47	
1992	Ds.	Dominator	H45/21D	1	Hull 132	Rby.
1992	Ds.	Lance	B45D	1	Ipswich 160	
1992	Ld.	PSU5D/4R	DP47F	1	Scarborough & Dist.236	Rby.
1992	Ld.	PSU5B/4R	DP51F	1	Cherry,Beverley 281	Rby.
1992	Ld.	PSU3F/4R	DP49F	1	East Yorkshire 234	Rby.
1992	Vo.	B10M-61	H44/30D	9	Cowie,N16 163-72	Rby.
1992	Vo.	B10M-61	B49F	7	Cowie,N16 855-61	Rby.
1992	Ds.	Dominator	H45/33F	4	Grimsby Cleethorpse 91-4	
1992	Vo.	B10M-50	B45F	2	Burnley & Pendle 24-25	
1992-3	Ld.	AN68A/1R	B47F	2	Basichour 2502,2591	Rby.
1992	Vo.	B10M-55	DP47F	1	Northampton 115	
1992	Ld.	PSU3E/4R	B51F	1	Stewart,St.Helens	Rby.
1992	Ld.	PSU3E/4R	B51F	2	Rossendale 78-79	Rby.
1993	Ld.	PSU3C/4R	B49F	1	Rossendale 77	Rby.
1992	Ds.	Dominator	H47/31F	4	Bournemouth 266-69	
1993	Ds.	Dominator	H45/31F	3	Mayne,Manchester 36-38	
1992	Ld.	TRCTL11/3	DP57F	2	Strathtay ST3,17	Rby.
1993	Vo.	B58-56	CH40/26F	1	Simmons,Gt.Gonnerby	Rby.
1992	Ld.	ON2R56C	H49/35F	2	Nottingham 481-82	
1992	Vo.	B10M-61	B51F	1	Allander,Milngavie	Rby.
1992	Ld.	TRCTL11	DP57F	3	Road Car 451-53	Rby.
1992	Ld.	PSU3	B51F	2	Blue Bus,Horwich 51-52	Rby.

1992	Ld.	AN68/2R	B46F	2	Catch a Bus, E.Bolden	Rby.
1993	Ds.	Falcon HC	B48F	9	Midland Red North 1211-9	
1993	Ds.	Lance	B45F	9	Grimsby Cleethorpes 1-9	
1993	Vo.	B10M-50	B45F	2	Burnley & Pendle 26-27	
1993	Ld.	PSU4D/2R	B47F	2	Rossendale 162-63	Rby.
1993	Ld.	PSU3E/4R	DP49F	1	Rossendale 75	Rby.
1994	Ld.	AN68/1R	B45F	1	Nottingham 555	Rby.
1993	Ds.	Dart	B40F	1	Blue Bus,Horwich 1	
1993	Ld.	ON2R50OC	H45/31F	2	Bullock,Cheadle	
1993	Sca.	N113CRB	B45F	4	Tayside 110-13	
1993	Sca.	N113CRL	B42F	1	Tayside 114	
1993	Sca.	N113CRL	B38D	1	Scania,Milton Keynes	
1993	Vo.	YN2RV18	H49/35F	2	Nottingham 483-84	
1994	Vo.	YN2RV18	H49/35F	5	Nottingham 485-89	
1993	Ld.	TRCTL11	B53F	1	Loch Lomond Coaches	Rby.
1993	Ds.	Dart	DP43F	2	Great Yarmouth 62-63	
1993	Ld.	PSU3F/4R	B51F	1	Bullock,Cheadle	Rby.
1994	Sca.	N113DRB	H49/35F	5	Nottingham 349-53	
1993	Sca.	N113DRB	H47/31F	1	Mayne,Manchester 14	
1993	Sca.	K93CRB	DP51F	3	S.B.Travel SS3-5	
1994	Ld.	TRCTL11	B55F	1	Hedingham L148	Rby.
1993	Ds.	Dart	B32F	3	North Western 150-52	
1993	Ds.	Dart	B40F	2	London & Country 503-04	
1993	Ld.	TRCTL11	DP57F	1	Road Car 454	Rby.
1994	Ld.	TRCTL11	B72F	1	Road Car 455	Rby.
1993	Ds.	Lance	B48F	6	Bournemouth 401-406	
1993	Ld.	PSU3B/3R	B55F	1	Weardale,Stanhope	Rby.
1994	Ds.	Dart	B33F	22	Midland Red North 502-23	
1994	Vo.	B10M-61	DP51F	2	Western Scottish V427,31	Rby.
1993	Vo.	B10M-61	B51F	1	Rhodes,Yeadon 302	Rby.
1994	Vo.	B6-50	B41F	4	Blackburn 533-36	
1994	Ds.	Dart	B40F	5	Lon.& Country 505-8,10	
1994	Ds.	Dart	B40F	2	G'ford & W.Surrey 509,11	
1994	Ds.	Lance	B41D	2	Ipswich 161-62	
1994	Ld.	PSU5/4R	B51F	2	Porthcawl Omnibus	Rby.
1994	Ld.	TRCTL11	B62F	1	Delaine,Bourne 115	Rby.
1994	Vo.	B58-61	B53F	1	Parfitt,Rhymney Bridge	Rby.
1994-5	Sca.	N113DRB	H47/33F	20	Midland Fox 4159-78	
1995	Vo.	YN2RV18	H45/30F	2	Bullock,Cheadle	
1994	Ds.	Dart	B34F	11	London Central DEL1-11	
1995	Sca.	L113CRL	B53F	5	Yorkshire Traction 295-9	
1994	Ds.	Dart	B40F	5	Derby 34-38	
1994	Ds.	Dart	B40F	1	Silcox,Pembroke Dock	
1994	Ld.	TRCTL11	B51F	1	Blue Bus,Horwich 71	Rby.
1994	Ld.	PSU3F/4R	B51F	1	Blue Bus Horwich 53	Rby.
1994	Vo.	YN2RC16	H44/30F	20	London & Country 685-704	
1994	Ds.	Dart	B40F	1	Blue Bus,Horwich 2	
1994	Vo.	YN2RC16	H45/31F	1	Bullock,Cheadle	
1995	Ds.	Dart	B40F	14	North Western 157-70	
1995	Sca.	N113DRB	H45/31F	2	Mayne,Manchester 10-11	
1995	Ds.	Dart	B43F	1	Davies,Pencader 260	
1995	Vo.	YN2RV	CH41/29F	2	Solent Blue Line 735-36	
1995	Vo.	YN2RV18	H51/35F	2	Delaine,Bourne 116-17	
1995	Sca.	N113CRL	DP42F	4	Midland Red North 1401-4	
1995	Sca.	N113CRL	B46F	1	Scania,Milton Keynes	
1995	Ds.	Dart	DP31F	1	Metopolitan Police	
1995	Vo.	B58-61	DP49F	1	Blue Bus,Horwich 61	Rby.
1995	Ld.	PSU3E/4R	B51F	1	Blue Bus,Horwich 54	Rby.
1995	Ld.	TRCTL11	B59F	1	Wake,Wincanton	Rby.
1995	Vo.	B10M	DP47F	1	DRM Coaches,Bromyard	Rby.
1995	Ld.	PSU4D/4R	B47F	1	Green Bus,Gt.Wyrley 6	Rby.
1995	Vo.	YN2RV18	H49/31F	3	Ipswich 40-42	
1995	Ld.	TRCTL11	DP57F	3	Road Car 456-58	Rby.
1995	Vo.	B6-50	B40F	1	Volvo,Warwick	
1995	Ds.	Dart	B40F	12	Bournemouth 451-61	
1995	Ds.	Dart	B40F	48	North Western 1217-64	

1995	Ds.	Dart	B40F	2	London & Country 525-26	
1995	Sca.	N113CRL	B45F	5	Clydeside 508-12	
1995	Sca.	N113DRB	CH43/29F	3	Midland Red North 1831-3	
1995	Sca.	N113DRB	H45/33F	2	Midland Red North 1834-5	
1995	Sca.	N113DRB	H45/33F	5	Derby 160-64	
1995	Vo.	B6-50	B44F	8	Road Car 321-28	
1995	Ds.	Dart	B30FL	4	London & Country 521-24	
1994	Ds.	Dart	B40F	3	Midland Red North 806-8	
1995	Sca.	N113DRB	H47/31F	1	East Lancs.	
1996	Sca.	N113DRB	Ch47/31F	1	Northumbria 381	
1995	Sca.	L113CRL	B51F	8	Clydeside 514-21	
1995	Sca.	L113CRL	DP45F	10	Northumbria 281-90	
1995	Ld.	TRBL10/2	DP49F	1	Rhondda 703	Rby.
1995	Vo.	B10M-50	DP53F	1	Rhondda 704	Rby.
1995	Sca.	L113CRL	B51F	7	LDT 693-99	
1995	Sca.	L113CRL	DP49F	16	LDT SE701-16	
1995	Vo.	YN2RV18	H51/35F	1	Delaine 118	
1996	Sca.	L113CRL	B51F	5	Derby 29-33	
1995	Ds.	Dart	B40F	3	London & Country DS19-21	
1996	Ds.	Lance	B49F	15	London & Country LS10-24	
1996	Ds.	Arrow	H45/35F	10	London & Country AD1-10	
1996	Ds.	Dominator	H45/31F	4	G'ford & W.Surrey DD13-6	
1996	Sca.	L113CRL	B51F	10	Midland Fox 2166-75	
1996	Sca.	L113CRL	DP49F	4	Midland Fox 2176-79	
1996	Sca.	N113DRB	CH47/31F	12	Northumbria 382-93	
1995	Ds.	Dart	B30FL	3	London & Country DS16-18	
1996	Ds.	Dart	B40F	3	London & Country DS22-24	
1996	Sca.	L113CRL	DP45F	10	Northumbria 271-80	
1996	Sca.	N113DRB	H47/31F	10	Brighton & Hove 751-60	
1996	Ds.	Dart	DP31F	9	Metropolitan Police	
1996	Ds.	Dart	B40F	10	Bournemouth 463-72	
1996	Sca.	L113CRL	B51F	4	LDT SE717-20	
1996	Ld.	TRCTL11	DP53F	1	Road Car 463	Rby.
1996	Sca.	N113DRB	H45/31F	4	Mayne,Manchester 1-4	
1996	Vo.	YN2RV18	H49/35F	2	Nottingham 490-91	
1996	Vo.	YN2RV18	H51/37F	6	Road Car 681-86	
1996	Ld.	PSU3E/4R	B45F	2	Bluebird 15,69	Rby.
1997	Vo.	B58-61	DP57F	1	Provence,St.Albans	Rby.
1997	Sca.	N113DRB	CH47/31F	4	Brighton & Hove 761-64	
1997	Sca.	N113DRB	H47/31F	13	Brighton & Hove 765-77	
1997	Sca.	N113DRB	H45/33F	2	Mayne,Manchester 8-9	
1997	Vo.	YN2RV18	H49/35F	2	Nottingham 492-93	
1997	Ds.	Arrow	H49/28D	9	Capital Citybus 417-25	
1997	Vo.	OLY-56	H51/28D	13	Harris Bus	
1997	Vo.	OLY-56	H51/35F	9	Harris Bus	
1997	Ds.	Arrow	H8/3F	1	Pyramids Playbus	
1998	Vo.	OLY-56	H51/28D	13	Harris Bus 360-72	
1997	Vo.	OLY	H47/25D	15	Metrobus	
1997	Vo.	OLY-56	H51/35F	1	Delaine 127	
1997	Ds.	Arrow	H45/28D	1	Capital Citybus 426	
1997	Vo.	B10M-61	H45/35F	1	Dunn Line,Nottingham	Rby.
1998	Vo.	B10M	CH45/35F	2	Dunn Line,Nottingham	Rby.
1997	Vo.	B10M-50	CH47/35F	5	Nottingham 336-40	
1997	Vo.	B10M-50	H49/35F	5	Nottingham 341-45	
1997-8	Vo.	OLY	H49/39F	15	Nottingham 466-80	
1997	Ld.	PSU4E/4R	B45F	1	Bluebird,Middleton 70	Rby.
1998	Ds.	Arrow	H49/35F	1	Aintree Coachline	
1996-7	Spa.		B53F	2	Yorkshire Traction 201-2	
1996	Ds.	Dart SLF	B28F	5	Rossendale 106-10	
1996	Vo.	B10M-55	B62F	2	Delaine 121-22	
1996	Ds.	Dart SLF	B31F	1	G'ford & W.Surrey DSL37	
1996	Ds.	Dart SLF	B31F	1	London & Country DSL38	
1996	Ds.	Dart SLF	B31F	11	G'ford & W.Surrey 39-49	
1996	Ds.	Dart SLF	B31F	1	Horsham Buses DSL50	
1996	Ds.	Dart SLF	B31F	2	London & Country DSL51-2	
1996	Ds.	Dart SLF	B31F	3	Horsham Buses DSL53-55	

1996	Ds.	Dart SLF	B41F	5	Midland Red North 131-5	
1996	Ds.	Dart SLF	B41F	4	LDT DE171-74	
1996	Sca.	L113CRL	B47F	6	North Western 1035-40	
1996	Sca.	L113CRL	B53F	3	Nottingham 640-42	
1997	Sca.	L113CRL	B49F	3	Black Prince,Morley 653-5	
1997	Sca.	L113CRL	B49F	1	Lakeland,Hurst Green	
1996	Ds.	Dart SLF	B44F	1	Nottingham 514	
1996	Ds.	Dart SLF	B39F	2	Strathtay 310-11	
1996	Ds.	Dart SLF	B44F	3	Dunn Line, Nottingham	
1996	Ds.	Dart SLF	B43F	2	Stuart,Dukinfield 135-6	
1997	Ds.	Dart SLF	B47F	1	Country Lion,Northampton	
1997	Vo.	B6-50	B40F	1	Nottingham 511	Rby.
1997	Sca.	K112CRB	B53F	2	Barnsley & Dis.157-8,	Rby.
1998	Sca.	K112CRB	B53F	2	Yorkshire Traction 203-4	Rby.
1997	Ds.	Dart SLF	B45F	2	Paramount,Malta	
1997	Ds.	Dart SLF	B37F	8	GCT MD1-8	
1996	Ds.	Dart SLF	B37F	1	East Lancs.	
1997	Ds.	Dart SLF	B42F	3	Ipswich 130-32	
1997	Ds.	Dart SLF	B37F	2	Bournemouth 473-74	
1997	Ds.	Dart SLF	B25D	6	Meteor,Heathrow	
1997	Ds.	Dart SLF	B36F	1	Town & Around,Folkestone	
1997	Ds.	Dart SLF	B28F	3	Rossendale 111-13	
1997	Ds.	Dart SLF	B35F	1	Smith,Prenton D54	
1997	Ds.	Dart SLF	B31F	8	Express Travel,Speke	
1997	Ds.	Dart SLF	B40F	2	Harris Bus	
1997	Ds.	Dart SLF	B40F	1	A1A,Birkenhead	
1997	Ds.	Dart SLF	B40F	2	Busy Bee,Birmingham	
1997	Ds.	Dart SLF	B37F	2	Strathtay 312-13	
1997	Ds.	Dart SLF	B39F	1	Yorkshire Traction 442	
1997	Ds.	Dart SLF	B40/41F	5	Yorkshire Terrier 126-30	
1997	Ds.	Dart SLF	B40F	4	Road Car 501-04	
1997	Ds.	Dart SLF	B33F	1	Merseypride,Bootle 90	
1998	Ds.	Dart SLF	B39F	2	Wolverhampton MBC.	
1997	MAN	NL222FR	B43F	1	MAN,Swindon	
1998	Ds.	Dart SLF	B44F	1	Dunn Line Nottingham	
1998	Ds.	Dart SLF	B39F	1	Ludlows,Halesowen	
1997	Ds.	Dart SLF	B40F	1	Busy Bee,Birmingham	
1998	Ds.	Arrow	H45/31F	1	London Traveller	
1998	Vo.	B10M-50	H47/31F	1	Northampton 122	Rby.
1998	Ds.	Dart SLF	B37F	13	Capital Citybus 705-17	
1998	Vo.	B10M	CH45/35F	1	Rodgers,Weldon	
1998	MAN	18.220	B57F	4	Southn.Educn.& Liby.Brd.	IRL.
1998	Vo.	OLY-4953	CH43/29F	4	Strathtay 955-58	
1998	Vo.	OLY	H47/33F	2	Road Car 687-88	
1998	Vo.	B10M	O55/41F	6	Guide Friday,Paris	
1998	Ds.	Arrow	H49/27D	28	Capital Citybus 427-54	
1998	Ds.	Dart SLF	B39F	2	Ipswich 133-34	
1998	Ds.	Dart SLF	B29F	5	Manchester Airport	
1998	Ds.	Dart SLF	B40F	1	Bluebird,Middleton	
1998	Ds.	Dart SLF	B40F	3	Pete's,West Bromwich	
1998	Ds.	Dart SLF	B37F	8	Bournemouth 475-82	
1998	Ld.	TRCTL11	B53F	2	Jim Stones,Leigh	Rby.
1998	Sca.	N113DRB	CH47/31F	4	Brighton & Hove 778-81	
1998	Sca.	N113DRB	H47/31F	1	Fowler,Holbeach Drove	
1999	Ds.	Trident	H51/35F	2	Nottingham 405-406	
1998	Ds.	Dart SLF	B39F	8	Road Car 505-12	
1998	Ds.	Dart SLF	B40F	4	Andrews,Sheffield 131-4	
1999	Vo.	B6LE	B41F	8	Yorkshire Traction 125-32	
1998	Vo.	B10M	DP53F	1	Dunn Line,Nottingham	Rby.
1998	Vo.	B10M	B53F	2	Dunn Line,Nottingham	Rby.
1998	Ds.	Dart SLF	B23D	2	Meteor,Mayfair 86-87	
1999	Sca.	N113DRB	H47/31F	4	Scania Stock	
1999	Sca.	N113DRB	CH47/31F	1	Dewhirst,Bradford	
1998	Vo.	OLY-4953	H45/30F	1	Blue Bus,Horwich 44	
1998	Vo.	OLY-4953	H47/30F	2	Blue Bus,Horwich 43,45	
1998	Ds.	Dart SLF	DP28F	1	Gatwick Parking	

1998	Ds.	Dart SLF	DP52F	2	Wolverhampton MBC.	
1998	Vo.	OLY-4953	H47/25D	13	Metrobus 846-58	
1998	Vo.	OLY-5639	H47/33F	1	Delaine,Bourne 128	
1998-9	Vo.	OLY	H49/35F	16	Nottingham 450-65	
1998	Vo.	OLY-4953	CH43/29F	4	Strathtay 959-62	
1998-9	Ld.	TRBTL11	B51F	2	Blue Bus,Horwich 72,74	
1998-9	Ds.	Trident 3	H55/31D	30	Hong Kong Citybus	
1999	Sca.	Various	B51F	3	Yorkshire Tractn.205-07	Rby.
1999	Ds.	Trident	CO47/32F	2	Brighton & Hove 819-20	
1999	Ds.	Dart SLF	B30F	3	Express,Speke	
1999	Sca.	N113DRB	H47/31F	30	Scania Stock	
1999	Ds.	Trident	H47/32F	18	Brighton & Hove 801-18	
1998	Vo.	B10M	CH45/35F	1	Dunn Line,Nottingham	
1999	Ds.	Dart SLF	Library	2	Durham County Council	
1999	Ds.	Trident	H53/35F	10	Nottingham 407-16	
1999	Ds.	Dart SLF	B37F	1	Avon Coaches S54	
1999	MAN	18.220	B57F	2	Southn.Educn.& Liby.Brd.	IRL
1999	Vo.	B10M	O55/41F	6	Cityrama,Paris	
1999	Ds.	Dart SLF	B35F	2	Southern National 824-25	
1999	Vo.	B10M	O55/41F	6	Les Cars Rouge,Paris	
1999	Ds.	Trident	H51/33F	9	Bournemouth 270-78	
1999	Vo.	OLY	H47/30F	2	Blue Bus,Horwich 41,42	
1999	Ds.	Trident	H51/30F	5	Mayne,Manchester 25-29	
1999	Ds.	Dart SLF	B39F	9	Road Car 513-21	
1999	Ds.	Dart SLF	B36F	3	Ipswich 135-37	
1999	Vo.	B6LE	B35D	15	London Traveller 501-15	
1999	Ds.	Dart SLF	B40F	15	Andrews,Sheffield 135-49	
1999	Vo.	OLY	CH80F	1	Dualway,Ireland	
1999	DAF	SB220	B40D	17	London Central 2001-17	
1999	Vo.	OLY	H47/33F	1	Delaine,Bourne 129	
1999	Dart	SLF	B37F	6	Southern National 830-35	
1999	Vo.	OLY	H47/33F	1	Morton's Coaches	
1999	Ds.	Trident	H53/35F	10	Nottingham 417-26	
1999	Ds.	Trident	H45/24D	15	Metrobus 401-15	
1999	Ds.	Trident	H47/27F	8	Solent Blue Line 742-49	
1999	Vo.	B6LE	B41F	12	Yorkshire Tractn. 133-44	
1999	Ds.	Dart SLF	DP43F	4	Strathtay 314-17	
1999	Ds.	Trident	H45/21D	9	Blue Triangle DL901-9	
1999	Ds.	Trident	H45/30F	7	Preston Bus 190-96	
1999	Ds.	Dart SLF	B30D	3	Wings,Uxbridge	
1999	Ds.	Trident	Edu.Bus	1	Lloyds TSB	
1999	Ds.	Trident	H49/30F	1	First Bristol	
1999-00	Ds.	Trident	H53/35F	10	Nottingham 427-36	

BODIES BUILT ENTIRELY AT NEEPSEND.

1963	AEC	Rt.5	H41/32R	2	Mayne,Manchester	
1964-5	AEC	Reliance	B34D+26	8	Reading 47-54	
1965	AEC	Rt.5	H41/32R	3	Mayne,Manchester	
1965	Ds.	Loline 3	H39/30F	6	Luton 181-86	
1965	AEC	Reliance	B42D	10	Chesterfield 43-52	
1966	Ld.	PD3A/1	H41/33R	1	Leicester 260	Roof
1966	AEC	Rt.5	H37/28R	4	Ipswich 65-68	
1966	Dr.	CRG6LX	H45/31F	13	Coventry Nc.	
1966	Ld.	PDR1/2	H44/33F	20	Sheffield 162-81	
1966	Dr.	CVG6LX	H40/30F	15	Bradford 226-40	
1966	AEC	Rt.5	H38/32F	3	Rotherham 129,130,132	
1967	Ld.	PD3A/2	H40/30F	15	Bradford 241-55	
1967	Dr.	SRC6	B49D	10	Chesterfield 71-80	
1967	Ld.	PDR1/1	H43/34F	5	Oldham 148-52	
1967	Ld.	PSU4/2R	B44F	2	Huddersfield 25-26	
1967	Ld.	PSU3/1R	B51D	5	Barrow 55-59	
1967	AEC	Rt.5	H40/30R	10	Southampton 393-402	
1967-8	Ld.	PSUR1/1R	B49D	10	Chesterfield 81-90	

EAST LANCASHIRE COACHBUILDERS LIMITED

SUMMARY OF NATIONAL GREENWAY CONVERSIONS

YEAR	MECH.SPEC.	SEATS	NO.	CUSTOMER & FLEET NOS.	NOTES
1991	NL116L11/1R		1	Development vehicle	1
1991	NL106AL11/2R	B41F	1	London Country SW 252	
1992	do.	B41F	1	C-Line SRG875	
1992	NL116AL11/2R	B48F	1	Hyndburn 52	
1992	NL106AL11/2R	B24D	1	London General GLS1	
1992	NL116AL11/2R	DP49F	1	Centrewest London GLS2	
1992	10351/1R	B41F	6	Scarborough & Dist. 255-60	
1992	10351A/1R	B41F	11	Kentish Bus 431-41	
1992	11351A/1R	B48F	2	Sheffield United 10,11	
1992	11351/2R	B44DL	1	Wilfreda Beehive 66	
1992	NL116HLXCT/1R	DP23DL	1	Northumbria 702	
1992/3	Various	B41F	12	London Country SW 335-46	
1993	Various	B49F	6	London Country 347-52	
1993	11351A/1R	B48F	1	Smith,Moreton	
1993	Various	B49F	2	Blackburn 423-4	
1993	10351	B41F	6	Blackburn 525-30	
1993	Various	B49F	2	Black Prince	
1993	10351/1R/SC	B41F	2	Crosville Wales SNG821-2	
1993/4	NL106AL11/2R	B24D	36	London General Nc.	
1993/4	do	B38D	5	London General Nc.	
1993	10351B/1R	B41F	1	Crosville Wales SNG823	
1993	1151/1R/2802	B49F	1	Jones, Bontnewydd	
1993/4	10351	B41F	8	Crosville Wales Nc.	
1993/4	Various	B41F	8	Eastern Counties Nc.	
1993	10351A/2R	B41F	1	Universitybus,Hatfield	
1994	Various	B49F	8	London Country 353-60	
1994	Various	B49F	10	Midland Fox 2156-65	
1994	10351	B41F	2	Blackburn 531-2	
1994	11351A/1R	B49F	2	Blackburn 425-6	
1994	NL116L11/1R	B49F	1	Kelvin Central 4138	
1994	10351A/2R	B41F	1	Parfitt,Rhymney Bridge	
1994	10351A/1R	B41F	2	London Country 361-2	
1994	11351	B49F	10	G'ford & West Surrey 363-72	
1994	11351	DP49F	5	G'ford & West Surrey 373-77	
1994	11351A/1R	B49F	2	Midland Red North 937,952	
1994	11351/1R	B52F	1	Willetts,Pillowell	
1995	11351/1R	B49F	3	London Country 378-80	
1995	11351A/1R	B49F	4	Blackburn 427-30	
1995	11351A/1R	B52F	8	Eastern Counties Nc.	

Notes.
1. Became Blackburn 423

KEY TO BODY LIST NOTES.

Rby. Rebody Rbd. Rebuild
Bru. Bruce Bri. Bridlington
Bond. Bond of Wythenshawe
P.Carr. Personnel Carrier

Neep. Frame to Neepsend.
AD Air Despatch
Nc. Non consecutive fleet numbers

INDEX

(Page-number entries in italics refer to illustrations. If the subject is also mentioned on the same page as an illustration, the number has not been duplicated.)

GOLDSBROUGHS
Finest Scotch Whisky
CAR CONFIDENCE
735
706
82